MR WRONG

Also by Mark Barrowcliffe

Fiction

Girlfriend 44

Infidelity for First-time Fathers

Lucky Dog

Non-fiction

The Elfish Gene

MARK BARROWCLIFFE

MR WRONG

MACMILLAN

First published 2008 by Macmillan
an imprint of Pan Macmillan Ltd
Pan Macmillan, 20 New Wharf Road, London N1 9RR
Basingstoke and Oxford
Associated companies throughout the world
www.panmacmillan.com

ISBN 978-0-230-70969-0

Copyright © Mark Barrowcliffe 2008

The right of Mark Barrowcliffe to be identified as the
author of this work has been asserted by him in accordance
with the Copyright, Designs and Patents Act 1988.

All rights reserved. No part of this publication may be
reproduced, stored in or introduced into a retrieval system, or
transmitted, in any form, or by any means (electronic, mechanical,
photocopying, recording or otherwise) without the prior written
permission of the publisher. Any person who does any unauthorized
act in relation to this publication may be liable to criminal
prosecution and civil claims for damages.

9 8 7 6 5 4 3 2 1

A CIP catalogue record for this book is available from
the British Library.

Typeset by SetSystems Ltd, Saffron Walden, Essex
Printed in the UK by CPI Mackays, Chatham, ME5 8TD

This book is sold subject to the condition that it shall not,
by way of trade or otherwise, be lent, re-sold, hired out,
or otherwise circulated without the publisher's prior consent
in any form of binding or cover other than that in which
it is published and without a similar condition including this
condition being imposed on the subsequent purchaser.

Visit **www.panmacmillan.com** to read more about all our books
and to buy them. You will also find features, author interviews and
news of any author events, and you can sign up for e-newsletters
so that you're always first to hear about our new releases.

TO JEREMY HANDEL

With some of my love

NEWCASTLE UPON TYNE CITY LIBRARIES	
C443529000	
Bertrams	02.07.08
306.709	£10.99

Store of ladies, whose bright eyes
Rain influence and judge the prize.

Milton, *L'Allegro*, 1645

If I speak in the tongues of men and of angels, but have not love, I am only a resounding gong or a clanging cymbal. If I have the gift of prophecy and can fathom all mysteries and all knowledge, and if I have a faith that can move mountains, but have not love, I am nothing. If I give all I possess to the poor and surrender my body to the flames, but have not love, I gain nothing.

1 Corinthians 13:1–3

Note to my daughter. Put this down. Right now. If you read it you can foot your own shrink bills.

Note to my family, particularly Mum and Dad. Please do not read this. I beg you. I know you will read it, but I can tell you that you'll really, really, wish that you hadn't. If you do read it, then remember that what goes on in this book is not unusual for a man of my generation. It's the fact that it's typical that makes the story worth telling. Everything here is normal nowadays. Having said that, don't read it. Really don't. Please. I beg again.

Thanks to Emily Smith and Sharon Tanton, as always, for their very helpful comments on the text.

All names have been changed here. If there ever was a Xavier Viana or Francesca X, for instance, they're not the ones mentioned here. Some biographical details have been altered too, so, if a person in this book fits the description of someone you know then you can be certain it isn't them.

1 HALF A PERSON

I saw the girl for me for the first time when I was fourteen. It was the Christmas of 1978, one of those electric-blue winter days that make the world feel clean, and she was walking across the bright snowy street in a hat, scarf and long black coat. All you could see of her was a shock of blonde hair and those eyes that had stolen their colour from the sky, but I knew straight away I was in love.

'Who's that?' I asked my mum.

'Shhh!' said my mum.

'Who is it?'

'We'll never bloody find out if you keep talking.'

The girl moved in and out of the sunlight, across the deep shadows of doorways and the smoke of the fires of workmen's braziers. I cracked another Brazil nut, sucked the last of the chocolate orange off my teeth and readjusted my behind on the brown Dralon.

'Julie Christie,' said my dad, reading the paper, 'playing the tragic Lara to Omar Sharif's Dr Zhivago. Bloody rubbish, I'm going to do the washing up.'

I stayed and watched the film and I formed the idea of what I might want in a woman. I didn't want Julie Christie; I wanted Lara. With a girl like that you would be swept up on the wings of war, lie in each other's arms in the Winter Palace while the tides of history raged around you, eat iced rowan berries in frost-enchanted forests and write poetry that would make a generation weep.

'Have you walked that dog?' said my mum as it finished.

'Yes,' I said, noting that the dog was trying to force his head through the door in order to get out.

'No you haven't. Out.'

So out we went, me and the spaniel. There was no snow but it was damp, dark and cold. I made my way up to the football pitches on the common near where we lived because they were overlooked by a big road and were reasonably light. That's when I saw Ady Smith from two classes above me at school. He was at the bus stop across the road with his girlfriend Dawn. It was Christmas Day, so there was no chance of a bus coming, but they were there to keep out of the misty rain and for the mild privacy the shelter would give them. Having seen the tragedy of Dr Zhivago unfold on a tram, then public transport seemed inextricably linked to romance for me and I felt a lump in my throat as I watched them.

The street was still and the couple were too caught up in each other to notice me. In those days the roads were almost empty on Christmas night, so all that separated me from them was twenty feet of tarmac and a veil of mizzle falling through the orange lamp post light.

I looked at Ady and Dawn kissing and realised that, for anything significant to ever happen in my life, I needed a girl. When I say 'needed' I don't mean like you might need food or water or something inessential like that. I mean need like you need air and I felt that if I didn't get a girl in seconds then I might just expire.

Ady and Dawn would be married soon, I thought. I had a vision of them putting suitcases into a car for a weekend away. I had no idea where they'd be going, or even where there was to go, but I was clear in my mind that a serious relationship with a girl was the key to a whole new world, and not just that of sex. Everything was happening for Ady, I thought, nothing was happening for me. I needed to change that and quickly. Ady was sixteen. If I wanted to be settled by that age I'd have to get going soon.

I was very clear back then that if you didn't make a match by the time you were eighteen then your chances of making one at all would be seriously dented. You'd have to wait until the divorces started around thirty before any women would become available. If I didn't get cracking then it would be a lonely twelve years.

Had I been able to see into the future, I might have been tempted to throw myself into the road and wait for the traffic to take me. If I'd known it would be twenty-six years before I got married, I don't think I could have stood it.

As I moved past Ady and Dawn onto the wet common, I felt a deep need bite me. My knees suddenly seemed to forget that they were meant to support me, ordinary things seemed bizarre and strange. What was that in my hand? The dog lead. What was that for? Oh, the dog, yes, that's right. It was as if a huge space had been cleared in my head and where other information had been – how to walk, how to talk, the need to eat, even – there was only want. No action would ever be casual again; cleaning my teeth, walking the dog, going to school – I was doing them all without a girlfriend and it made them torture.

What did I expect this girlfriend would bring? What Lara brought Dr Zhivago – a total escape from the mundane. When I was a small boy I had a book of pirate stories. It showed a handsome pirate captain, sword drawn, surrounded by his crew. It wasn't the life on the high seas or the danger of adventure I was drawn to, though, but the exotic and strange cast of friends that the captain had. I was ambitious for interesting friends. I wanted to know people like the grinning black man, in ear-rings and feathers, or the squat mate with his bandolier of powder charges and the pistols in his belt. Most of all I wanted what the pirate had on his arm: a beautiful girl. She lolled backwards as if on a couch, a cascade of dark curls behind her and her eyes were fixed on the pirate as if it was her regard that gave him his authority. That picture showed what I expected from a girlfriend – everything. She would be the key to an interesting life and the proof that I had achieved it. I thought she would transform me.

Of course I expected that I'd have sex with a woman too, but this was highly abstract. My fantasies about women weren't, on the whole, sexual at that point. That's not to say I didn't have sexual fantasies, I did, strangely featuring a situation I'd seen in the comedy *On The Buses*, where the driver, played by Reg Varney, is trying to seduce a girl on the sofa. This was my only clue to what it might be like when it happened to me: a dark room, a sofa and a fish tank in the background, or it might have been a lava lamp. There is an innocence to all this, I concentrated less on the sex and more on the strange undersea glow of the light. It would be a year or more before the deflowered would begin to feel like a glamorous club from which I had been excluded.

If I did fantasise it was about companionship, about having a girl to go places with and to be my friend. I imagined my normal life with a girl – playing wargames with her at my side, going to the swimming baths and kissing her chlorined lips in defiance of the pool regulations, having coffee in a café in town with her as I'd seen other couples do. I even imagined imagining things about her – going to school and wondering what she was doing, lying in bed at night reading one of her love letters and knowing she was thinking

4

of me. Of course, I also fantasised about being seen with her, about having evidence I could present to my friends and classmates that I was grown up.

I couldn't even guess my future back then, thank God, and thought I could get the whole life partner business wrapped up within an afternoon. The next day I resolved to pay a call on Kate O'Riordon. Kate had been the best friend of a girl I'd been interested in at junior school, in the years before I was sentenced to do my time at the gulag archipelago of the all-boys Woodlands Comprehensive.

That was the blonde and beautiful Karen Macgregor. She and Kate made quite a pair, one elfin and pale, the other dark haired and bonny, with a cheeky grin. I'd spent some time chasing after Karen when I was ten, but had never had any luck. Other boys in my class had girlfriends, but they weren't for me, I'd concluded. Something about me meant I'd never be able to get a girl.

All the boys I looked up to at school had girlfriends and the most attractive girl went out with the most attractive boy. I didn't have anyone, but it seemed like my destiny – I didn't get picked at football, I didn't get picked by a girl. There was no point in feeling bad about it, it was just the way the world was.

However, Karen looked at me occasionally and had no other obvious boys around her so I made her a sort of secret girlfriend, so secret that not even she knew we were going out. In my final year of junior school I received a Valentine's card and I was sure it was from her. It was a handmade thing in red felt, shaped like a heart and completed in childish writing. I kept it in my bottom drawer and it often made me feel good that at least someone loved me, even if I didn't know who they were. I think I took it out about once a fortnight and felt a mixture of comfort and frustration that somewhere there was a girl who loved me. If only I could find out who it was.

Thinking about the card four years later I'd come to the obvious conclusion. The reason that Karen hadn't been interested in me wasn't because she didn't fancy me, or that I'd never even given her any indication that I fancied her beyond a sort of embarrassed moon-faced loitering in her company, it was because she hadn't wanted to upset her friend. Kate was obviously mad on me and, though I regarded her as second best, she was second best to the best so that was still pretty good.

I'd go round to Kate's house immediately and ask her to go out with me.

I was quite exhilarated that I'd finally got a girlfriend. I didn't see any impediment to us getting together. I hadn't seen her for four years, I'd never actually spoken to her, only watched her from the other side of a classroom, I wasn't even that sure where she lived and had no idea if she had a boyfriend or even had emigrated to Australia.

I returned home and primed my flares. The rest of creation had cut theirs down to drainpipes a year before, but I, discovering the world of heavy metal, had demurred and stood up for 'proper clothing'. In this case 'proper' meant torn bell bottoms that I had to protect from my mother by steely negotiation. She would insist on washing them and I would insist that clean jeans would make me look a complete fool in front of anyone who mattered. My mother's point of view was similar, in a way. She believed that allowing her children out in dirty clothing would reflect badly on her and the family and that 'people would talk'. Some of the pairs that I owned were more hole than trouser, a collection of stains held together by a few threads. I would have loved to have worn my choicest pair round to see Kate, but my mother had conducted a purge the week before and I'd returned home from school to find only two pairs of relatively intact trousers remaining in my drawers. The rest had gone, though my mum didn't admit to throwing them away.

When I say I primed my flares, what I mean is that I took them off and kicked them around my room for a while, scrunched them up and sat on them. My mum had an annoying habit of ironing my jeans and, to a nascent biker, creases down the front were social death. I then fished my favourite T-shirt out of the washing basket, where my mother had flicked it using the wrong end of a broom. The fact that I'd been wearing the Motorhead T-shirt for a week previously didn't faze me. In fact I thought it good that this girl, who was bound to be a heavy metal fan because, well, she just was, would see how committed to the lifestyle I was.

Then it was just a matter of cycling over to her house. Wherever that was. Today I might have found this a daunting prospect but, at the time, my path seemed clear. I would simply start with girls whose address I knew and work round to Kate by asking about her.

Accordingly I set off for Julie Smith's house. She lived on the council estate down by the brook and I knew her house because I'd visited it when I was eight. Her mum and my mum had been work colleagues.

I left my racer at her gate and made my way up the path. This was the first time since I'd thought of contacting Kate that anything like trepidation had intruded. I thought I'd have to make it absolutely plain that I wasn't interested in Julie right from the first because I was afraid she might get the wrong idea.

As I got to the step I could hear an argument going on inside, the words 'lazy fucking bastard!' being particularly clear. I rang the bell. The top half of the front door was in wire glass so I could see shapes moving behind it.

'. . . another think coming!' said Mrs Smith, to someone inside. 'Yes?'

She didn't seem to recognise me.

'Is Julie there?' I said.

'Julie!'

There was some clumping from upstairs and down came a girl I didn't recognise at all. Julie Smith at eight had worn thick NHS glasses and was extremely plain, as far as I recalled, in a gawky buck toothed sort of way. This girl, who appeared dressed for a nightclub in a Christmas-gift fresh white jump suit with a gold head band, was an attractive young woman.

She looked me up and down with alarm.

'Do you know where Kate O'Riordon lives?' I said.

'No,' she said and closed the door.

I stood on the step. 'I don't know who it was, why don't you go out and ask him?' I heard from behind the door. A man's voice said something like 'cheeky little fucker'.

I knew she did know where Kate lived because they'd been friends at school. I was within my rights, I thought, to insist that she told me.

I rang again. This time Mr Smith answered. He was a big dark man wearing a colourful jumper that made him look bigger.

'Yes?' he said.

'Julie won't tell me where Kate O'Riordon lives,' I said.

This seemed to puzzle him. He clearly needed some warming up on the theme, perhaps an introduction, but I saw no reason for that. However, Mr Smith was clearly in some sort of protracted conflict with his daughter and welcomed any stick with which to beat her.

'Why won't you tell this lad where Kate lives?' he said, as if she had been entirely unreasonable.

'I don't know who he is,' she said, 'or if she wants to speak to him.'

Even Mr Smith had to concede that this seemed a fair point.

'Who are you?' he said.

'Mark Barrowcliffe,' I said.

'Really?' he said, peering at me, 'Doreen, it's Ann Barrowcliffe's kid.'

'Really?' said his wife. Both she and Julie emerged onto the step to look at me, with that expression on their faces like people have in front of certain paintings when they say, 'I think it's supposed to be birds circling a tower block. Look, you can see the shape of one there.'

We stood looking at each other for a bit. I had a quiet pride in my appearance, so obviously gone to the wild side, no longer the little boy they had known.

Julie's dad read my T-shirt slowly. 'Mo-tor-head,' he said, 'are you a punk rocker now?'

'Fuck off!' I said.

I'd forgotten that Mr Smith was a hot tempered sort, but he only went for me in one of those 'dad going for a teenager' ways that give the teenager plenty of time to escape. He chased me down the path and out down one of the alleys that led to the brook, allowing me to escape once we got to the field. I had to sneak back for my bike half an hour later.

I was at square one and then inspiration struck. The phone book was full of people's addresses. I could look up O'Riordon in that and see which one lived nearest to us.

I returned home and circumspectly took out the phone book. If my mum saw me using it she might suspect me of making a call. I was allowed to make calls occasionally, but certainly not to anyone who lived within cycling distance, and then only briefly. Incredibly, it seemed to me, there was the address: 33 Riverside Close. I had all the information I needed and was ready for action.

I decided to walk to Kate's house as it wasn't far at all. I would open with a conversation about Lemmy, the warty bass player of Motörhead or, failing that, tell her that a friend of a friend of mine was a Hells Angel. If that didn't swing things, well, I'd just have to wing it.

Kate lived in a tiny modern house in a network of alleys down towards the brook.

I'd mentally prepared myself for another ring on a door, but when I arrived at the house a woman I took to be Kate's mother was sweeping the small front yard, scarf on head, fag in mouth. It's a look you don't see too much any more.

Suddenly I felt quite scared. I couldn't bring myself to speak to her. It occurred to me to just nod at her and then ring the bell in a nonchalant fashion but, unfortunately, I wasn't feeling nonchalant at all, more chalant, really.

I walked past her, then back again, then again and again. She caught my eye.

'If you're looking to break in son, all you'll get round here is practice,' she said.

'No,' I said, 'no, I'm, er . . .' I didn't know what I was.

'Are you Mark Barraclough?' I wasn't yet inured to the habitual mangling of my name.

'Iffe!' I said.

'If what, you either are or you aren't,' she said.

'Barrow-cliffe,' I said.

'Are you Mark Barrow-cliffe?' she said, copying my slow enunciation.

'Yes,' I said.

'And you've come to see our Kate?'

'Yes,' I said, not realising the obvious, that Julie had alerted Kate to the fact I might be on my way.

'Why?'

'Well, I, er . . .' I wanted to show I wasn't a fly-by-night sort, 'I was thinking of settling down with her.'

'Is that so?' said the woman, tossing the haft of her broom from hand to hand in a vaguely threatening manner.

'I was going to ask your permission!' I said in that teenage 'get off my case, daddio,' way.

'Oh, good,' said the woman.

There was an uncomfortable silence.

'Is Kate there?' I said.

'Yes,' said her mum, nodding slowly.

'Can I see her?'

'No,' said her mum, shaking her head equally slowly.

'Why not?'

'Because she doesn't want to see you.'

'How do you know?'

At that moment I heard a girl's voice from inside the house.

'Tell him to piss off, Mum!'

'Watch your language, Kate O'Riordon,' said her mum.

This was a blow. Still, I went to an all-boys school. There's only one way to respond when attacked – attack back.

'I didn't want to go out with you anyway!' I shouted, 'I always fancied your mate Karen more.'

'She didn't fancy you!' said the voice.

'Yeah, resort to lying,' I said, 'I happen to have a Valentine's card that says rather different.'

'Piss off, smelly!' I still couldn't see her. It was like a consultation with an abusive oracle. 'By the third moon dark of spring, blood will flow on the Athenian plain. You bollockhead.'

'Kate!' said her mum.

'You shouldn't swear!' I said.

'Piss off,' said her mum.

So piss off I did. I went back home, took out the Valentine's card and sat on my bed studying it. I imagined Karen at home sticking down the red felt with glue, cutting out the picture of cuddling teddy bears from a birthday card, scenting the envelope. I wondered if it was worth going round to her house, if she still felt the same. However, I didn't even know it was from her. I didn't want to risk making an even bigger fool of myself.

I took the card downstairs. My mum was in the kitchen and I casually made towards the bin.

'Yeah,' I said, 'I'm just throwing this card away. I wonder who it was from; you didn't see anyone deliver it did you? A blonde-haired girl.'

'When?' said my mum.

'About four years ago. Around Valentine's Day.'

'Oh that old thing,' said Mum, 'I made that to cheer you up. I didn't want you to feel left out.'

I stood mute. It was as if all hope had drained from me that second, as if for years I had been living a lie. I wasn't just a sad case, but someone whose mum thought he was a sad case. I felt utterly taken in and humiliated. To be humiliated normally requires a third party, but I managed to be humiliated in front of myself. It was as if a bit of me had always known that I was unworthy of a card and that it was mocking the naïvety of the rest of my brain.

There was no way of making sense of it. I went upstairs and put the card back in my drawer. I felt like crying, but then I realised what had happened. My mum, I concluded, had probably got confused and hadn't made it at all, or made one for someone else. That was it. It was most likely from

Karen. For years afterwards the card would continue to give me solace.

It would be two years before I got another girlfriend. I say 'another' because at the time I really did regard my very brief exchange with Kate as a sort of mini relationship, albeit one conducted without ever seeing each other.

This was to set the pattern for my future dealings with women. I have made every mistake it is possible to make with them; everything you can do wrong that doesn't involve wilful cruelty or black eyes, I have done wrong. I have been too keen, too cool, too talkative, too silent, too silly, too serious, too wild, too boring, too self-centred, too focused on them, too assertive, too much of a doormat. I have pressed forward when I should have laid back; I have failed to call when I should have deluged roses. I cannot possibly think of an error, within the bounds of legality, that I have not made. Not a one.

As an experiment I picked up the agony page of a magazine the other day and ticked off the complaints women have against men. 'My boyfriend just wants to be with his mates.' Sorry Ella. 'My man won't give me any space.' Sorry Catriona. 'He makes it so difficult to finish with him.' See Francesca, and Ella. 'He wants sex all the time.' Guilty. 'He never touches me,' guilty again, sometimes with the same woman who was complaining about the unceasing demands for sex. 'He finishes with me every week but always makes up again.' Sorry Suzy, and everyone else. If a girl's going to cry when you split up with her then only a brute could go through with it. Or someone who doesn't want to spend his life with the wrong person.

Only a shakingly insecure man has to number his girl-friends. I have been out with around forty. Of those, I have had thirty-nine failures. When I say 'been out with' I am using the definition that would take in Kate, who I never saw, and Ella, someone I got engaged to and with whom I bought a house.

I know this casts the net pretty wide, but it does so for a reason. So much of what happens in relationships happens in our heads. I may not have 'gone out' with Kate in any meaningful way but, in the weeks leading up to me going round to her house, she was my girlfriend in my mind. And the mistake I made with her – forming a little fantasy of her – is the same mistake I've made with virtually every woman I've been out with, my idea of who they are or what they should be butting up against the stubborn fact of the real woman.

Not that this fantasy was limited to the women in my life. I've also, for years, borne an incorrect image of myself, and that has influenced the way I've related to women, particularly in expecting them to take away my own insecurities and inadequacies.

If one thing sums that up it's the Valentine's card. In no way did I allow reality as it was to intrude on reality as I wanted it to be.

It's only faith in these fantasies, though, that gives us the endurance to go on, the idea that the one who makes it all OK is just around the corner, or that she's actually there and, if only your girlfriend would behave a little more like Uma Thurman in *Pulp Fiction*, then it would all be OK.

To me, it seems that I've been out with a lot of women – certainly a lot more than I would have chosen to – but I know there are some men who would think I was practically celibate, others to whom I would appear hugely promiscuous. What strikes me, though, is the amount of time I have managed to spend alone in my life.

I had my first girlfriend at fifteen and met my wife when

I was nearly forty. In twenty-five years, then, my average was roughly two girls a year. If you consider that many of those were one-night stands, that about three of them were relationships that existed only in my head, and that my six serious relationships consumed around twelve years between them, then I have spent thirteen years doing very little else than search for a long-term partner. That's over a decade of wanting, much more when you add the years I spent in bad relationships wishing I was with someone else.

The want hardly ever went away. On the good days it felt like a mild hunger, an acid feeling in the stomach and a light tightness in the throat. On the average days it was like how you feel during the first hymn of an hour-long wedding service, as you will the choruses to evaporate faster and hope the readings will be short ones. On the bad days it was like when the postman is late with the exam results that could change your life. It's not just mental turmoil, it's as if the body is full of some strange and undesired chemical, halfway between a poison and a stimulant. You hope for a good outcome, you dream of success, but more than anything you just want the waiting to be over. If someone offered you someone else's results for a different exam that would take you to a different destiny then you'd refuse. With lovers, though, sometimes there is no guarantee that one is coming with the second post, so you'll take any one just to end the waiting.

It may seem strange that, given I have been absolutely committed to finding one life partner since I was fourteen, this book features quite a lot of casual sex. The reason is that I'm a man and that, when casual sex has been available to me, I've seen very little reason to turn it down. Sex is more than what men do, it's what they're for. There's nothing wrong with casual sex and a lot to recommend it. The only pity is that it so rarely occurs. I can think of only two occasions where I've been to bed with a woman when there has been absolutely no expectation on either side that things will go further and so no capacity for disappointment or one person being left feeling cheated. When the sex has been genuinely casual, it's been marvellous.

More inexplicable are the number of short relationships I've had, but I think this is because I've been doing something known in sport as 'forcing the game'. It happens when you put so much effort in to, say, hitting a ball that you actually hit it worse than if you'd just relaxed and taken things easier. I so much wanted to move on to the next stage – that of a permanent, committed relationship – that I was very often willing to lie to myself and the woman I was with that there was a future for us. We'd both have been better off if I hadn't called after the first time – but I usually did.

In the 1980s there used to be a nightclub dress code that said 'casual but smart'. I think that's the sort of sex I've had a lot of – casual but smart – and, like the dress code, it didn't combine the best aspects of a relaxed and a formal approach but the worst. I very often ended up in some half-committed state that lacked the honesty of casual bonking or the rewards of being in love. If my sex life was a hairstyle it would be that grisly compromise we call the mullet.

I haven't been unusually promiscuous, I think, and have never gone looking for one-night stands. It is actually quite difficult to remain chaste nowadays. I have a friend of my age who is wholly committed to long-term relationships, would never be unfaithful and who abhors the idea of a one-night stand. He veers to the uncommon end of picky, despite a naturally swarthy and unwashed visage that should mean he is grateful for anyone who will look at him. He has slept with more than thirty women while actually trying not to.

This is a new form of promiscuity: the promiscuity of failure. Every woman he goes out with he views as a prospective life partner; he wouldn't be interested otherwise. Every time it fails he has another notch on his bedpost but it doesn't feel like that. It feels like a scar on his heart. In my twenty-five year search for someone to settle down with, I felt exactly the same. This is far from a joyful rake's progress; genuinely promiscuous men I have known have been with nearer the three hundred mark; those aided by fame or stunning good looks even more.

All I ever wanted, though, was love. In that I am just an average man. Most psychologically stable men aren't really looking for a life of promiscuous sex. They might find it momentarily alluring, but mostly they're after 'the one'. Everything else is just browsing.

This is a story of how a typical character was formed by love and by the idea of love. It's also about the dark corners you can find yourself in when you don't find much coming your way.

2 MISLAYING MY VIRGINITY

When I was fourteen, sex seemed like a far off myth that I only half believed. By the time I was fifteen, my virginity lay like a weight on my chest and I knew I could never breathe freely until it was gone.

Humanity, to the adolescent male, falls into two categories – those who have had sex and those who have not. The sexually experienced are enchanted beings, their lives spent smoking cigarettes from holders in gleaming casinos, staking it all on a throw of the dice, and winning, before driving home in their open-topped sports cars to their villas over-looking the sea.

The virgin, however, is a sticky creature who goes around with the feeling of having spilt treacle down his neck; his temperature is never right, always too hot or too cold, his shoes don't quite fit and his hair feels tight on his scalp. He is damp at the arm pit and the groin, but dry in the mouth and at the hands. Nothing flows for him, nothing good ever happens.

To me, having sex was not a condition of happiness, it was a condition of having a future. Nothing could really begin until that landmark had been reached. Experience knew no shades or differences. Going to school, playing records, hanging around with my friends, it was all the same, all just not having sex. The only thing that terrified me more than not having it was the prospect I'd be offered it. I simply didn't know what you were supposed to do.

I was already fifteen when I got my first proper girlfriend, Jane, who I met at a heavy metal disco in Coventry city centre. I'd been headbanging next to her for weeks. This is, of course, a heavy metal dance that involves shaking your head wildly. It has distinct advantages for the shy in that it's perfectly OK to do it alone and to close your eyes while you gyrate. Every sixth or seventh shake, though, I'd come up like a crawl swimmer for breath to catch a glimpse of where Jane was standing, measuring her attraction by how near she was and if she was headbanging too. It's quite difficult to make eye contact, even if you want to, while you're both headbanging and doing so depends largely on timing and luck. She was dancing with me, though, her long hair bobbing up and down next to mine. To the outsider we must have looked rather like an Afghan hound bouncing and hopping at its own reflection in a mirror.

We danced like this for weeks, before she became worried that if we continued, we'd end up as punch-drunk cabbages. She caught me by the ears on an upswing and put her tongue into my mouth.

This first French kiss was in many ways more memorable than the first time I had sex. In many ways it *was* having sex. People speak of becoming 'turned on'. That's how it felt, as if I was some newly built android with electricity coursing through its circuits for the first time. It was delicious and I didn't want it to stop: a little rush of nausea at the start as the tongue went in, followed by an odd sensation of nourishment, as if my skin was undergoing strange dilations and contractions, coming alive like a garden under the spring rain.

I arranged to meet her the next day, Saturday, at the end of Andrews Lane at 1 p.m. In my haste to write down the details, I forgot to ask which end. Andrews Lane is about four miles long.

That didn't cross my mind. An end appeared, I got off. I sat on a wall, wondering which direction she would come from, moving away from the bus stop so people would see that I wasn't waiting for a bus but for a girl. I lounged in the way I imagined a man waiting for a girl would lounge, floppy and casual but alert. However, lounging isn't really lounging when you get up every five seconds to see if you can see her on the horizon.

At ten past one I asked a passer by 'Is this the end of Andrews Lane?'

'It's one of them, son,' he said.

'It has two ends?' I said in the manner of a Medici pope learning that the earth went round the sun.

'Ye-eees,' he said.

'Oh, God, why didn't anybody tell me?' At the time it felt like rotten luck. Now, of course, I can simply see that – in the case of straight roads that do not span the earth – it's a mathematical law. Everything was against me, I decided, even geometry.

In a panic I boarded another bus and willed it down the lane, scanning the streets for signs of her. I had blown it, I thought, and may well have to wait another fifteen years before securing another girlfriend.

There were other anxieties too, connected with her presence rather than her absence. Jane was two years older than me, small and pretty with short blonde hair and a boyish figure. Being two years older than me, that meant only one thing, that we would be having sex. When I say it meant just one thing, it meant just one thing to the boys in my class, to whom I could say 'Yeah, she's seventeen,' with everything that implied.

Of course, the frightening thing was that, being seventeen, she might actually want to have sex. I was ready, ready like a downhill skier poised at the gate, but not prepared, like someone looking down Tortin at Verbier and wondering if it might have been wise to invest in a couple of lessons before taking it on. I definitely wanted to go for it, but wasn't actually sure how to proceed.

In these days of freely available internet pornography it seems inconceivable that a fifteen-year-old should lack knowledge of the female anatomy. I, however, had only seen one or two relatively demure top-shelf magazines and wasn't entirely sure what I would find, should I be called upon to debag the girl.

I had fantasies about sleeping with girls, for sure, but they lacked any great detail and normally focused on kissing someone very pretty, rather than sex.

The night before, when she'd first grabbed me by the ears, I'd been wearing a stained cut-off denim jacket over my leather jacket and a pair of jeans that my mum would have considered too far gone for dusters. That was clearly what Jane had been attracted to, and any deviation from this might cause her to see me in a different light. I was really nervous when I had to take off one of my badges, in case my mum saw it, and I couldn't remember exactly what angle it had been at when she'd kissed me. Would she notice if the 'John Peel's a Cunt' was at ninety degrees to my lapel rather than seventy-five?

For my meeting with Jane, I wore the exact clothes, down to the underpants, that I'd had on the night before. This was a kind of superstition, but also a sort of idiot science. To me women were like a cross between goddesses and, although it pains me to say it now, fish. Just as you might have to summon a goddess in an occult ceremony by wearing the right robes, burning the right incense, then there were strict parameters of dress and behaviour that girls found acceptable. Deviate from them and end up in the bin. Similarly, my childish experiences of angling had taught me that you needed a certain kind of bait, a certain hook and, more than that, a certain feel if you were going to catch a fish. Once you'd found the right combination you just repeated it exactly and filled your keep net.

On the bus to the other end of Andrews Lane, I was kicking myself. I was by now fairly sure that Jane had only been winding me up the night before, probably put up to it by some of my friends. For a second I thought I would get off the bus at the other end of the lane to find a gang of five or six of my mates jeering at me and laughing.

There were other anxieties, too. I had to go upstairs on the bus and sit at the back because I was a biker. You may think it strange that a biker should be on a bus at all and not on a motorbike. So did I and the self-consciousness forced me to go up the stairs and sit in the hard lads' seats. If Jane saw that I'd come from the lower deck then she'd drop me on the spot, I was sure, as it was effeminate to sit downstairs. I was terrified, as I got on, in case there were actually any hard lads there – or even hard girls who I might be forced to try to talk to – but luckily there was only a bloke in a donkey jacket smoking away.

As I sat down he wafted his hands in front of his face, said 'Jesus' and went and sat at the front of the bus. At the time I was pleased, I thought he was scared to sit next to a biker in case I started anything. In fact there were more mundane reasons.

At this point my hygiene hadn't really come on at all since before puberty. Then I'd had a bath a week – Sunday nights – and I did the same aged fifteen. I pity those who had to sit next to me. Not that they would have smelled any sweat. At the time hippies, freaks, bikers and others of the long-haired community had a mania for patchouli oil. Not wishing to be viewed as a lightweight, I'd tipped a bottle of it all over my clothes. Even a man whose sense of smell had been encased in the tar of a lifetime's Old Holborn smoking couldn't bear the niff.

The bus pulled in to the terminus and there, just by the stop but walking away, was Jane. I flew down the stairs, but had to wait while a 25-foot-wide old lady got off the bus with her shopping. I wanted to call after Jane, but I thought it would be more romantic to sneak up behind her and pretend to mug her. I don't know what I was thinking either.

One of the weird things you encounter when writing about your past is that you have to look at your behaviour and your thoughts and to say 'I did that', even if you now have no idea of why or, more to the point, how you came to act like such an idiot. I really do think I've changed, that I have so little connecting me to that oafish boy on the bus, but have I? I had to go to casualty the other day and have a pain-killing injection. 'This will hurt,' said the nurse, 'just try to say a few rhymes over in your head, it takes your mind off it. I bet you know a right few dirty rugby songs don't you?'

'I'll venture a few lines of Dryden,' I said. 'Do you know "Song to a Fair Young Lady, Going Out of the Town in Spring"?'

'Is that like "Four and Twenty Virgins"?' she said. 'Come on, sing along, you know it. "Four and twenty virgins went to Inverness, when the trip was over there were four and twenty less, singing balls to your father . . ."'

To me, I'm a sort of Vicomte de Valmont figure from *Dangerous Liaisons*, or at least a younger better-looking version of him off *Curb Your Enthusiasm*. I'm someone cool and intelligent, anyway. To her I was clearly just another bar-room boor. Who's right? I feel I've changed entirely from the person I was at fifteen but could I be wrong? I had some photos taken the other day and, rather than the slightly effete poetical figure I'd expected to emerge – think the young Aubrey Beardsley, perhaps with a nod to Brando in his prime – I resembled none other than Eugene Terreblanche, the far right-wing Afrikaner. I looked as though I'd been carved from ham. Still, I've been running twice since, so I more than likely resemble James Dean circa *Giant* again now.

I dodged round the old lady and made towards Jane as softly as I could in my size-11 Docs. I can recall now that she was kicking along looking quite depressed, but I didn't register this at the time.

I clapped my hand on her shoulder, and shouted 'Give us your money!' at the top of my voice. She, screamed 'Fuck off!' and went to hit me and so our relationship began.

Jane found my joke funny, as only a teenage girl really could, and I think was relieved that she hadn't been stood up.

'Hi,' I said, 'I saw you from the back of the bus, where I was sitting. Sorry I'm late, buses confuse me. I was born for bikes.' I made a little brum brum and gave a twist of the wrist to show I meant motorbikes, not the pedal variety.

'Hi,' she said. In fact, she only got half the 'Hi' out, short word that it is. I instantly dived at her, tongue first like an obedient child readying itself for a spoonful of medicine or like a dry bulldog heading for the waterbowl.

We stood snogging for about ten minutes. This wasn't a 'Gosh I'm pleased to see you' snog or even a 'Wait until I get you into bed' snog, it was snogging for snogging's sake, a 'Snogging! Isn't it great!' snog, or even a 'Look, I'm snogging! Me! Imagine!' I even did it with no hands at one point, but decided that might be considered showboating and placed them back on her shoulders. The novelty of it was overwhelming.

I was stuck, for once, for anything to say, so I just held her hand as we walked down the street. I felt transformed, as if everyone was looking at me and thinking 'There's a chap who's made it in life, I wish I was him,' despite the fact the street was empty.

Part of me wanted to walk around a bit with her, just to be seen, but another part of me wanted to go back to her house. I wanted to get to know her better, to see how this exotic creature who came from an area miles and miles away from my own – five at least – lived. I really thought that this was it and that I should get going with meeting my future in-laws.

The desire to be seen with a girl was quite unfocused at this time of my life. It didn't matter to me if she was good looking, ugly, fashionable or geeky, what she wore or even what her personality was like. Just being female, my age and holding my hand was enough.

My entire effort was spent getting girls to like me. However misguided, that was what my biker guise was about and why I danced in a certain way or mouthed the lyrics to any song I liked when I wasn't on the dance floor just so I could be seen liking it and benefit by close association with such a cool tune. Girls asked a question and it was up to me to shape my life to provide the answer. It never occurred to me until later – aged twenty-eight or so – that I could pick too. The only thing I was looking for in a woman was a willingness to have me. That barrier seemed so formidable that anything else was a bonus.

Jane was attractive and full of life. That was pure luck however; I hadn't picked her, she had picked me. I'd have had anyone. A few months before I had had a brief fling with – that is I had talked to at the shops and invited back for coffee – a girl of about nineteen who was so ugly and 'common', to use the pejorative of the day, that my mum had burst into tears when she saw her.

My mum held the assumption that whoever I went out with was a potential bride. Actually, that was my assumption too. 'I don't want you settling down too soon,' she told me, when I was aged sixteen. I think you could reasonably describe that as a misplaced fear.

I often thank God that my culture does not support arranged marriages. I shudder to think who my mum would have picked for me. I could guess 'honest, a grafter, the girl next door type'. If I wanted a girl next door it was the girl next door to Andy Warhol.

My mother always assumed that all I needed to do was click my fingers and a girl would marry me. In subsequent years – one, then two, decades later – she would say 'You won't get away with this forever, you know. Sooner or later you'll have to settle down.' Once, when I brought one girl back to meet her, she asked if we would be getting married.

'No,' I said, 'why would we?'

'You'll get a disease!' said my mum. 'Now then!'

Her assumption was that I was avoiding commitment because I was promiscuous. How can you tell your mum that you've been on a 25-year trawl through nightclub, party, workplace, night school, sports club, pub and friends' circles of acquaintance, that night and day the identification and attraction of a life partner has been your only endeavour – and still you have drawn a blank? Better to let her think that you have some commitment problem. Actually I did have a commitment problem – women wouldn't commit to me.

The young woman I met at the shops, with her ninety per

cent clean mini skirt as tight as Band-Aid over her bare legs, her gold slingbacks and her fur jacket, was not what mum had imagined as a daughter-in-law.

The girl, whose name I can't remember, had stood in our kitchen shaking her head at me and saying: 'I don't think I've ever heard anyone talk as posh as you.' Even at that age, I knew she needed to get out more often. My dad tested telephone systems at the GEC factory and my mum was a secretary. They weren't exactly the Bowes-Lyons.

My mum had firmly barred access to my room and there was no way I was going around to the girl's house because her brother was a notorious local heavy who had once accepted £50 to hammer someone's knee. He'd gone to the pub, attacked a man, discovered it was a case of mistaken identity and become so angry when he found out his mistake that he'd done the other knee as well to teach the bloke to be the person he was looking for in future. I was in no hurry to make his acquaintance. Just knowing someone like that brings its own trouble in a neighbourhood like the one I grew up in. You have to say hello to him in the street if you see him. But what if he doesn't want to say hello? What if you bump into him six times a day? What if he wants to borrow some money off you? What if you haven't got any money? Those types are, in my experience, best avoided entirely.

However, despite the fact that she had a potentially lethal brother, was ugly, charmless and four years older than me, she was a girl so I was willing to go out with her.

I saw her to the bottom of the path, my mum insisting that there were about nine hundred things that needed doing in the house right then and so I couldn't possible go down the brook with her. I couldn't kiss her with my mum just the other side of the door and the neighbours – in my imagination at least – meerkatting from behind the curtains.

I said that we should meet up the next day.

She, however, doubtless struck by the yawning chasm between our social classes, as represented by the three hundred yards she lived from my front door, said she'd see me around.

'Where then?' I said.

'Just 'round.'

'Like down the brook?'

'Nah. I don't go there much.'

'Where then?'

'That's for me to know and you to find out.'

'I'm finding out by asking you. That seems reasonable.'

'There you go with them long words!' And with that rather puzzling comment she left. I never saw her again, or her brother, which was a relief. I did hang about the shops a bit, but couldn't wait there for too long because wandering nerks may have taken upon themselves to kick my head in. I felt I'd missed an opportunity, until I met Jane. Then, I decided to make up for lost time.

When you have a flat of your own or even a room in halls of residence, sex can be a take it or leave it thing, something to do in between conversation and coffee. Denied these luxuries, it's simply what you do the second you are out of adult company, no matter that there are twenty other teenagers around you. Of course, I had no clue what I was doing. This didn't spoil things, though. At age fifteen, there's a combination of factors operating that guarantee that the sex you have is bound to be absolutely terrific.

There's something in the structure of your relationship at this age that forces the erotic upon you. It's not just that there is enormous social pressure on the girl to take things slowly for fear of being known as a slag. I found it a bit of a relief myself. I was acutely aware that I was a learner in these things. There is something about sex that puts you in touch with the reality of who you are. A year later a friend would ask me if I could drive. He'd been drinking, I hadn't, and he wanted me to drive his car home.

'Sure,' I said. I'd watched my dad drive, how difficult could it be? Quite difficult, as it turns out, though I mildly congratulated myself that on my first ever outing in a car I had managed the stunt manoeuvre known as a handbrake turn. I had no such misplaced confidence when it came to sex.

Jane would let me kiss her but no more on that first encounter. It was enough for me. I wonder at my endurance back then. If you asked me to kiss someone now for three hours at a stretch, I think I'd retire with face ache. It's actually sad to say that I wouldn't even want to if I could. Back then it was no problem. I found it bore an enormous erotic charge.

We had the sort of sex that is simply unavailable to anyone over the age of nineteen, at least that's what I thought until I bizarrely started having it again aged about thirty-eight. This involves trying to stroke someone's breasts through a set of heavy dungarees and perpetually having your hands removed.

I enjoyed it, much more than I enjoyed the sex I had at the other end of the scale on the Greek island of Ios eight years later. That evening, aged twenty-three, I'd met a beautiful German girl at a café and talked about books, Thomas Mann to be precise (my knowledge of whom was gleaned by reading the back of her copy of *The Magic Mountain* upside down). I'd gone back to our campsite with her and had been looking forward to reliving the worst excesses of the Weimar

Republic when she said she just had to nip into the loo. She did not emerge and, half an hour later, I had to concede that she'd had second thoughts and had climbed out of a window.

I was bitterly sucking on a roll-up next to my tent when a well-built Australian girl approached me.

'Got a light?' she said.

'Yes,' I said.

I lit her cigarette.

'Fancy a fuck?' she said.

'Yes,' I said. I was going to ask her if she was from the department for reinforcing cultural stereotypes, but thought better of it. They were the only words I exchanged with the girl other than 'Goodbye'.

It was thrilling in its way, but nowhere near as thrilling as three hours of trying to get my hand beneath a dungaree bib on the sofa with Jane.

'You're a desert nomad!' said Jane, unclasping my hot paw for the fifth time.

'What do you mean by that?' I said, thinking she was referring to a bike gang.

'Wandering palms!' she said.

There is, of course, the question of whether this constitutes having sex at all. I think it does, in that sex is the total focus of your activity. In fact, it's more having sex than some actual intercourse I've had, when the focus of my thoughts has been exactly why my sodding computer won't print, rather than the curve of my lover's back.

After a couple of hours her mum returned from town, as did her older sister, and we had a very welcome break forced upon us. The sexual tension had been unbearable and, even though I was never going to get any further than feeling the outline of Jane's breast beneath her blouse, it was relieving to know that I could desist from trying to get a finger into her bra.

'What have you been up to?' said her sister.

'Reading poetry,' said Jane.

'It's made your mouth all red,' said her sister.

'Purple prose,' said Jane.

I hadn't noticed that. Jane looked a bit like a toddler who had gone mad with the Ribena and I guess, after three hours of snogging, I must have looked the same.

Jane and her sister were the only experience I'd had of girls since my junior school, I was almost as fascinated to talk to the girls and to read Jane's *Jackie* magazine as I was trying to get her top off. Reading the problem pages of Jackie, I was drawn to a conclusion that had never even occurred to me before – women were interested in sex too.

I have only brothers and went to an all-boys school. The only women I encountered were the elf maidens of fantasy novels or the girls on heavy metal album covers. It never occurred to me before that women had an interest in sex, any more than a Rubik's Cube does in being solved or – as I thought at the time in my vaguely alarming fashion, than a horse does in being ridden.

The horse might not like to be ridden at first but, if you approach it correctly and proceed step by step then it can eventually be made to enjoy a trot in the country. *Jackie* seemed to indicate that horses all over the land were rattling their stable doors demanding to be saddled up, so to speak.

Even back then, and even though the second we were alone we fell to necking as if a starting pistol had gone off, sex was only part of what I was discovering.

The experience of being admired by a girl, for instance, was totally new. Jane had a good sense of humour and she seemed amused by me. That is, she wasn't amused by anything I said or did, and she certainly didn't laugh at me, but she was just amused when I was there. I now think that she saw through my pretensions as a hard man biker or, paradoxically, super brain, but liked what she saw underneath.

I can't remember what we talked about exactly, though we did talk a lot. I did, I'm sure, fill her in on the doings of the wonderful Black Sabbath and indulge in that perennial teenage Coventry conversation 'who's harder than who', but there were other things on offer too.

The nearest I'd had to the experience was speaking to my nan. My grandmother was the main female influence in my life. She told me stories of her past and some of the girls at her work – she was a cleaner at a Teacher Training College – but, thank God, shared very little of her emotional life with me. If there was ever a problem between her and my granddad, or if she was upset about the neighbours or work colleagues, I never knew.

Although the subject matter was very different, there was something of the feeling of my conversations with my nan in those with Jane and her sister. It could have been the calm. My own house, with three boys, a mad dog, and two on-the-go parents was always in some state of riot. There were old things at Jane's house, things that had been allowed to bed in and eventually wear out – a fading armchair, a slightly stained coffee table. This would never have been tolerated in my house and shiny new replacements would have been bought the second anything started to look shabby. This left the place looking very tidy and pristine, but it lacked a sense of stability, reference points or symbols of home.

This air of comfort could have been to do with my status as a visitor. The tea and the cakes would be produced, people would be on something like best behaviour, and the conversation would start against the soft hum of the gas fire on a low burn.

It was only about girls they both knew, or about her sister's plans for a holiday, or even what I hoped to do in the future, but it was of a different quality to what you get with boys, which is all jokes and put downs and stories about how mental someone is. I did feel I'd missed out and was often torn between wanting to hear more of Jane's sister's talk of the life she shared in her flat with her boyfriend – a flat in which she could presumably bonk like Billy-o night and day – and wanting her to go so I could try to bonk like Billy-o myself.

For the first time, and through these women, I had an idea of what my life might be like when I moved home. Jane's sister told me that her boyfriend – a biker – had installed a tropical fish tank. The position of the tropical fish tank in my subconscious sexual make up would no doubt be a meaty topic, were I ever to trouble an analyst. To me such a tank represented the height of sophistication, although if I think of tropical fish now I imagine them behind toddler-smeared glass at a doctor's surgery. At fifteen, though, I pictured myself in my own flat with such a fish tank and maybe the inside of the room done out like a tent – as owned by sheikhs of the desert rather than as erected by the Boys' Brigade at Camber Sands.

I thought I could see a future with Jane, but there again, I didn't want to get tied down. Jane was far from unattractive, but neither did she look all that much like one of the heavy metal heroines, all bulging bikinis and gleaming swords, as featured astride a dragon in one magazine I had. I thought I might meet one of those up the shops and take her back to my flat with the tropical fish to play her some records on my LED-adorned music centre.

This is one of my first recollections of an idea that would poison many of my future relationships – that of the perfect woman. Perfect women were, I knew, attainable, just as – with a little effort – I could become a world-class martial artist, poet and the fastest motorcyclist alive. I thought these were ambitions for their own sake, but, of course, they were really dreams of acceptance. My peer group valued tough, fast bikers, so I imagined myself as one. Women, I thought, valued sensitivity, so I would be the paragon of sensitivity – a poet. I'm just not the type who aims to keep fit, enjoy motorbiking in the country and listen to his girlfriend. For me then, as for years after, it all had to be at the top of the dial. The image had to be complete, with no cracks where insidious doubts could creep in. Perfect me required a perfect she. Anything else was falling short.

Still, Jane would do in the meantime. Our sexual life proceeded together according to the timeless prescribed pattern – snogging, tops (the schoolboy word for feeling a girl's breasts) with blouse on, tops blouse off, bottoms jeans on, bottoms jeans off and after that the promised land.

There were impediments along the way. Most notably was the fashion of the day – tight, tight, jeans for girls. Jane would lie on the floor while her sister reached over her shoulders and put her fingers through the belt loops. Then, in a series of bottom hops, Jane would wriggle into the jeans. There was no way she was taking these off because of the amount of time it would have taken to get them back on again if her mum came back. God knows how anyone ever went to the loo in them.

This forced an extended period of rubbing and writhing on us, which was fine by me.

I wonder if these early experiences shaped my future erotic life. Jane was willing to yield bit by bit to me doing things to her, but she wouldn't do anything at all to me. Although I had thought of her as an older woman then, she was still very young herself and inexperienced. Accordingly, there was no way she would touch me. She seemed almost frightened of my penis, which is not of terrifying proportions, and simply wouldn't touch it for most of the time. She wouldn't go down on me and wouldn't let me go down on her, even though I was eager to try, as much for a closer look as anything. This wasn't so much a sexual thing as a biological one – I still wasn't sure what things looked like down there.

Even though I was in the grip of a painful sexual tension – and at that age it really is painful, a solid ache from thighs to belly as if your penis is some blunt spar upon which you are impaled – it never occurred to me that I might find some relief by seeing to the problem myself while she was there. I thought masturbating in front of a girl would be an immediate turn off for her. Who knows, I might have been right.

However, these impediments aside, it was to Jane that I lost my virginity. Sort of. I think.

We had three goes at it. She made a great show of making me wait until my sixteenth birthday. I was very keen to avoid waiting that long, for two reasons. The first was that I didn't want to wait that long, plain and simple; the second was that I didn't want to be accused of being a late starter. If you had to hang around until you were legal, then you'd admitted that you were a wimp and a ponce, I thought.

The first time was at my house. My mum and dad had gone away for a holiday with my younger brothers. I didn't want to go. They'd agreed that I could stay, but they had taken the very wise precaution of confiscating my key and dispatching me to my nan's for the week. However, for the investment of 50p, I secretly had another key cut and so had my own pad for a whole seven days.

Jane was a bit reluctant to come upstairs into my room with me. I don't think – though I could well be wrong – that she feared getting pregnant, but I think she feared getting pregnant by someone who was under sixteen. It was impossible, though, for me to buy condoms. There are two sorts of boy in the world. There are those who stand in the pub toilets waiting for their friends to come in before they ostentatiously buy the condoms and who then nod to those friends saying something like 'Nodders, I tell you, she wants it all the time, I can hardly keep up. Though I definitely can.' Then there are those boys like me, to whom the machine seems to fizzle as if wired to the mains. It was as if, should I have touched it, an alarm would go off in the bar, and a large sign would light up saying 'He has sex, with a girl, the dirty pouf' when I came out again.

Actually, there is a third category, represented by one chap I knew at school – that of a decadence as premature as it is utter. Steve was one of those larger than life figures who seem to look about twenty years older than their age, and not an easy twenty years either: twenty years in the Flying Squad, whisky and late-night stake outs, fighting nights in the pub where you shag the stripper out the back on your way to the kebab house, that sort of twenty years. He approached me one day.

'You've got a girlfriend haven't you Spaz?'

This was my less than respectful nickname.

'Yes,' I said.

'Can I ask you a question?'

'Go ahead.' I felt quite flattered. Steve had a long-term girlfriend, one I fancied quite a lot. He had been going out with her for years.

'You know when you're holding your piss?'

'When I'm what?'

'When you're holding your piss to increase the pleasure of shagging.'

I looked blankly at him. He continued as if I was being wilfully thick.

'When you drink loads of pop until you're both dying for a piss and then you have a shag.'

'Oh yes,' I said, not wishing to look stupid. The use of the word 'pop' seemed a grotesquely childish note in the context.

'Do you think there's any harm in it? My mum says I could rupture myself.'

He had been discussing this topic with his mother. I paused a while and drank that information in. I couldn't bring myself to admit to my mother that I was even interested in girls.

'I think you'll be fine, Steve,' I said.

I was light years back from this level of operation and, even if I'd overcome my embarrassment, there was also a practical reason I couldn't approach the condom machine at the Lanch disco – the only bar I could get into, given my age. What if I couldn't work the machine? What if I put money in and it just swallowed it? No, that was out.

There was always a chemist's, of course, but I associated going in and asking for a packet of three with the same level of shame as if I'd gone in there led by a handsome and naked erection and said to the lady behind the counter, 'Could you just slip one on there?'

So contraception wasn't going to happen, one way or another. Luckily, myth and misunderstanding came to the rescue. They really did. I don't know where I got the idea of anal sex from. I hadn't even done it the regular way and I certainly didn't have open sexual conversations with many of my schoolmates. I can never recall talking to anyone about it. I think it might just be one of those ideas that is in the ether when you're fifteen. You don't know where it comes from, all you know is it's there.

At various times in my life I have been swept up by anal sex mania, particularly in the weeks following the first time a girl asked me to 'play Pooh sticks' with her. At that moment, though, it was a matter of indifference to me. I hadn't really given it any thought. All I knew was that you couldn't get a girl pregnant by doing her up the wrong un. It was the practical choice.

Jane and I spent our customary hour necking before, finally, we were both naked. She looked, I thought, fantastic, her small breasts set off beautifully by one of the then-fashionable ribbon collars she was wearing.

'We could do it, but I don't want to get pregnant,' she said.

'I'll do it from behind,' I said.

In English lessons certain boys used to sneer at fine distinctions of language, saying that as long as people knew what you meant then you didn't need to be exact. The trouble is that people don't always know what you mean. When I said 'I'll do it from behind', Jane thought I was suggesting it doggy style, a method by which she presumably thought it was more difficult to get pregnant. But I didn't mean 'from behind', I meant 'up the behind'.

And so it was that the first time I tried to enter a girl it was up the bum with no lubrication.

'Jesus, what are you doing!' she shrieked, leaping off the bed at a rate of acceleration more usually associated with human cannonballs.

'Just what we said,' I said.

'Ahhhh!' she said. This was frustration, not pain. She was having one of those moments where you vacillate between blaming yourself for being such an idiot and blaming the other person for exactly the same offence.

'It's, it's . . .' It was no good. She was speechless and the moment was lost. I think it brought it home to her that she could get pregnant by a fool. Weirdly, I think she had a fear of getting into trouble with the law if she did, though in the 1970s no one was going to prosecute an older woman for sleeping with a fifteen-year-old boy. The policeman would have simply doffed his hat to the child, although if the situation was reversed he would have thought nothing of giving an older man who slept with a fifteen-year-old girl a very unpleasant time in the cells.

The next time we tried was less traumatic, but equally unsuccessful. She was houseminding for some friends of hers. On the bus down there Jane had given me the green light by ostentatiously counting on her fingers.

'Ten, eleven, twelve, that was Thursday, day fourteen Friday, yes Saturday, that's OK, it'll be fine.'

'What?' I said, gormless.

'Just counting,' she said.

'Yeah, well you've got to be counting something, so what is it?'

'You don't know, do you?'

'No.'

She blew out heavily, and then she explained the details of the rhythm method to me.

'Yeah, right,' I said, 'and you can't get pregnant on your first time or if you do it during a full moon either.' It sounded to me like a complete myth. It's in fact not a complete myth, only a partial one. Talk of the rhythm method always recalls the old joke to me:

'What do you call people who practise the rhythm method of contraception?'

'What?'

'Parents.'

We took off our clothes and got into bed. I felt all those fresh and amazing feelings of having a naked girl next to me underneath the duvet – or continental quilt as it was then called. My skin seemed to tingle where we touched, her perfume overwhelmed me – I think it was the brand Tramp by Mayfair. That's one of those labels that didn't prosper when the rock 'n' roll seventies turned to the uptight eighties.

Despite the fact that I was shimmering with a sort of sensual overload – when I look back I imagine myself lit up like they did the Eiffel Tower around the millennium, little points of light bursting all over me – I managed to behave like a bull at a gate.

Unusually, we'd hardly touched each other before getting into bed. It was amazing to me to see her strip off and hop in. I hadn't had to take off her clothes myself, which I found hugely exciting – roughly the opposite situation to that in which many married couples find themselves.

So we got into bed, I went all shimmery in synapse and nerve and then I just immediately tried to go for it with no preliminaries. Again, she shrieked, 'You really haven't a clue, have you?'

'Well, no,' I said. I didn't find this humiliating or offputting. It was simply a statement of fact. Again, Jane pulled back from the moment and I was into another extended session of pawing at her. That suited me very well, but I'm not sure it did much for her. I was absorbed in what she felt like inside, or the slightly surprising revelation that her tits didn't produce milk when I sucked them. I didn't know that women only produce milk after they've given birth. What she got from it I don't know. To me the clitoris was a foreign country, it could have been a Greek island for all I knew. It wasn't that I didn't know of its existence, just that I didn't know quite where it was meant to be or what to do with it if I found it.

It's terrifying to relate, but my only guides for anything approaching sexual technique were other boys. It was well known at my school that you had to 'finger' a girl. The more fingers you could put inside them, the more they would enjoy it. This is the level of chilling ignorance that young girls have to correct in men. It's scary but it's also OK. You can't learn what to do from some DVD where a painfully thin man with a German hairstyle lights candles and incense and goes to work on his mottled wife. Everyone wants something different.

The final time was more successful, though I didn't so much lose my virginity as mislay it. It was my sixteenth birthday. I was due on a school trip to Switzerland the next day – my first ever time abroad – so I felt the world was really opening up to me.

Jane was babysitting for her next-door neighbour. I met her round there and I immediately knew that something special was going to happen.

For a start, Jane was wearing a skirt, a long cheesecloth hippy thing. She never wore a skirt. In my mind it was designed for one thing – easy access. The couple she was babysitting for were really nice. They could only have been about twenty-one themselves, but the man called me into the kitchen before I went.

'Here' he said, opening a drawer. Inside was an enormous box of condoms – at least forty packets of three. 'She's a nurse,' he said, 'gets them from work. Help yourself tonight, they're free.'

I went red to my boots but said 'Thanks very much' nevertheless. How I'd break this to Jane I didn't know.

Strangely it seemed she knew about them. We fell to it with abandon and then – I think we were both a bit scared of what might happen – spent ages leading up to the main event. Aware that I was going away for two weeks the next day and that Switzerland could have been full of willing women, Jane gave me the most extensive set of love bites I have ever seen on one neck. If I was going to meet someone else then she wasn't going to make it easy.

'Go and get a contraceptive,' she said, at about 9.45.

The problem was that Jane's house was two buses away. If I didn't catch the ten o'clock I wouldn't be able to get home. Normally I'd have said 'Sod it' and walked the five miles, but with the Alps on the horizon this was out of the question. I had fifteen minutes to fit a condom, lose my virginity and get to the bus stop.

The trouble is that I had never put a condom on before and neither had she. I tore one trying to get it on. Then she tore one. Then one panged off to somewhere beneath the coffee table.

It was 9.55. 'I've got to go,' I said.

I tried to leave but I couldn't.

'Oh, come here,' I said.

At 9.56 on July 13, 1980, I actually had intercourse with a woman for the first time. I was all of two thrusts in when the clock clicked to 9.57. It was now or never for the bus.

'I'm really sorry,' I said, 'but my mum will kill me if I'm late tonight.'

I had no time to waste, I pulled up my trousers and ran for the bus, hampered by a hard as a fossil erection and leaving Jane to watch the rest of *Juliet Bravo* on her own.

When I got home that night I wanted to go straight to my room to deal with my throbbing cock, but my mum made me go through and check everything I was taking on holiday to make sure I hadn't missed anything. I don't think I've ever experienced that level of sexual tension since. When I finally managed to see to it, a good hour and a half after the point at which it had become painful, I'm surprised I didn't go spinning round like a Catherine Wheel.

So this leaves the vexed question of whether that counts as me losing my virginity. I don't know. At the time I was sure that it did, but now, not that it really matters, I'm not so certain.

3 COMPETITION

I can't really remember anything about the Alps. For me they were not the main feature of our Alpine walking holiday.

We went to a small village just outside Interlaken in Switzerland and stayed in a run-down hotel that specialised in school parties and serving entirely inedible food. I survived the whole week on bread rolls, chocolate and Café Fertig – a local variant on Irish Coffee which featured copious amounts of rum.

It remains, however, one of the happiest times of my life. I was away from parental distraction, accepted by my peer group (an entirely new experience for me) and I had the memory of my five seconds with Jane (I'm being generous on the timing). I felt I'd been given the keys to the house of fun.

The mountains seemed dull next to the closer distractions – a party of girls from Aberdeen who were sharing our hotel. Normally their presence would have caused me some disquiet. I was one of the runts at school. I was one of the youngest in my year and had an almost unbearable enthusiasm for learning and answering questions in class. In short, I wasn't at all socialised into the world of an all-boys comp.

A party of girls would have meant one thing for me – more scorn from my schoolmates as I went red and chewed my hands in the shadows while they, banners streaming, took their conquests off into carpark and broom cupboard.

Switzerland, however, made me feel free. I was away from my family for the first time and had teamed up with some boys who seemed to share my sense of humour, which involved spending much of my time acting out a caricature of what we imagined a Rhodesian farmer to be. Rhodesia had become Zimbabwe the year before and the TV had been full of such farmers decrying the awful practices of the terrible 'blecks'. We had no sense of the politics of this whole thing and just thought the farmers talked funny. So anything that went wrong, anything that did anything, would be greeted with the response 'I blame the blecks' and variations upon it. The joke might seem a bit dodgy by modern standards, but if anything, this was actually anti-racist. The farmers seemed to accuse the blacks of everything from corruption to bad weather and we felt they couldn't be responsible for it all. Soggy crisps? The blecks. Sudden sprouting of spots? The blecks. Stale bun at dinner? 'I blame the blecks.' This is the sort of sense of humour that is utterly unbearable to listen to if you get stuck next to it on public transport, but if you're a young sixteen and involved in it yourself it seems like the funniest thing you've ever heard.

I was rich too. In those days you were allowed to sign on between the end of the fifth form and joining the sixth, so I had £15 a week flowing into my coffers. It was more money than I'd ever had in my life and I really had no idea why anyone would want to work.

Also, by joining the prevailing cult of Heavy Rock – rather than sticking insistently to the Bonzo Dog Doo Dah Band as I'd done when I arrived at school – I'd earned some respect from the other pupils, made myself understandable to them.

Everything was going right for me. Even when the pinball machine in the hotel got stuck, I walked up to it, gave it a sharp knock and it started working again. 'Fonzie!' said someone. It was a better nickname than Spaz. Unfortunately it didn't stick.

The holiday, for me, was all about going out at night. We'd do the Eiger railway during the day (forgot sunglasses, saw nothing; crisp packet swelled up in lower air pressure, which I saw as a large compensation), but come the evening we'd hit the nightspots of Interlaken.

That's where I met Chrissie. I don't think she'd normally have looked at me twice, but the holiday had forced some changes on me. For a start it was a school trip and there was no way that I'd be allowed out at night wearing my full-on biker gear. Accordingly I'd borrowed a denim jacket from one of the other boys, put on a normal T-shirt and clean jeans and looked somewhat human. Secondly, even I had to have a shower after a day's hiking. This wasn't through choice, we were actually forced into it by the teachers. At that time a good proportion of boys viewed washing as somewhat effeminate.

So I was clean and my dress was subdued when I met Chrissie in the nightclub. It was week two of the holiday so the love bites had faded and with them Jane's hold over me. Chrissie was with the party of Scots girls who were sharing our hotel. She was dark, very, very pretty and had a real sparkle to her. I'd regarded someone from five miles away as exotic, she with her clean Aberdonian vowels and non biker-ish way of dressing seemed like a beautiful alien. I think part of the reason for me trying to be a biker was that I wasn't very confident of my looks. This is a surprise because I was better looking then than at any time in my life. I still have a bus pass photo from that era and I can't believe it's only me who would see the resemblance to the young Jim Morrison. Well, perhaps it is.

I allied myself with a youth cult that despises beauty and celebrates ugliness – have you seen Motörhead? – because I thought women from that cult saw how shallow it was to value looks and that I'd have a chance.

Chrissie looked recognisably 1980s: baggy trousers tapered at the ankle, short hair with a big bow in it. I recall her wearing a polka dot scarf, but I might be wrong about that. Jane dressed much more seventies, like a Status Quo groupie. In fact, Status Quo's groupies probably didn't dress like that. Jane dressed more like Status Quo themselves in her faded jeans and denim jacket.

Normally I'd have been too frightened to talk to her but, trailing behind a couple of friends, talk to her I did. There were a number of girls and I found myself in competition for Chrissie with only one other boy. This isn't because she was the least attractive, far from it. It's just that the seating arrangements dictated who we could speak to. If another boy had wanted to talk to her he would have had to move, which would have shown her that he fancied her, which would have blown his chances, he would have thought.

We did have boys who would have been bold enough to make their intentions plain, but relatively few at that age. Luckily no one like that was with us.

So I was up against Jeremy Hall. Jeremy was in several lessons with me and was notable for being more unpopular in his day to day school life than I was, though it was a close run thing.

I think he was one of those boys whose parents gave him too much praise: he never had any sense that anything he ever said would ever meet with disapproval. From hissing 'Sir, Sir, Sir!' like a steam train in lessons to attract the teacher's attention to trying and failing to enlist interest in bullying others – presumably to deflect attention from himself – Jeremy made every mistake possible.

He'd got himself a job somewhere – he had actually officially left school but, because we didn't have to sign on for the sixth form for another few weeks, he was allowed on the trip – and he was very, very proud of it.

He had already alienated many of the boys on the holiday by rabbiting on about the job, how school was for kids (well, yeah) and how much he was going to be paid. I can see him now, sitting back in his chair like a northern industrialist and saying 'Thirty pounds a week', in deep satisfaction. 'Forty hours a week for not even double the dole,' was my thought.

I've never showed any sophistication in picking up a girl before or since, but I did that night. When Chrissie went away to the loo Jeremy collared me.

'I'm in here, Spaz,' he said, 'what do you think I should say next?'

My level in the school pecking order can be deduced from the fact he didn't even consider me a rival. Why he wanted my advice, then, I don't know.

'Well, you could always tell her about your job, Jez,' I said, 'you know women like to feel secure.'

So when Chrissie returned Jeremy did go on about his job and about how he'd have a Ford Escort by the time he was nineteen, and maybe even his own home by the time he was twenty-five. Gratifyingly, I saw her eyes go to the ceiling at certain points and then to me.

When Jeremy went to the loo – which took a while because we were all holding on as long as we could because we couldn't believe you had to pay to go – I just went for it, although I didn't actually know how you were meant to go for it – Jane, after all, had pounced on me. A lot of men have a line they use for this sort of thing and I certainly developed a couple later. Back then, though, Chrissie looked at me, I looked at her and it just happened.

When we were children we would often speculate what kissing someone is like. I suppose the obvious answer is that it's always different. It's influenced by temperament – some people seem to go at it with an excess of teeth, lacerating lips, chewing on the cheeks, some go at it like a convalescent camel might attempt to poke out the stone of a date with its tongue before swallowing it. To some it seems a great pleasure in itself, to others a rather annoying formality that needs to be overcome before getting down to the real business. It's also influenced by bone structure. Some women seem narrow and constricted, it's like trying to get your tongue into the top of a pen, the faces of others seem almost like inflatables, as if you're pressing your lips into a water wing. There is skin texture and perfume, eyes open or closed – a combination being favourite – and, crucially, angle of head.

The human body has its preferred ways of arranging itself – just try sitting on a sofa with your knees curled to one side and then placing them to the other side. It feels weird and unnatural. Similarly, the head has its preferred orientations, left or right, up or down. When this is compatible with your partner's preferred then it's fine, when it's not someone risks losing a contact lens with a nose in the eye.

Still, this is the exciting bit, the accommodation and adjustments you need to make to be comfortable with a new partner. It's often imagined that men dislike the preliminaries of sex and are all baying to get on to the main event. I don't think this is true at all. I could have sat there kissing Chrissie for hours, enjoying it for itself with no immediate thought of progression. In fact, I think, I did.

When Hall returned from paying his Schilling to the purse-rattling waiter at the loo, he was incandescent. Not only had he been usurped but he'd paid for the privilege.

He was utterly furious with me. When I recall it I see him sitting an inch from us, the top of his head loose and rattling like a lid above the boiling pot of his brain.

It became popular in the 1980s for feminists to discuss how men objectify women, discount their personalities and treat them as possessions. I have to say, they had a point. To Hall's way of thinking – and to all of us – what Chrissie wanted was entirely irrelevant. The only reason Hall was not tickling her fillings at that moment was that I had jumped in when his back was turned. The fact that Chrissie didn't fancy him would never have occurred to him. It was as if he'd left his packed lunch on the table and come back to find I'd eaten it – Chrissie had no more say in the affair than would the contents of his Tupperware.

I'd be lying if I didn't say that stealing Chrissie from under Hall's nose didn't make the experience all the more enjoyable. It's like at sport, I always prefer to play bad losers. Seeing someone storm off the pitch or start arguing with team mates adds a little tingle of pleasure to any victory.

It may appear distasteful to compare these amorous encounters to sport. However, to young boys and even to men, that's how it feels. It doesn't *just* feel like that, of course. There are other elements to it, the softer sentiments, but at this early stage of a relationship a man isn't looking at a woman as a soul mate or even, in most cases, as a human being. All that comes later. In that first instance he sees courtship as a competition, first against himself, then against her and then against other men. This is why the language of love – which has been written largely by men – is full of 'conquests' and 'winning' the woman.

All the elements you face in a real sporting contest – self-doubt, fear of the quality of the opponent, fear of the emotional crash of losing, excitement at the prospect of winning – are all there. There's also its effect on other men, who certainly regard your ability to attract a woman as akin to a game.

I was never any good at sport at school. A combination of being a slow developer, the youngest in my year and having the sort of central nervous system that was phased out with the brontosaurus saw to that. I was always mildly resentful that otherwise socially inept individuals who happened to be able to run the length of a rugby field quickly – just running the length of a rugby field would have been the extent of my ambition, never mind quickly – had a charmed passage through school. Everything they said was funny, what they wore was great, stories about their deeds and their brilliant repartee abounded. 'And then he turned to the man giving him the prize and said "Thank you". Just like that. Great eh?'

'Getting off' with Chrissie saw an instant, if temporary, promotion for me into this world. Suddenly I was OK, one of the chosen. A day later I would actually hear the story of our night out – several of the other boys copped off too – related back to me in awestruck terms.

Hall boiled, but there was nothing he could do. He wasn't the fighting sort and, even if he had been, he would have had to expose himself to Chrissie's scorn by thumping me. This wouldn't have stopped some boys, but it stopped him. It didn't prevent him trying to take his revenge though.

A notable member of the school rugby team was Alan Myers. Alan was another of those boys who had gone directly from being ten to being thirty-two with no apparent intervening period. He was enormous and frightening and came from a family of notoriously tough brothers. He also suffered badly with spots. I had a bar of Clearasil soap and, the day before, he'd asked if he could borrow it. If Alan Myers asked to borrow something from you then it well behoved you to lend it. I'd given up hope of ever seeing the soap again, but was sanguine about it, this is the school weed's life. However, the afternoon after Chrissie and I had got together, Alan came back in to return the soap, apologising that he'd forgotten to bring it back after he'd used it the night before.

Jeremy Hall had just returned from the shower and was laying things out on his bed. One piece of information had passed me by, thank the Lord. If someone had told me that Alan had earmarked Chrissie as the girl he would try to seduce that evening I don't think I could have stayed in Switzerland. I'd have run for the French border and seen if any safe houses were still operating from which I could be smuggled home. The information had not passed Hall by.

'Al,' he said, as the looming Myers went to pass me my soap, 'Spaz got off with Chrissie last night.' Alan seemed to freeze, that immobile pose – an English classic really – that could be photographed, framed and hung on a wall to the title 'Hard man hearing news of a diabolical liberty'. The interesting thing about people like Al is that, when something displeases them, their countenance hardly changes at all. The jaw may tighten, the eyes may narrow, but only by imperceptible margins. It's the world around them that changes. Things seem to totter, as if on the edge of a pit, the air departs, noise creeps away.

What he did next absolutely amazed me. He crushed the bar of soap in his hand. I have tried this on a number of occasions since and I can't even make an impression on it. He then – again with that spooky flat expression – stepped forward, took a hunk of my hair at the back of my head, drove the soap into my face and rubbed it in as hard as he could – which was hard, believe me – until I resembled a lady in a face pack.

Hall could not contain himself. He was in hysterics, lying on the bed writhing out his squealing laugh.

What he couldn't have known was that waves of relief were crashing down on me. If that's all I was going to suffer then that was fine by me. I could wash the soap off. I had seen what Alan Myers had to hand out in a scrap and I did not want some of it.

When he had finished wiping the last of the soap off his hands onto my T-shirt Alan went out onto the balcony.

'Chrissie! Chrissie!' he shouted up. Chrissie came to her balcony and looked down. At least I presume she did because I heard her reply.

'I hear you're going out with Spaz here.' I'd introduced myself by my nickname. She was going to find out anyway and you may as well make out you're in on the joke.

'Yes,' she said. That felt good. I was going out with two girls. 'Just how cool am I?' I wondered as I looked at my soap-ingrained face in the mirror. I didn't want to start washing it off until Al had gone because I thought that might make him angry.

Alan, who was years ahead of me in confidence, went on.

'You wouldn't prefer to go out with me?'

'Er . . .' I think Chrissie was suddenly alive to the peril she may have been placing me in.

'Go on, you won't get him into trouble if you say no.' These were the harsh realities we were dealing in. The only thing keeping me in or out of trouble was Al's say so. I felt no sense of injustice. To complain about it would have been like complaining about the weather – it might have made me feel better, but it wasn't going to change anything.

'No then.'

'Right,' said Al, 'that's OK. We know where we stand.'

He turned and came back into the room. I actually felt

my knees go as I saw his face. Al was scary enough when he looked impassive. Angry, he was truly terrifying. In fact it wasn't quite anger, it was a sort of cross between rage and incomprehension, as if each of those emotions was fighting for expression-time on his face.

I think he was grappling with one of the strange adjustments boys are forced to make when they start to go out with girls. The old certainties that have served them so well all the way through school will no longer do. The fact that you're captain of sports, have your school colours, that all the other boys respect and fear you and that you've always been top dog in every way suddenly counts for nothing. It's the first sliver of an idea that you may be going to a destiny other than the one you had envisaged and that in future, you will be playing by different rules. Sure, there are girls that will be impressed by sporting prowess or even some by your skill in a scrap but they might not be the girls you want. Those may be more interested in whether you're good looking or not or whether you can make them laugh. In later life this can cause resentment. The sports Billies think it unfair that dorks should be allowed to walk around with beautiful women. Hard luck, sports Billies.

Myers addressed the room.

'He,' he said, pointing at me, 'has pissed me off. I fancied that girl. However, he's made an honest mistake and I bear no grudge. At least he's not a fucking grass.'

I think it was at that point that Hall's giggling abruptly stopped. Unfortunately for him he was still bare-chested, which is what may have given Al the idea. It could just have been that Hall's belt was the first thing that came to hand. Anyway, Myers went for Hall like the Marquis of Queensberry after a tardy hound, gave him a sound whipping and that was the last I heard from either of them on the subject of Chrissie.

It's no wonder that, against all this, things felt intense. Holiday romances are intense anyway, when you're a teenager you're intense, first love – and that's what it felt like – is intense. Each day when we climbed an Alp – or a bit of one – I felt as though I'd been torn from her, each evening when we met it felt as though we were stealing moments from eternity. (I wrote that in my diary at the time. Sorry.) When I glimpsed her heading to her day-trip bus in the morning I felt like Dr Zhivago glimpsing Lara on the tram.

In between snogging in the carpark, we talked about how we would overcome the 400-mile distance between us when we got home. I think that one of the teachers – an avuncular Welshman – became convinced that I had some magical effect on women. He'd noticed my love bites at the start of the holiday and commented on them when I got on the bus.

'What happened to you?' he said.

'I walked into a door,' I said, having picked up on Jane's habit of offering unlikely explanations with a cheeky twinkle.

'Both sides?' he said.

'It was a revolving door,' I said.

Now he stumbled on me kissing in the carpark.

'Christ, boy, you can't leave it alone, can you?' he said, as I unfastened myself from Chrissie's face to say 'Good evening, Sir.'

Neither Chrissie nor I thought that the relationship was doomed, as it was sure to be. I said I could get the train fare to see her. It was £40, it later turned out, over a week's wages for the enjobbed like Hall, weeks of pocket money and abstinence for me. She, however, had an uncle who lived in Coventry and said she could get down to see me. It seemed possible.

Where did Jane fit in, in all this? I didn't know. It had never occurred to me even for a second to be faithful to her.

That didn't mean that I wasn't serious about her, just that I lacked – and would continue to lack for years – the maturity to see what faithfulness was for. The only question in my mind was 'Is Jane likely to find out?' The answer was clearly 'No'. Even if she had been likely to find out, then I don't think it would have bothered me. I could envisage the future as pictures – me and Chrissie living in Aberdeen together, or going out at night with all her classmates who seemed to me to be the most tremendous hoot, but I couldn't envisage it as a series of related events that might actually occur, like Jane finding out, then crying, then leaving me.

I'm sure this is a condition that affects many people. The standard complaint of the betrayed is 'How could you do this to me?', but it doesn't feel as if you're doing something to anyone other than the person in front of you at the time. I had the classic conviction of the cheat – that in some undefined way everything was going to sort itself out and be all right.

Of course, in the event the worst thing possible happened – everything did sort itself out and it was all right. That, I thought, was the way it was always going to be.

4   TO THE DEVIL A DAUGHTER

Jane finished with me two weeks after I got home. She hadn't seemed all that fussed about seeing me when I'd returned from Switzerland, and I wasn't all that concerned about seeing her. I think she said she was going on holiday herself, which was code for 'I'm trying out another boyfriend'.

There was something about Jane that had made me uncomfortable and, at the time, I didn't know what it was. Looking back I can identify it clearly. I was beginning to have an idea of the sort of girl I wanted. In 1980 I would have said someone more like Chrissie. Now I can see that I wanted someone who, like me, was destined for the middle class, A levels, university and whatever happened after that. I was never too clear on what you were meant to do when you finished education. A job was clearly out of the question, so I guess I thought I'd just work things out when I got there.

Jane was from the same working-class background as me, but – or so I assumed at the time – likely to stay there. For all I know, of course, she may have gone to university eventually and followed the same route I did, but back then it seemed she was going to remain in the culture she grew up in. Of course, I didn't actually think any of this, it's just my later interpretation of my motives at that time. I didn't have any ambitions, as such, beyond getting a motorbike, so I wonder what, exactly, I was after. I had no vision of myself with a job, that's for sure, or a desire to have a flashy car or expensive clothes or anything like that. So in what sense do I mean I wanted to be middle class? I think culturally. For all Jane's joking that we were 'reading poetry', that was the sort of thing I wanted to do.

I wish I hadn't felt like that and I wish that I didn't feel like that now, but it's an uncomfortable truth about my psychological make up. Girls of my own class and background are OK to go out with. I'd only be interested long term, though, if they were looking to escape that class and background. I can no more excuse this attitude than I can change it.

In the short term I was too busy thinking about Chrissie to worry much about Jane, writing her letters and making abortive phone calls to her. I tried to call her from the city centre from a phone box, but we only got a minute and a half into the conversation before it had eaten my money. Back then the pips would go when the phone was running out of cash. On long-distance calls this would happen about once every ten seconds so the conversation would go:

'How are you?'

'I'm missing bleep bleep bleep'.

'What?'

'I said I'm missing bleep bleep bleep.'

'I can't hear you, the pips keep bleep bleep bleep.'

'I love you!'

'I bleep you bleep too.'

No more money. I'd have to see if I could put aside a pound next week to repeat the experience.

I'd asked my mum if I could take on the Bolivian national debt, remortgage our home and sell my brothers into slavery, but she had said no. Of course I didn't really ask these things, I asked to phone Chrissie in Aberdeen, but that was what my mum heard.

In 1980 long-distance calls were simply not made by the

likes of us. My mum would allow me a minute once a fortnight. Now I can see it from her point of view. Calls were expensive back then, we weren't made of money and she didn't feel like paying a week's grocery money for me to sit mooning on the phone to a girl I was bound to break up from anyway.

The second reason was that I'd met another girl. At the time I believed it was always going to be that easy.

This girl was the utterly beautiful, bewitching rock goddess Debbie. When heavy-metal lyricists slaver, and slaver they do, over women, when they say 'Seventeen, dat girl a nature's queen, oh brother, know what ah mean?', it is to women like Debbie they are referring.

I can remember my father's reaction to meeting her. He had seen the girl from up the shops, he had met Jane who was pretty but unlikely to stop traffic. Debbie elicited a 'Good God!' the first time he saw her.

'Enjoy it while it lasts, is my advice to you,' he said. The implication was clear. I had scored well out of my class.

Debbie was small and dark, but really was the kind of girl who could have gone unmade-up straight onto a rock album cover. Not that they'd have let her go on to a rock album cover without make-up, but there you are.

She had a terrific figure, which you could see even under her leather jacket and cut off, curvy but not too curvy, slim but not thin. It was her face though that was her crowning glory, framed by her sable curls. She had nothing short of an angelic quality to her – not model-type good looks, severe and angular, but cherubic and almost heart breaking.

She would make old men cry and curse their years, braggarts tremble, gigolos blush and avowed atheists throw away the Darwin and declare that such as she could only have been made by God. At the time I thought she was beautiful and, in a way, she was. Beauty though, I think, belongs to older women, not teenagers. A better description might be incandescently pretty. What in the name of the living Christ she was doing with me I really don't know.

The living Christ is an apt deity to question here. Debbie's father was a charismatic preacher in an evangelical church, the sort that involves you flinging yourself at the altar and declaring your faith in a very unEnglish way.

Debbie had been stifled by her upbringing, had developed a Meatloaf obsession ('Bat out of Hell', you see. That'll show you Dad!) and become a bikerette, much to the delight of bikers everywhere and, in particular, bikeless bikers like me. I said at the start that I didn't know what she saw in me, but I think it could have been that I was dripping in Satanist regalia.

Having given my earlier explanation of how I was looking for a girl with whom to leaf through the TS Eliot, buy a clapped-out Volvo and eventually set up an organic bee farm near Exeter, then I must add a caveat. Things seem a little different when confronted by ship-launching good looks. The unidentifiable disquiet I'd felt with Jane was nowhere, despite the fact that Debbie had left school without any exam passes and worked in a cake shop, where she intended to stay until pregnancy or death intervened.

Jane called to say she didn't want to see me any more and I said 'Fine'. I didn't feel at all dumped even though, reading between the lines, she'd met someone else. It didn't occur to me then that this was any sort of comment on me. I was more psychologically stable at sixteen than I'd prove to be for the rest of my life.

The incredible thing about going out with Debbie, though, was the effect it had on other boys. I very rarely encountered jealousy, more a sort of 'hats off!' respect. That's not to say I didn't encounter jealousy and, when I did, it felt wonderful.

I bumped into one of my classmates when I was on my way into town with her. Pete was a terrible materialist, an only one who had formed a mutual admiration society with his own dad, Pete Senior. I can well remember him going through all the things his plumber father had bought him for Christmas when we'd been at school and comparing my gifts unfavourably to his. British people divide into two camps – those who would love a personalised number plate and those who wouldn't have one if you paid them. Pete Dawson was firmly in the former camp. Pete would sneer at me for going on holiday to Norfolk when he, so much richer, went to the Canary Isles. I wish I'd known at the time that the Queen goes on holiday to Norfolk. Don't look for her scrapping with the Germans for a sun-lounger in Fuerteventura, though.

Pete had his first girlfriend early, and at fourteen was very fond of describing the exact sexual favours she allowed him. On the bus down town one Saturday night I met him with her. She was as plain as porridge. That sort of thing doesn't really matter, of course, and she may have been a wonderful person, but who are we kidding? Debbie and I sat down in front of him and I said Hello. He looked as though he'd been punched.

'Is this your sister?' he said.

'No, it's my girlfriend Debbie,' I said.

Pete went quiet after that. I could tell he would have liked to have laid into me, but, awed by Debbie's attractiveness, he kept his mouth shut. At school on the Monday he made his feelings clear.

'How can a girl like that go out with a twat like you?' he said. He was right. Who was I? A disaster at sports, hugely uncool throughout most of my school life and still uncool despite being into the then-popular heavy rock because I overdid things, a scardey cat when it came to fighting, spoddily clever in a Mr Logic sort of way, greasy and vile, who was I? My dad had never even given me a mini motorbike or bought me a ride in a helicopter or taken me on holiday to the Mediterranean. Who *the fuck* was I? I was the kid who was going out with the gorgeous Debbie, that's who, and so better than him in every way. For a boy of that age, and much after, nothing trumps a beautiful girlfriend, nothing. Pete had lost, utterly, and on his own terms as well. After five years of putting up with his showboating, I think I was allowed to gloat.

He finished with his own girlfriend a week later. I think she got off lightly.

It didn't last much longer with me and Debbie. To me, Heavy Rock was the preserve of intellectual sorts who disdained the uncomplicated banalities of pop and punk in favour of the delicious intricacies of forty-five-minute drum solos. However, in large parts it was still the preserve of blokes who had 'Kev' tattooed on their knuckles and who were drawn to it for the image of toughness it still conveyed at that point. These were the sort who were Debbie's friends, the sort who invited you to come 'on the rob' with them and who spotted me for the fake I was.

Debbie and I didn't talk much. We hung around with her girlfriend Sue in what Al Myers referred to as a 'beauty and the beast' combination. Her friend looked like a much spottier version of John Lennon. Her similarity to the Beatle didn't stop there. She was funny and bright and a good pianist. In fact, I would have much preferred to have gone out with her, but funny, bright and talented lose out every time to good looking, especially when you're sixteen. My seeing Sue wouldn't have left Pete staring hollowly at his father's swimming pool, clacking forlornly at the balls in his snooker room, taking disconsolate swings on the driving range; in fact he would have thought funny, bright and talented were the sort of consolation prizes I was going to have to put up with for the rest of my life.

Debbie's good looks helped me ignore the fact that we were fundamentally unsuited. She was a quiet, straightforward girl who accepted life as it came to her, apart from the oppressions of her family. I'd grown up in a very liberal family – that's not liberal as in 'We choose to be like this because it's cool and have a "Nuclear Power Nein Danke" sign on our car', but liberal as in making despairing attempts at being disciplinarian but failing to make any rule stick for more than ten minutes and so giving up. To me it was intolerable that her dad thought he had the right to tell her what to do. However, I saw the value in pleasing him in small ways – being back on time, being polite, tidying myself up for my visits and appearing to take what he said about God seriously – in order to get him off our backs for ten minutes so I could sleep with his daughter. Not that I ever did.

We stayed together until the half-term holiday, which seemed a long time, but I couldn't have gone out with her for more than a couple of months. Still, it was exciting while it lasted. Sex was played for enormously high stakes, or so it felt. She had one record – 'Bat Out Of Hell' – which we played again and again with half an eye on the door for her dad to descend on us like the Lord upon Gomorrah, which he was wont to try to do. It was slightly preposterous – I don't mean that he kept coming into the room some time between every three and every seven minutes, or that he didn't even attempt to disguise what he was doing, just saying he was 'seeing everything was going smoothly', but that under those circumstances we still attempted to have sex. Obviously we were limited to anything that could be done fully clothed, hands had to be withdrawn from jeans and beneath blouses in a snap when we heard his tread approaching the door, but we still got by OK. I don't know why her dad didn't simply forbid us to go to the back room, or make us have the door open. I think there may have been some tension between him and her mother on the subject of how much privacy Debbie should be allowed and so they came to a ludicrous compromise that saw him hopping in and out of the room.

The end came one Friday night when she was visiting. We were up in my room on the bed. Some readers of this book may think by the end of it that I've slept with a lot of women. Some will think that I've hardly slept with any at all. One thing, though, is indisputable. The number of women I've failed to sleep with is truly staggering. In fact there have been situations when by far the easiest thing to do would have been to have sex. I wanted it, the girl wanted it and still I have contrived to avoid it by a variety of inventive and subtle methods known only to the very biggest idiots in the land.

Debbie definitely wanted us to have sex. I infer this from her statements such as 'Come on, let's do it' as she sat naked from the waist up on my bed with her hand down my trousers. It was just that she was so good looking that I assumed she wouldn't, no matter what she said. I think I was a bit scared too. Unfortunately I had a Dungeons-and-Dragons-influenced view of women back then, one that implied working up through the levels. So I'd started with the girl in the sticking plaster skirt from the shops, worked up to Jane, then Chrissie, now Debbie. The problem, in gaming terms, was that I was a third-level boyfriend whereas Debbie was a fiftieth-level girl. I was intimidated by her beauty even when she was taking off her jeans and getting into my bed.

Also, it was the night of the Heavy Rock disco at the Lanchester Polytechnic in town. It was seven o'clock and we had to be there by half past.

'Do you want to go down this disco or not?' shouted my mum up the stairs. My dad was to give us a lift, one that my mother was keen he give us soon in order to forestall my chances of having sex. I don't know why mothers don't want their sons to have sex. I think it's something more than a fear of early pregnancy. Maybe it's a desire to hang on to their childhood. Whatever, my mum didn't make it easy for us and very often found questions she needed to ask me that would necessitate her coming into my room, but she did leave us alone more than Debbie's dad.

Debbie took my penis out of my trousers and began to stroke it while keeping full eye contact with me. It was quite literally the stuff dreams are made of, and was the subject of many of my dreams for a good few years thereafter. It was too much like a dream, though. I wasn't up to the reality.

'Yeah!' I said, 'we'll be down in a second.' I apologised to Debbie and said that we'd have to go because I knew she'd really enjoy it. She was understandably a bit annoyed, but went down there anyway. I didn't know it would be my last night with her, but it wouldn't have made that much of a difference to the way I behaved anyway. I wanted to have sex with her, for sure, but I wanted to be seen with her more.

I said earlier on that it wasn't primarily sex that I was looking for in women. It was self-esteem. At the Lanch disco, buying Debbie a drink, introducing her to my friends, I felt on top of the world. Nothing, I thought, could touch me. Then she dumped me.

5   BLIND ME DATE

Debbie left because we had nothing in common, I'd refused to have sex with her and then shown her off like she was a flashy car to all my friends. No reason at all, in other words. Some women would regard that as grounds for marriage.

Of course she didn't say this, she just said she didn't want to see me any more, that I lived too far away. A few months later I heard she was pregnant by a Hells Angel, which must have pleased her dad. It might not be true, though – rumours breed freely in teenage mouths.

I put on Black Sabbath's awful 'Changes' song and sat enjoying a new sensation – basking in the misery. I really did relax into the experience of it, feeling very adult to be mildly upset over a girl and actually pleased that the song now meant something to me on a deeper level.

At that time in my life I saw myself as living in a story, one that I was sure would have a happy end. In fact most of what I was doing at that point was just 'early days' material that I'd use in interviews when I made it big in a band. My friends conspired in this. The most trivial incidents would be built up into stories, as we sought to mythologise our lives. Anything would do, an incident where one of us was slightly cheeky to a shopkeeper, for instance, would be retold time and again: 'And he said, "Can I see some ID?" and I said "I'm in MI5, of course you fucking can't."'

This isn't a verbatim quote – I'm not even sure that 'ID'

had arrived in England at that point, but it's very much the sort of thing that was said. It was as if my life was an under-attended party and I was the host, desperately trying to jolly everything along into a memorable time.

I think I felt briefly sad when Debbie left and did think of trying to get her back. I took a handful of Prellies a chap we'd met at a pub had given me – these were the same slimming pills the Beatles had favoured in Hamburg – and, awake at five in the morning, considered inviting Debbie and her friend to start a sex magic cult with me. Luckily the appeal of the idea had faded by the next day.

I had no insecurity about meeting anyone else and felt sure that I would hook up with another girl very soon. This is very far from the feeling that would begin to dominate the next twenty years of my life – that I was unworthy of having a girlfriend and that I had to cling on to anyone who came my way or I faced a life alone.

I did want to find a girlfriend quick, though. My sexual courage returned as the threat of actually having to have sex receded and I was keen to make up for what I had missed with Debbie.

So it was that I went on the blind date from hell, organised by a friend's girlfriend. She had already sorted out one of my friends with a blind date – John was introduced to Patsy this way. I think that one can be termed a success, as they are now married with two children after over twenty-five years together. Patsy was very pretty, I thought, and I couldn't wait to see who I'd be introduced to.

I was very disappointed to meet a girl I didn't fancy at all, but nowhere near as disappointed as she clearly was. I'd been told to dress smart as that was what the girl was like. The trouble was that I had no smart clothes at all and so had to borrow them off my dad.

My dad worked in a factory and almost never went out in the evening so he hadn't bought anything new in ten years – the ten years between the big-collared seventies and the angular designs of 1980. Accordingly I turned up in a large-flower-patterned shirt, flares and shoes that didn't fit me. I was crippled with pain, but the shoes were smart – 1960s slip-ons.

We were introduced and, as I hobbled forward like a psychedelic Quasimodo, I recall her saying something like 'awwww!' and looking to the heavens.

The fact that I didn't fancy her even slightly, and she plainly didn't fancy me, in no way prevented me from trying to get off with her. Why would it? I think my subconscious had a very clear understanding of odds at that age, a view of male-female relationships in almost commercial terms. Yes I hoped long term for a very different sort of girlfriend – one not wearing head to toe burgundy would have been a start – but the burgundy girl was in front of me, had expressed an interest in me (or at least had one expressed for her) and so qualified as 'female most likely to' for the evening. I was in no way deterred that the second she saw me she took on the expression of a houseproud mum walking into a student flat, nor that I didn't actually want anything to do with her. She was there, she was a girl and potentially available. I had no idea that there was any other way to respond. In the computer language of my brain the program was written: IF GIRL = THERE then GO FOR IT.

The beginning of our encounter went badly. Compared to what happened in the rest of the evening, though, the first meeting could be regarded as a giddy success. I term what followed my 'Taxi Driver' moment, as in the Robert De Niro film of the same name.

We had decided to go and see whatever the popular film

was at the time – *Kramer vs Kramer* maybe. Unfortunately that was full. No problem, we were at Coventry's Theatre One, an early take on the multiplex. So we went to see a film that had just come out. I chose it because it appeared to be a historical epic and I wanted to reassure this girl she was with an intellectual. I know, I can see the error of my ways now. Here's a little slice of the film's blurb.

> CALIGULA *may very well be the most controversial film in history. Only one movie dares to show the perversion behind Imperial Rome. Not for the squeamish, not for the prudish, Caligula will shock and arouse you as it reveals the deviance and decadence beneath the surface of the grandeur that once was Rome.*

Critics at the time were briefer: 'unadulterated wacko porn', summed up the tenor of most reviews. It remains among the most pretentious and least likeable films featuring dwarf sex I have ever seen. The scene where Caligula's sister buys him a slave with a 12-inch penis to sodomise him for his birth-day made me take a very different view of being bought an inappropriate sweater. I tried to crack a joke with my blind date:

'Oh no, my sister's bought me a bloke to bugger me. I didn't want buggering, I wanted a record. Never mind, I'm going to have to let him bugger me anyway or she'll be upset.'

'Shhh!' said someone behind us.

Obviously they were enjoying it.

The girl just leaned even further away from me than she was leaning already, which was far. Still, it was an education. The idea of fisting hadn't even occurred to me as possible before I saw that movie and certainly not as a form of rape on a bridegroom on the day of his wedding.

The film really is remarkable in that it manages to feature nearly three hours – that's right, it's nearly as long as *The Godfather* – of wall-to-wall depraved porn without once becoming even mildly titillating *to a sixteen-year-old boy*. That takes more than talent, it's virtually scientifically impossible and deserves investigation by our finest minds. Even my classmate Pete, he of the rich (Coventry-rich) dad and appalling taste, complained that the only bit worth watching was the extended lesbian scene just after the interval.

I'd forgotten that. That film contained an interval. Why we stayed I really can't say. I think it's that teenage thing – we'd paid to get in so we were going to get our money's worth. It reflected the date as a whole, we'd started so we'd finish.

The burgundy girl and I laboured through *Caligula* and caught the bus home together. She explained how very hard her brother was and I sat itching to get out of my dad's shirt. Then, two stops before I had to get off, we had a snog. I cannot explain it. She definitely didn't fancy me, I didn't fancy her. What was going on? I think it was just so that we could both get out of the date with some dignity. We'd had a snog and so we were both attractive, official, if not to each other.

It was the same when I met a girl at my Venture Scouts – Squirrel. I was attracted to rock climbing, despite being very scruffy and nominally anti-monarchy. We spent the evening snogging at her birthday party, something that continued even when her parents got home. My flesh crawled as her tongue explored my cavities while her mother poured herself a cherry brandy and asked if we'd enjoyed the night. Squirrel appeared to regard it as normal. I was surprised when I found out she wasn't interested in going out with me. Why had she spent the best part of two hours kissing me then? I wasn't sophisticated enough to realise that sometimes a girl is prepared to spend two hours kissing someone who she would never consider as a partner.

However, in the lower sixth form, I regarded my love life as a desert. Approaching seventeen, it felt like a long time since the golden period less than twelve months before when I could do no wrong. I didn't know I was about to begin my first serious relationship.

6 SERIOUS

The parties at the Polish Club in town began. These were typical of the period, where discos played the basic after-wedding fare with a little of something for everyone: one punk record (normally 'Teenage Kicks'), one Heavy Metal (we used to ask for 'Freebird' – twenty-three minutes long and inevitably truncated by the gulping DJ after three), lots of chart stuff, 'Oops Up Side Your Head' with everyone doing the rowing boat and 'Hi Ho Silver Lining' to finish, arms on shoulders, cancanning in a ring.

Blond wedge haircuts shook back and forth like miniature show dogs perched on the burgundy or pastel platform of the shoulders, white socks flashed from above moccasins, and half-sovereign rings adorned fingers. Unless you were me, of course, when you dressed as a cross between a Hells Angel and Coco the Clown.

It was the end of the disco and I was indulging in the time-honoured teenage fashion of swiping any drinks that had been left in order to become as plastered as possible.

I didn't really notice her. I just saw a table with more drinks than people at it and so I made towards that. Clumsiness is often seen as a burden, but sometimes it can bring a reward. As I zoomed in on the drinks, afraid that some other roving nerk would get his hands on them first, I tripped over something and fell almost directly into a seat right next to Sarah and her friends.

It was obvious I'd fallen, but I decided to make the best of a bad job.

'Sorry to drop in on you,' I said, 'the name's Barrowcliffe, Mark Barrowcliffe.' I then deliberately fell off the seat. It wasn't exactly Omar Sharif, but it had the desired comic effect and Sarah laughed.

She was a goodlooking girl, dressed in the Top Shop smart of the time, fashionable without submitting to gimmicks like the rah-rah skirt, which I think was just coming in. Normally I wouldn't have thought I would have had a chance with her.

I can't remember what was said between us, some sort of amiable goofing on my behalf I think, but I did establish that she went to the all-girls counterpart to my own school, Tile Hill Wood, and that she was in the sixth form. I was entirely unself-conscious, mainly because I hadn't been intending to chat her up when I went over there, so it didn't occur to me to try.

All the mistakes I might have made, the ones I would make with lots of other women and would eventually make with her – talking solely about myself being the number one killer – I avoided. I did drop into the other trap that so often awaits a man – that of behaving like the girl's personal stand-up comedian – but Sarah was young enough that it was still fresh to her.

She had a friend with her who I found pretty too. I was surprised to learn she was the sister of one of the boys in my sixth form, a studious lad who I didn't like because he was a 'smoothie'. Whether he had any idea he was a smoothie, I don't know, but he didn't belong to any recognisable youth cult and he washed, so this marked him out as a sort of wannabe Radio 1 DJ in my mind.

Boys – and for all I know girls too – make a calculation

in instances like this and don't always go for the one they fancy the most. In fact, they sometimes go for the one they fancy the least if they think they have a better chance of success with them.

If I picture this scene in my head, I actually get the shivers. I was an oafish boy and, although I could be funny, it was a lumbering, too pleased with itself wit. There I was gurning through my routines, pulling their legs, winking and teasing while they, well there's no other way of saying it, seemed to enjoy it.

Sarah's friend Philipa was a shy girl who, I think, had had little male attention before. I think this was one of the first discos she'd attended. I can still see her now, moving her head in that Princess Diana way, giggling and going red. It was all a bit sick, but none of us could see that then. It wouldn't have been surprising to have seen a latter-day Hogarth sketching away in the corner.

It was Sarah who I found most attractive, but I would have gone for her no matter what because she expressed the most open interest in me. Women can gain a lot by holding back, by making the man come to them, but not in every circumstance. When you're evenly matched in looks, and the boy is desperate – or sixteen, which is saying the same thing – then it's a case of getting your tray into the queue first.

Before I knew it, I had her number written on my hand and, in for a penny, leaned across the table and snogged her before she had to go for her dad to pick her up. Philipa sat blushing and twisting her hair as we kissed.

'What,' I thought, 'are the chances of me shagging both of them at the same time?'

This is a question that will enter the heads of all young men from time to time and, as a service, I here provide the answer: 'none'. At least for the vast majority of cases. If you know differently then . . . I can't think about that.

On another note, this says something about the nature of being male. I hadn't even had proper sex with one person yet, and yet there I was wondering if I could have it with two. I can't fault my ambition, just my sense of reality.

I walked home from the club on my own. Normally I would have walked with my friends, but I wanted to take plenty of breaks and to go slowly, to lower the risk of sweat making the biro number on my hand run. I must have resembled a Hindu pilgrim, soft shoeing at a snail's pace with one hand in the air.

I felt fantastic. A new and attractive girlfriend makes a man believe that everything about his life is right. All the doubts I had about the way I looked, the things I said, the views I held, evaporated. If I was wrong then I wouldn't have been able to get Sarah's number, would I?

I carefully transferred the number to a pad when I got home – in fact to one pad, one piece of paper and the inside of the *Yellow Pages*, just in case some freakish act of fate destroyed one of them. I preserved the writing on my hand anyway. It felt special. At that age I believed in fate, and the fact I'd met Sarah in the only five minutes of my teenage life when I hadn't been looking for a girl indicated to me that she could be the one.

I'd played the field, I thought, and was now ready to settle down. Playing the field, I knew, was an essential part of a young man's life. I'd also read, I don't know where, that the average number of sexual partners in a life was four. Whether the girls I'd met so far were actually sexual partners was open to debate, but not in my mind. I hadn't had sex in the Bill Clinton sense, but I had had it in the Mark Barrowcliffe sense.

I've since discovered that Bill Clinton's is also the sense in which many women use the word 'sex'. One of my girlfriends used to tell me she'd only had sex with about four people in her life. It then transpired that, if you included blow jobs, the number was nearer fifty. At the time I thought this was just her idiosyncratic take on the definition of 'sex'. Asking around, though, I've discovered it's a very common view among women.

I'd had three relationships in which sex had featured in some way, if only in my mind, and now this was my fourth, and so I could relax and make it the last and permanent one.

It was important to me to at least achieve the average in this department. Even as a pre-pubescent, when reading the sex education books my parents had given me, I'd been mortified in case I fell at the low end of 'average'. I remember one that said 'Sex can last anything from two minutes to two hours.' I took this absolutely literally. It was a source of some anxiety that my first sexual experiences with Jane had been so brief, certainly shorter than two minutes, shorter than two seconds actually. However, I'd concluded that the book might have been referring to the whole thing, from first kiss to cigarette, so I was in the clear and there was no need for a visit to the doctor's. But there again, I'd spent more than two hours kissing. Was that normal? Was it even medically advisable?

Mostly, though, the anxieties I had regarding sex were not great at this point in my life. Had I managed a full session of certified intercourse I wouldn't have had time to develop any worries about it. I'd have been too busy phoning the skywriter in order to let the folk of Coventry in on the good news.

At the time, I didn't know what I didn't know but, there

again, I've never really developed too much angst around the act itself. I'm not concerned that my performance will be up to it and I am arrogant enough to believe – sometimes very wrongly – that the woman will always enjoy it. When she doesn't enjoy it I assume it's her fault, even when it's obviously my fault. My fears, the ones that were to develop during my time with Sarah, centred on securing and retaining someone to have sex with and, more than that, to love me.

Sarah made me nervous and so we got off to a very good start because I was cautious and polite. My world at that age was still very small and, though her house was no more than a mile from mine, heading up the hill towards it felt as if I was entering a foreign country. I'd been into the big dip that led to her home, but never the two hundred yards up the hill. I actually wondered what might happen up there. I didn't exactly expect to see antelope and zebras, but I wouldn't have been entirely surprised if they'd appeared.

There were no exotic animals, though, just more of that anonymous 1960s housing we seem to love so dearly in England, pale yellow bricks, storm porches and a hollow look in the inhabitants' eyes that is a yearning for replacement windows. Stone cladding was the rage at the time and every third house seemed to have been encased in icing sugar biscuits like the witch's cottage in *Hansel and Gretel*.

I'd been careful about what I wore for this first visit. In the case of Jane and Chrissie this had meant that I'd tried to out-biker the bikers, making up for my lack of motorcycle by encasing myself in band logos and wearing my jeans with a beer towel sewn into them. Thank God I got the idea that this wasn't going to work with Sarah. I also realised by now that 'smart' wasn't just a category and that any shirt – floral with a large collar – or any trousers – flares with a go faster stripe – just wouldn't do. Accordingly, I wore the only smart shirt I had, one that I hadn't considered before – my Venture Scout uniform.

This isn't as bad as it sounds, though it is bad. I hadn't put any badges on the shirt just then and so it appeared as a rather oddly styled beige shirt to the untrained eye. I put on a pair of new jeans, much to my mother's relief, and polished up my Docs. Of course I still wore my tasselled leather jacket, but that was good quality and new. I looked like a nice lad going through a bit of a biker phase rather than someone who had fallen off a motorcycle, been concussed and had just emerged after three days in a ditch.

So there I was, normal, knocking on the front door at Sarah's house, not knowing that everyone always came in by the back. I was extremely wary, I have to say. Her brother Dave had been two years above me at school and, though a quiet sort, was definitely not to be crossed. Dave had beaten up Big Foot, a virtually Neanderthal youth in his own year. No one beat up Big Foot, he was known for throwing a couple of PE teachers over during one bait, yet Dave had, producing all seven shades if accounts were true.

'Hello,' he said, as I came in.

I'm in an unusual position with Dave. I know roughly the number of words he spoke to me across the whole time I knew him, almost exactly. I think I visited Sarah's house about two hundred times in the year I knew her. Dave said 'Hello' each time. Sarah and I inevitably sat in the back room, and I would leave just sticking my head around the door to say 'Goodbye'. Dave, though, did not reply to this on the whole, not wanting to look up from *Tenko*. So Dave said about two hundred words to me in all the time I was going out with his sister. Apart from one conversation, that is.

'Dave's going to Ibiza, aren't you?' said Sarah.

Dave puffed out his jowls slightly, like a beefy hamster who would prefer to be left alone so he could go back to his seeds.

'That must be interesting,' I said, 'I bet there's lots of things to see there. Spain has a fascinating history, in some ways as much African as European.'

'Dunno,' said Dave. 'Going on the piss.'

And that was it. Our only exchange. This makes it sound as if I think Dave was thick. He wasn't, I'm sure, it's just that he took one look at me, decided I was an idiot and that he didn't want to speak to me.

It was interesting to me to observe Dave's life back then. It seemed that he went to work, came home, watched the TV and went to bed. I found this odd. I had to be out every night, staying in was impossible, literally impossible. My head would feel as if it was buzzing unless I found something to do. I couldn't imagine watching an evening's TV other than at gunpoint.

I have no clue what Dave's politics and philosophies were, but he managed to convey that they were a way removed from mine by just looking at the telly as if he was going to hit it when I entered the room.

There may have been one other factor at play here. I don't think Dave was jealous of me at all, but I think my presence, and that of the friends I began to bring to his house with me, was a sort of reminder of a life he wasn't living at that point. With the benefit of hindsight, I think he might also have been a bit shy at that age. This thought would never have entered my head. Dave was tough, he was a good rugby player, of course he couldn't be shy. I have to say, I may be completely wrong here. I was so self-absorbed that Dave may have been the centre of a giddy social whirl, a sort of muscular Madame de Rambouillet figure hosting his latter-day salons, and I wouldn't have noticed.

The problem with long-term relationships when you're still living with your parents – you aren't just going out with your girlfriend or boyfriend, you're going out with their family too.

In Sarah's case this meant her dad – an Irish man who seemed to me absolutely enormous. When he'd been younger he'd been a very good hurling player. For those who don't know, hurling is the national sport of Ireland and appeals to people who find bare-knuckle boxing a little effete for their tastes. It's basically armed rugby, a cross between hockey and an uprising. Here's a taste of the rules, from Wikipedia.

'Players may be tackled but not struck by a one-handed slash of the stick; exceptions are two-handed jabs and strikes.'

'What's wrong with you, writhing about on the floor after a mere two-handed jab in the ribs with a stick wielded by a two-hundred-pound peat cutter? Get up and play like a man.'

In this game, the loss of an eyebrow, and the attendant flesh, is not deemed worthy of comment.

Sarah's dad was a very genial man, but he was also a devout Roman Catholic. He knew what boys wanted from girls and he was going to make bloody sure I didn't get it from his daughter. If Chrissie's dad had caught us at it, then I would have been banned from seeing her and she would have had to go to church every day for a month. If Sarah's father had caught us, I would have had to go to church once – for my funeral.

When I picture him now it's like a bigger, slimmer version of Tony Soprano and, to my teenage self, he had a similar mixture of charm and menace.

Sarah's mum seemed to me even tougher than her dad.

My parents weren't strict at all, but Sarah's mum managed to convey, without ever saying it, that her home ran to firm rules and I would do well to respect them. Which, of course, I didn't, but that all came later.

On that first meeting I was polite and deferential. Sarah and I were allowed to sit in the narrow back room, similar to a conservatory but actually part of the house.

Even though we'd kissed on our first date, I felt nervous about going for it again and so we talked, perched on separate seats a few feet apart. Her father had a decorative shillelagh on the shelf above us. 'Greetings from Sligo,' it said on the side. I had no idea what it was so I asked Sarah.

'It's an Irish club,' she said.

'What for?' I said.

'For knocking heads.'

'Right,' I said.

She put her hand on my knee, but I withdrew as if it was a viper. It would be a few weeks before I was confident her father wasn't going to come through the door and knock my head with it.

The result of this slightly oppressive atmosphere was that we talked, as opposed to kissed. I can remember now how awkward I felt, as if any movement I made might be judged and evaluated. With other girls, I'd felt that their approval was like a hoop of fire to be jumped through. Once you were on the other side then you could do what you liked. In that room with Sarah, the club above my head, I had the first inkling that there was more to it than that and that a woman's favour might need ongoing attention.

When I finally managed to take my eyes off the shillelagh and move beyond talking, there were other barriers in our way. There was no sofa in that back room, or if there was, we didn't sit on it as it would have been too much of an admission of our intentions, so we'd have to kiss from seats a few feet apart and with one eye on the door in case her dad came in.

Unfortunately both the seats were on wheels, so we'd constantly drift away from each other, as if we were trying to kiss from separate rowing boats. Some nights one of the chairs would go suddenly, leaving me grasping at the air, reaching out to steady myself.

One night her dad heard the noise and was in in a flash.

'What are you doing?' he said, looking at me lying on the floor. Sarah was in hysterics, half off her chair herself, having grasped for me as I went.

I pointed my finger at her outstretched hand. 'Re-enacting the scene on the ceiling of the Sistine Chapel, I thought you'd approve,' I said. 'Get yer brush, you can paint us.'

'You'll get my brush in a minute,' he said, before returning to the TV.

These sudden partings are funny the first time they happen, but when they become a condition of your togetherness they become a little wearing. I half suspected her parents of polishing the floor, particularly when we asked for some castor cups and her dad said 'No castor cups!' as if I'd just requested a packet of three.

It was becoming increasingly obvious that some sort of sexual activity was going on between us. The tension rose to a point where you thought you might be able to slice it from the air and serve it up with sprouts and gravy.

Sarah had bought some stockings and a suspender belt. Doubtless Sarah's mum had considered, and her God-fearing father considered even more closely, that she wasn't just wearing this get-up because she found it comfy. I was helping Sarah put out the washing one day and, as boys will, trying to make her laugh by nibbling at the suspender belt, which was on the line and saying 'I shall ravage you, ma cherie,' in a stupid French accent. Her father chose that moment to come into the garden. He said nothing, in a way that seemed to draw all the moisture out of the washing, but it was the last we saw of that particular item of lingerie. I couldn't help noticing too that, when I returned to the house, the shillelagh had been moved to a different spot. I had a picture of myself with 'Greetings from Sligo' stamped in mirror writing on my forehead.

Sarah's school was more progressive than mine, which still left it plenty of scope to be unprogressive, but there you go. The sixth formers were allowed to come home to study on their free periods and this meant Sarah had two or three free half days a week.

I'd bunk off school and we'd spend delicious mornings in bed. It was exciting, heading off in my school uniform but knowing that I was off for a morning of fun beneath the sheets. Having said that, we never did go all the way. My reluctance to buy condoms, combined with her natural hesitancy at doing it for the first time and fear of going on the pill meant that we had a whole year of spooning with no end product.

It may seem strange that she should be wary of going on the pill, but Catholic girls know the penalties if they are discovered. Handbag diving is a papally sanctioned sport for Catholic parents. I've been out with a lot of second-generation Irish Catholic girls and, sooner or later, there's always a confrontation – normally with their father. One, not Sarah's dad, told his twenty-two-year-old daughter, 'Every man in the town will know where your house is', after finding a pack of pills in her bag. What he expected to find in a young woman's bag, I don't know. A rosary and a copy of the catechism, perhaps.

7 FIGHTING REALITY

Men often try to turn their partners into extensions of themselves. There are some women who fall in with this sort of thing more readily – who suddenly become yachties, hill walkers, cyclists or football fans on taking up with a hobbyist, but Sarah was more her own person.

I had become convinced I was a hippy. I wore the duffel coat and the beads, the CND badges and the kaftan, and I expected her to do the same. Sarah joined in in a half-hearted kind of way, buying a cheesecloth top and a padded coat from Top Shop that had a flower on it, but that was the extent of her embrace of the Summer of Love look.

This led us into some conflicts. She was bought a second-hand bike and I said she should paint it in flowers and call it the Cycle Delic. She preferred that it should remain plain and be known as 'my bike'.

I found this mildly irritating as I thought my girlfriend should reflect the sort of person I was. If the reverse idea had been suggested to me – that I should have dressed better or behaved slightly differently in order to please her – then I would have been outraged by the idea. However, she did try to indulge my hippy leanings, as did her parents, to an extent.

Calamity befell us at Christmas when they asked me what I wanted and I said a record – Gong's *Angel's Egg*. I hadn't realised, and neither had they until they examined it on Christmas Morning, that its cover shows a story where a hippy goes on a trip 'through the quim of the moon' – said quim being amply illustrated. No one mentioned this all of Christmas and we were still not mentioning it by New Year. We weren't doing anything else or talking about anything else, just not mentioning it. That's all. When I tried to speak Sarah's Dad would raise his eyebrow at me, indicating that the time when the 'not mentioning' could end and normal life resume was not yet over.

In my efforts to construct my personality – hippy, mystic, poet, druggy – I actually forgot who I was. I really did try to construct it as well, in clothes, attitudes and records, I was always defining who I was, even if others were bored to distraction with listening to me do so. Mind you, I don't think I'm alone there.

The most usual conceit at this age, of course, is acting tough, but there are a few others that come in too, some of which outlive adolescence – the flash car bought on a crippling loan, the book of slim verse open but unread as you smoke Gitanes at a pavement café, the financial adviser who wants to talk to you about his rock band.

Men lie to themselves about who they are all the time and it's not always a bad thing – ambitious people do found great businesses, write great literature, and perform fantastic music. Others, however, get into debt, use the fact they've read the dust jacket of *Ulysses* to look down on people, and play guitar looking like a golf club captain in sunglasses rather than Keith Richards.

I have only a fleeting sense nowadays of the kind of person that Sarah was. She was kind and intelligent, I know, but I can't really remember anything she said. I think this might be because I never really listened to her and was just off in my own thoughts for the whole year.

Having a girlfriend had been new to me with Jane and with Chrissie and so I'd been more careful. With Sarah, I was taking her for granted and testing her limits within a couple of months.

One wet day we were coming back from a walk, crossing a muddy gateway. The only way of avoiding ending up in mud was to clamber around the gatepost, carefully placing your feet on a tiny island of dry ground at its bottom. Sarah didn't find this easy and ended up fighting for balance while clinging to the post. I pretended to go to push her in.

'You wouldn't dare,' she said.

' "Dare" is not a word one should use to a captain in the cavalry of the British queen,' I said, gently removing her one supporting hand and allowing her to fall. She emerged from the puddle – perhaps small pond is a better description – filthy and soaked to the skin. I really couldn't work out why she was angry, not at all. Any of my male friends would have found it hysterical. Actually, you can say that shorter – any of my friends. I had no female friends, I hadn't spoken to a girl from the time I was eleven until I was fifteen so nothing had prepared me for people who didn't find being thrown into cow shit amusing. When you've grown up in one long episode of Jackass then you're not equipped to suddenly make the move to *Pride and Prejudice.*

That said, the good times we had were great – the proper first romance stuff. We went on a picnic on our bikes with my friend Andy and his girlfriend and romped around in a cornfield before cycling home in the pouring rain like something off *Butch Cassidy and the Sundance Kid* or, at least, a Flake advert. We began to socialise as adults in pubs and had wacky, memorable nights of kissing, cheesy disco music and fights. Kissing and kick-ins are what this period of teenage life is all about and we wore our stories on our skins, marked out in love bites or bruises.

I fell, bizarrely, under the protection of soap-crusher Alan Myers, to whom I seemed almost wedded at that point. We were standing outside a disco, waiting for my dad to pick me and Sarah up, when a couple of youths in sports jackets – the 'smoothie' uniform of the day – decided that someone in a floppy hat and cloak should not be allowed to go out with a pretty girl. Sarah had made me a cloak from a length of black cloth, proving that either she had taken leave of her senses temporarily, or that she really did love me and was prepared to go out with me no matter what I wore.

The night she completed the cloak, I went to pick it up. I really have no idea what her parents must have thought was going on. To get back to the pub where my friends were, I had the choice of either going through the underpass beneath the A45 or nipping across the road and climbing down the bank the other side. As I always feared what sort of violent nerks might be in the underpass, I took my chances on the road and hopped off the bank to get back onto the path.

The cloak had rather gone to my head, however, and instead of just walking down the bank normally I jumped from about four feet up and landed, I am sad to report, with a vampiric hiss.

'Ahh! Ahhhh!' screamed a figure I had narrowly missed, 'don't hurt me!' It was none other than Alan Myers. I had nearly jumped the toughest boy in the school.

'Oh, it's you,' he said, looking out from between his fingers, 'I thought you were Dracula.'

'I might be Dracula,' I said.

He actually looked a bit scared at this. Then he recovered himself.

'No you're fucking not,' he said, squinting at my teeth just to be sure.

I shrugged. Had I found Alan Myers's weakness? Could I gain control of him by casting a spell on him? It probably wasn't worth the risk if I was wrong.

Still, I did have him at a mild disadvantage. He made me swear that I wouldn't tell anyone he'd been cringing like Igor beneath Frankenstein's hand. For virtually the first time in my life I kept a secret. There was only one way the story would get out – if I told it. I didn't want to have to account to Alan for making him look foolish.

In the carpark with Sarah, I was just about to get beaten up – and it might have done me some good if I had – when I saw a familiar permed colossus looming behind my potential attackers.

'Any trouble, Stewart?' said the giant Myers. Alan never actually knew my name, always referring to me as 'Stewart'. I wasn't going to argue with him, if he wanted to call me Stewart, he could. However, I went to Alan's school. That meant, in his mind, that my trouble was his trouble. Also, I had the Dracula incident up my sleeve. I don't know if that was a factor in his thinking, but it might have been.

My potential assailants had to readjust their minds in an instant. One second they were about to limb an idiot who had dressed as if for a pantomime, the next they were taking on Alan 'Bonecrusher' Myers. In the school slang of the day, to him they were Weetabix – that is he'd have them for breakfast.

The conversation went something like: 'You can't be friends with this twat,' followed by Alan telling them he'd be friends with who the fuck he liked and offering – this was a fashionable expression of the moment – to knock the youth's teeth down his throat so far he'd have to stick his toothbrush up his arse to clean them.

I include this story in order to give a flavour of the time.

That period of my life was all about girls and narrowly avoiding getting beaten up. Some nights it seemed that all the emotions had been turned up – fights, snogging, dancing, we were all running on high octane. I can't remember a disco that didn't have a fight, or several fights. It all contributed to the febrile atmosphere of the era. And yet, at school and at home, the days seemed interminable.

It wasn't all scrapping. I discovered a love of Van Der Graaf Generator, a ridiculously wordy – or as lead singer Peter Hammil might say, sesquipedalian – prog rock band and spent days discussing the meaning of their lyrics with my new best friend Grahame Matthews. The band were almost perfect for an arty teenage boy, like having the clever, complicated companion you'd always dreamed about, but one who was unsophisticated and therefore accessible. Now I look back on song titles such as 'I Once Wrote Some Poems' and 'A Plague of Lighthouse Keepers' and I shiver. At the time I thrilled. Were the band saying we were fundamentally alone in life? I reeled as I pondered the implications of this banality.

The end for me and Sarah was abrupt. She went away to Ireland for two weeks and promised to write. I got a letter on day one and then no communication for the rest of the holiday. She said she'd call on the Saturday night but didn't.

Even then the penny didn't drop, I just thought it was too expensive for her to phone. When she returned she seemed distant. We were due to go up to a local pub with all our friends in the evening but, walking there, she didn't want to hold my hand. Still it didn't click. I assumed she didn't like it that I wasn't wearing the Gong Flying Teapot poncho she'd embroidered for me. It just didn't go with the yellow loons and beads I was wearing.

Then, on the way home, she told me – she didn't want to

see me any more. This was virtually the first thing she'd said to me in six months that had actually sunk in, that hadn't prompted some wannabe comic monologue about myself or deliberately contentious statement designed to cause a heated discussion and mark me out as an unusual individual.

I couldn't believe it. To me it seemed to come out of the blue but, for all I know, the signs may have been there for months. I wasn't paying enough attention to read them. I thought at the time that she must have met someone when she was on holiday. It was worse than that, although I didn't discover it for a few weeks.

She may have said why she finished with me but I can't recall it. Perhaps she'd just asked herself the question the kids in the sports jackets had asked, the one many of my school-mates asked and the one even my own mum had occasionally voiced when exasperated by my attempts to dress for Middle Earth rather than the upper sixth: what a girl like her was doing with someone like me.

When other girls had finished with me I just assumed there would be another one along in a minute. This time, though, I went through the classic reverse in self-esteem of the jilted male.

One second I was full of it, a visionary marked out for a special destiny. The next, I was no one. It was as if she was the prop underpinning all my pretensions and without her they fell to ruin.

I did consider going up to the A45 and throwing myself under a car to 'show her'. What this would have shown her, I don't know – possibly that I was an even bigger fool than anyone had suspected.

Instead, for the first time I did something that would become a pattern in the coming years – I immediately set out to find another girlfriend. When I say immediately, I don't mean the next day or the next week, I mean that second. As I walked home through the suburban night I looked at bus stops, by shops, down driveways, under the orange lights of the culs-de-sac and beyond the white ones of the highway. Was my girl speeding down the dual carriageway in a car, looking out of her window and wondering when she would meet someone like me? I thought another girl might be getting off a late bus or walking back with a friend. Maybe I could make eye contact, get talking and then start again. There were no girls, though, and there wouldn't be again for a long, long time.

The night after we split up I went to a party near her house and had to make a hasty exit when I became embroiled in a fight. A group of boys was searching for me and somehow, I ended up hiding in her back garden. I could almost feel the comfort coming from the other side of the door, the cosy world of conversations and kisses in that long thin room. I remembered the parting chairs, the shillelagh, the little book case, the sound of the TV coming from the lounge. It all seemed tremendously comforting and precious and I felt torn from it.

At the time I thought that I had finished up back at Sarah's because I knew their garden gate would be open. There is another interpretation, though. This behaviour wasn't far off the suicide attempt as a bid to get the girl back. It was a way of saying 'Look what you've done to me. See the state I'm in; how can you be so cruel? The world is conspiring against me, and you, who should be my friend, can only join in.' Maybe I was hoping to be discovered there. I have tried the 'pity me' ploy on a number of occasions since, sometimes unconsciously, sometimes deliberately. Each occasion has been different, each with its own flavour. There is one thing to be said for this strategy, however: no matter how it is executed, it never works.

Despite what some men think, women on the whole do not want a man they have to look after. In my experience they are drawn more to confident men than they are to blubbing wrecks. If a girl has rejected you when you were a polished and urbane lounge lizard who stared in the devil's eye and laughed, why should she suddenly start liking you when you're blarting like a four-year-old who's dropped his lolly?

I'm sure there were other forces at work here. Fundamentally, I felt safe at Sarah's, that's why I ran back there. I was ignoring the fact that it was a haven no longer open to me.

Things did not improve following the party. I tried to drown my sorrows with my friends. One of them, the golf-playing Ady Redmond, was very sympathetic.

'She was a lovely girl,' he said.

'Yes,' I said.

'Girls like that don't come up very often,' he said.

'Yes,' I said.

'This may sound insensitive,' he said, with a little click of his teeth, 'but would you mind if I took a pop at her? You do admit that her sort don't come on the market too often and you have to strike while the iron is hot.'

This is actually the male equivalent of offering a shoulder to cry on – turning the situation to a joke. It doesn't really work but, for a second at least, it makes you laugh.

Mysteriously, my friend Grahame Matthews was not available for consolation. I was in my magic mushroom phase at the time and decided a really good way of coming to terms with being dumped was to take a large quantity of hallucinogens. For those who have never taken magic mushrooms, I might point out that a major effect of the drug is the emotional torrent they release in the mind of those who have eaten them.

At eleven, I left the pub in which I was colouring in my sorrows. I could have left at 10.30, I could have gone to the loo and left at 11.05. However, in one of those coincidences that seem personally organised by God, I left at eleven, just as Sarah and my friend Grahame were walking by.

They didn't see me at first, or pretended not to, and I followed them down the road. I couldn't believe what I was seeing and thought that the vision of them hand in hand must have been produced by the mushrooms.

Realising that one of my best friends – who I had invited to come to Alton Towers with me and Sarah, with whom I had exchanged Van Der Graaf Generator records and who was a fellow Venture Scout – was going out with Sarah had a more warping effect on my brain than any drug. I don't know if he'd been lining her up throughout our friendship, or if she'd been lining him up, but his behaviour wasn't on. He was my close friend and he had betrayed me. Also, he had a car. How could she prefer that on a rainy day to my largely reliable motorbike?

I followed them down the road for about half a mile surreptitiously, as surreptitiously as a six-foot man high on a cocktail of mind-bending drugs and alcohol can when wearing a cloak, cowboy boots and a fair bit of his mum's eyeshadow. Just in front of the turn down to her house, Sarah spun round and asked the pertinent questions: 'What? What do you want? What are you doing?'

Her approval felt only an inch away. It was as if I could say 'Well, that's what it would be like if Sarah finished with me and went out with you, Grahame. Thanks for your participation in the exercise, I'll see you tomorrow. I'm back off to Sarah's house for a snog.'

I didn't understand why we couldn't just reset – say 'OK, forget the last four months, let's go back to when it was all such fun.'

I couldn't reply to Sarah's questions. I just couldn't take it all in. Somehow I ended up in that little room at the back of her house. This time they sat in the chairs where Sarah and I had always sat and I plonked myself down on the floor.

I tried to express about twenty different emotions at once – hurt, betrayal, bewilderment . . . but also love. Without the magic mushrooms these wouldn't have seemed so sharp or intense or identifiable, but they would still have been there. I wanted to tell them I cared for them both, but what I had failed to grasp was that what *I* felt was now irrelevant. Whether I cursed or blessed them, it didn't matter. Their lives were now proceeding without me.

'Have you taken something?' said Sarah.

'Yes!' I virtually sobbed. I don't know if I expected an arm around the shoulder. I didn't get it.

'I think you should go,' she said.

I then said one of those things you can only say when you're an adolescent, or a character in a soap opera.

'Look after her, Gray,' I said, and went into the night with a tear.

Later I would represent this incident to friends as a sign of my maturity, although I think that might not be right.

How would I have handled this now? I may, it has to be said, have socked Grahame in the eye. This isn't because I'm violent, far from it. It's just that, like morals, certain codes of behaviour have evolved down the centuries specifically to handle certain situations. A sock in the eye relieves the hurt the jilted lover feels, but it also satisfies the treacherous best friend. He knows he's done wrong and guilt nags away at him. A shiner is simply the currency in which he must pay for his misdeeds. That done, he can look to the future with a clear heart and with a woman to kiss him better. Everyone benefits.

Still, this sort of behaviour isn't really me, so I just prided myself on my reasonable response.

I didn't know at the time that I am capable of treacherous behaviour. In fact, I think many men are capable of it. They convince themselves that the girl is special, that she's the one, that they weren't that good friends with her ex anyway and then they dive in.

It would be easy to say that this is because all male relationships are competitive. They are, to an extent, but I think it's more than that. A good relationship with a woman is what most of us aspire to, above success at work, at sport or with friends.

We're almost forced to get to know our friends' girlfriends as people, rather than as objects of desire, and so it's unsurprising we should think we have established some deep connection with them.

When a woman we think we could make a go of it with becomes free, the desire to have her as a partner simply outweighs all other concerns.

I don't know if I loved Sarah; I doubt that I did. I was fond of her, but I was too wrapped up in myself to really recognise her as a person. She was a great girl, but fundamentally different from me. I had become used to her, though, and she was a prop to my self-esteem. Just as I'd felt justified and validated by her approval when we'd first kissed, I felt her rejection on a wider level. If she didn't want me, then no one did. By choosing one of my friends she was saying he was better than me in every way and that every aspect of my character was worthless. I'd lost a badge that said to the world that I was OK. It was a shattering blow and I would take a long time to recover.

I did see Sarah and Grahame again: once when they visited the semi-squat I moved into at eighteen, and once at their engagement party.

They came round to my house because they had heard I was renting a place and wanted to find out how it was done. Sarah had rowed with her family and wanted to move away. She wouldn't say why and I leapt to the conclusion that her father had discovered she was on the pill. I was inwardly very glad this had happened, despite having no evidence at all that it had.

As she and Grahame sat against the damp walls of my house I had the hideous feeling that they thought we'd all moved on. I hadn't moved on. I had gone off the rails after she finished with me, dropped out of school and moved out of home. I hadn't had a sniff of a girlfriend since either. My confidence was shot and my spots had gone wild, not improved by the lack of baths and poor nutrition of a life on the dole.

I hadn't forgotten her and still imagined she might come back one day, saying it had all been a terrible mistake, so it was very hurtful to see her popping up like that.

Instead of being pleasant, cordial and clearly above the whole thing, I gave them a long list of all the cool things I was doing that they weren't. I was in a band, we were recording, I'd rediscovered punk, I'd . . . They weren't interested and who can blame them?

Suddenly, in my house with ice on the insides of the window, facing a six-mile walk to my nan's in order to get something to eat, the world of replacement windows and kitchen extensions I thought they were destined for seemed very appealing. I put it out of my mind.

Shortly after, I heard they were getting married. I have no idea what led to this decision, but it seemed rushed to me. She certainly wasn't pregnant, but I think that Grahame, who was no looker, was keen to secure exclusive rights to her. She wasn't the last woman to leave me and get married in short order. It is possible that almost anyone looks brilliant by comparison to me.

I turned up at her engagement dressed bizarrely – combat gear head to foot. Combat stuff was popular then, but, in retrospect, I can see what my attitude to the evening was when I went dressed more for 'Desert Storm' than a night out dancing. 'Confrontational' might cover it.

But seeing them together, taking the last dance, opening cards, I had the opposite feeling to the one I'd had in the cold of my rented house, and a sudden picture of who I was and what I wanted to do came to me.

Everything was stopping for them, I thought. Marriage, to me, was a one-way ticket to a small house on a modern estate, a good job at a factory, badminton in the evening and then kids. Kids, I thought, would make you irrelevant in your own life, suddenly you were displaced as the focus for your ambitions, and would be content with wall to wall carpets, loft extensions, car ports and other things that symbolised a slow, rotting death. For the record, I'm glad I don't feel like this now and would actually love a car port.

Even as I felt lonely, I didn't envy them. Marriage is often represented as a success but, at nineteen, it would have seemed to me a total and complete failure. A long-term partner would have been great, but, in my mind, there was something about being married that meant you had to stay in suburbia among the UPVC windows and pinky yellow brickwork. I wanted something else; to live in a garret in Paris, perhaps. That was my ambition: to live in a French loft extension, not a British one.

I think this is what is meant by 'fear of commitment' in men. This is a pure fear, for a nineteen-year-old, the dread of a life change happening too early. It persists for some men for many years, but I don't think it's quite as prevalent as many believe. When a man has 'commitment issues' at thirty-five it's because he thinks he has better options than the woman he's currently with. At the bottom line, he finds her too ugly or too irritating to envisage a life with her, but not ugly or irritating enough to finish with. He is confident he could do better, but not confident enough to try. Instead he'll just stay with her, inwardly blaming her for her failure to live up to his ideal.

The girl I was looking for – witty, literate, beautiful and clever – did not seem ready to appear. Then, watching the TV one day, I saw her. Something had happened at Sussex University – some politician had been covered with egg, I think. They interviewed a student, asking her what she thought of it. I didn't hear her opinion, only looked at her: duffel-coated, pretty, intense. In the background other women moved. The place seemed full of them. I needed some A levels, I decided, and I needed them in a hurry.

8 FRESH

I was in my room preparing for what I considered the most important event of my life – the Freshers' Ball, Sussex University, at the end of my first week there. I was buzzing, my body humming with expectation of what lay ahead of me. It was FAF week – fuck a fresher – and, should the disco contain predatory third-year females in low-cut tops who smoked gold-tipped cigarettes and who were casting about for innocence to stain, or if it held the gamine, intelligent girl who looked like her off Jean-Luc Godard's *A Bout De Souffle* and who was ready to marry me and complete me, then I was ready. Like a racehorse in the gate, I was ready. My life, I felt, was about to begin and everything leading up to it had simply been a preparation for that disco.

There was a high tension to my preparations – I wanted to be thorough but I wanted to be quick. Who knew what I might be missing in the time it took me to talc my nuts and administer three squibs of the Paco Rabanne aftershave I'd had since I was seventeen – added pheromones for guaranteed attraction to the opposite sex, so the rumour went. I saw myself bitter in twenty years' time, saying 'If only I'd just done two squibs, then I would have got to the girl of my dreams before she met *him*.'

Who *he* was I had no idea, but one thing had entered my mind very deeply. I was in a competition for girls, it was cut-throat and it was played for the highest possible stakes – happiness. I had a small idea of my nightmare competitor

– arty, pretentious, privately educated, full of stupid ideas. Exactly like me, in other words, but posh.

I had no doubt I was now playing the endgame in terms of meeting a girl. Yes, there would be promiscuity, one-night stands, flings, flips and all manner of affairs while I was at university – that was what I had gone there for, after all – but somewhere out there, among the student body was the girl who was going to make me happy. The idea of me making her happy had not yet occurred to me.

I looked into the mirror to see a sort of pale, gangling troll. I went through my good luck ritual – first fill the tiger-skin Y-fronts my nan had bought me as a Christmas present a couple of years before with talcum powder down the front. Then tap them hard, sending a snowstorm rushing up from my pants. It caused a terrible mess but that was part of the plan. If you suffer, so you shall be rewarded. I was smeared from belly to nipples in white powder and appeared, I thought, much as the early Britons might have to the Roman legionnaires – as a painted savage. I was actually quite pleased with that.

I was, I think, a reasonably good-looking young man but disfigured by the times. This wasn't so much by the haircut – though it was bad, a sort of half-hearted Mohican – but by the attitudes of the day. I held my face in a washed-out hollow way designed to look like Ian Curtis, lead singer of Joy Division, but looking more like the early Rik Mayall from *The Young Ones*. I'm not sure it was a conscious thing, just a look picked up from the faces of other young men I admired.

Each decade has its way of holding the face, a fashionable expression that maybe once looked good on a pop star or model, but has been passed on in a series of visual Chinese whispers and comes out subtly wrong on the chops of the hoi poloi – like a tune played by someone who has only heard it hummed. So in the sixties there was a sort of blissed out gawp, or cheeky and keen as done by Paul McCartney; in the 1970s, the Bolan pout, the Mungo Jerry trucker's leer or the Johnny Rotten sneer; in the 1980s the Hooray Henry Hooray, the 1990s the Nirvana half awake or the therapist head tilt but, some time after 2000 the youth learned to look beautiful.

It's only recently that young people became beautiful. Today there are style magazines, fashion supplements, internet sites and a whole host of places telling you how to look and dress. You don't have to refer to your friends to know how to look. There is a whole industry set out to help you. In 1984 there was less support. Back then a hairstyle was considered optional.

My friend Mickey was from west London and he had a hairstyle. I didn't have a hairstyle, I had some hair that had been cut by a man who didn't like me. My hair is a law unto itself and I hadn't washed it because it had set in a way that I regarded as acceptable some time during the afternoon. To touch it would have been to provoke it, so it seemed wiser to let it lie.

'Hello,' I said, to my reflection, 'what A levels did you get? Where are you from. Would you like to buy me a drink?'

Did that work? I thought the 'Would you like to buy me a drink?' was a neat reversal of gender roles, something that would go down well in the hyper-PC environment of the day. Did it just sound mean, though?

This was the mid-1980s, Sussex University, the most politically correct place at the most politically correct time of the last century. I'd endured a hair-raising introductory seminar to my 'Gender and Politics' course, which I'd signed up for with the intention of getting a few lines to use on girls.

'Of course,' said the tutor, 'all heterosexist sexual inter-course can be regarded as rape. In fact, courtship rituals can be seen as part of the process, themselves a violent and aggressive positioning of the woman.'

'So if I smile at a girl across a bar, that's rape?' I said.

'Well, yes, it's within that discourse, so yes,' said the tutor, as if I was being wilfully difficult, 'Dworkin is helpful here.'

'I've never dworked, how might I go about it?' I said to icy silence.

This was the thinking, but I knew that I would have to swallow it. Accepting the ultra-feminist orthodoxy was not only politically fashionable, but the key to getting laid. The coffee rooms buzzed with right-on conversation. You walked along a knife edge as you approached a girl. You didn't want to seem indifferent, but you had to seem indifferent because to look keen was the same as rape: putting on nice clothes – preparing your trap, rapist; asking her in for coffee – do you feel I owe you something because you've given me a luke-warm cup of Nescafé, rapist? There were only about three women on campus who actually felt like this, but you never knew who they were. It made me wonder what they were going to say about an actual rapist.

On top of this were the normal anxieties facing a young man on a big night out. Was I wearing the right thing? I'd put on my newest jumper, that had to be OK didn't it? It had been knitted by my nan in a honeycomb pattern in super-heavy wool for extra warmth. I don't think it ever occurred to my nan that jumpers were to look at, and that insulation is not the main quality one requires in a discotheque. To be fair, it hadn't really occurred to me, either. I would have found the idea of not wearing a jumper to the disco abso-lutely mind blowing. It was freezing, for a start and, beyond this, I had a mortal fear of doing anything that smacked of preparation to meet a girl. What if I met a girl, all went well and then it came time to leave and I had no jumper, no coat. 'It's cold, where's his bloody jumper?' she'd ask herself. 'I'm with a sodding poseur who thinks he's got big arms so he wants to show them off. Bye bye, loser.' Even a thin jumper might inspire these thoughts. To be fancied I had to show total disregard for being fancied.

On my feet were the post-punk fashionable monkey boots and my trousers were a pair of jeans cut like combat trousers. I'd spilled a bit of cheese pasty on them earlier in the day, which had refused to come out. Never mind, I thought, it would give me an insouciant look. I had a Killing Joke T-shirt, should I be called upon to shed my jumper and, I shiver to relate, an ear-ring featuring the comedy and tragedy masks. It was the kind of get-up that Jude Law might have looked at and said 'You're expecting me to pull in this? No way!'

Still, like I said, we were all ugly back then so it didn't matter so much. I was the second one into the disco. I didn't know at the time that Sussex was stuffed with trendy Londoners who regarded it as too, too boring to go out before nine o'clock. Brought up in the Midlands on early closing and weak beer, I went earlier. The start time was seven. I was fashionably late at about 32-seconds-past, having forced myself to circulate in the entrance hall looking at invitations to protest about virtually every flavour of injustice known to humanity. I was just beaten in there by a weedy-looking man in an open-necked shirt. He was a mature student and must have been at least twenty-six.

'Hi!' he said, as I came in.

I nodded and went to the bar. There was no way I was becoming friends with someone dressed like a weekend-ing banker. He looked an idiot, I thought, as I checked the mirror behind the bar to make sure the neck of my jumper was lopsided. I didn't want to look as though I'd made an effort.

I lay against the bar, trying to look as if it was the most natural thing in the world to be kicking back on my own in a room designed for about two thousand people. Then, nightmare. They only put on Joy Division's 'Transmission'. I was going to have to dance wasn't I? What would happen if the friends I would have for life or the girl of my dreams came in and formed the impression that I didn't like this song because I was standing at the bar? They might believe that the music wasn't a reflection of my doomed, elegant soul. Who would watch my pint while I danced? For a second I thought I could just get away with leaning against the bar, mouthing the words and pointedly tapping my feet, but that was never going to do. She, the one who would be with me forever, would expect to see movement.

I took the floor and danced for three minutes in the middle of an empty room. Then the bastard put Cabaret Voltaire's 'Nag Nag Nag' on, so I had to dance to that as well. The DJ saw he'd been successful in getting someone onto the floor with the post-punk fayre so he put on 'Totally Wired' by The Fall. How could I not dance to that? Then, just as I was about to sit down the bastard put on 'King of Kings' by The Pack. I could have sat down to anything else, but this was a pre-Theatre of Hate, pre-Spear of Destiny Kirk Brandon, as any watching girl surely must have known. This was very rare stuff, I'm not even sure it was ever a single, it might have just been a bootleg tape of some sort. To go utterly mad to this was to mark yourself as one of the cognoscenti. I went dutifully berserk. Less than ten people were in the cavernous hall by the time it finished, one of them sniffing at my pint. I reached it just in time and stowed my jumper. I was already sweating heavily and there wasn't really anyone in there.

Then the DJ, who I thought was taking the piss, put on Killing Joke's 'Follow The Leader'. I was wearing a Killing Joke T-shirt. If I didn't dance then they – 'they' being my shorthand for everyone I was looking to impress – might think that I'd just bought it because I wanted to get the kudos for liking Killing Joke but I didn't know the music. If they didn't put on something rubbish soon I risked talking to no one the whole night. I started prioritising in my head – it was essential to dance to The Fall, Magazine, The Smiths, Psychedelic Furs, Bauhaus, The Cure, The Birthday Party, Theatre of Hate, Test Department, Foetus, Public Image, Devo, Echo and The Bunnymen, The Velvet Underground and any punk that happened along – if I was to represent myself as the person I truly was. If they stuck The Sisters of Mercy on, I could have a rest because they were rubbish. What about borderline stuff, though? I didn't like The Teardrop Explodes but they *were* weird. Did I dance to something I didn't like just to point out my dangerous similarity to nutcase lead singer Julian Cope? What was wrong with the DJ? Hadn't he got any Wham!, so I could march off the floor in disgust and meet the girl of my dreams?

The ruptured guitars of Killing Joke burst onto the dancefloor and out I went again, like a boxer fighting the tenth round when he'd only trained for five, going reluctantly utterly mental lest anyone think me a fair weather fan. I windmilled, doing the 1977 punk dance in case anyone should think I was a new convert to this music, which I was. Then things got worse. The man in the open-necked shirt directed his moccasins and white socks onto the floor and began dancing with me in the manner of a young Christian getting down and getting with it. So, as the potential friends and girlfriends filed in, I was hopping about soaked in sweat in an empty room like someone who the fire brigade had made a semi-successful attempt to extinguish after his arse had caught fire – next to a trainee accountant. It looked like the tie-break dance-off in the Twat of the Year competition.

In came the women. The Killing Joke finished and on went Lloyd Cole's 'Perfect Skin'. At last, I was free. I strode to the bar to finish my pint and order another, pleased that whoever was watching had seen my disgust at this cappuccino pop. I turned from the bar to see about eight girls dancing in the spot that I'd been thrashing about in not ten seconds before. Once again, the rules, it seemed, were changing.

I had only really known men before, despite my girl-friends. I'd been to an all-boys school, played Dungeons and Dragons obsessively, only really listened to boys, only valued their opinions. I'd been to punk and post-punk discos where the DJ said things like 'If you've come for music, forget it' before putting on a record that involved three art students failing to make a synthesiser work and a fourth blowing the top of a milk bottle. To me, girls existed as boys' satellites, reflecting their boyfriends' tastes and attitudes. Teenage boys in the late 1970s and early eighties respected nutters. So girls must too, I thought, or at least the sort of girl I was looking to attract, the sort that ... hang on ... looked like the beautiful, dark-skinned, twinkling beauty swaying away to Lloyd Cole. Actually, I thought, he wasn't that bad a lyricist, was he?

At any disco, for the single man, there is the vexed question of how to approach a girl. It would take me another fifteen years at least to work out that the answer is 'Just go up and say "Hello"'. No. Women were all-powerful, capricious and unguessable. If you showed a girl you liked her, that would be taken as a sign of terrible weakness and she would never look at you again.

The hall started filling up and some people I'd met on my courses came in – other boys, naturally. We clung to each other like shipwrecked sailors floating in a sea of self-doubt. My friend Mickey, fresh out of the Richmond rich-kid scene, was wearing a paisley shirt, fashionably long hair and a touch of eye liner.

'A bit trendy isn't it?' I said.

'Damn right,' he said.

He was proud of being trendy, proud of following rather than setting a fashion. There was something new.

When I look back on it now, it's as if everyone was carrying placards, announcing my future, marching around the room in some sort of demonstration against the mistakes that I was to make: Charlie, who said he thought James Dean was handsome and who I therefore took to be gay – how could you tell if another man was handsome if you weren't – with a sign saying 'I know I wasn't what you envisaged, but I will be your friend forever. We will never do anything else but argue, nor knowingly say anything nice to each other before we are past forty'; Mickey with 'I will find you fascinating, oik, but eventually I will tire of you'; Mad Bomber Harris with 'Hold onto your hats, it's going to be a bumpy ride!'

Then there were the girls: Fleur with 'The fact my father is a famous poet will blind you to the fact you do not like me'; Masie with 'You won't make me happy and I will die young, apparently. Charlie will hear the news and forget to ask how it happened.' There was Ella, above all Ella, in the power and glory of her youth, her beauty breaking on me like the sun through stained glass, with 'It will take us ten years, nineteen break-ups, lots of smashed crockery. We will lie for years immobile on the sands of our own insecurities while the waves of misery wash over us again and again. No problem: eventually we will be friends.' Then there was Sue, 'You should have asked me earlier if you had wanted her to join us in bed'; Angie, 'forty-three is too old for you, as you will realise when I take my clothes off'; Anna, 'Deep, serious, fascinating. You will fall in love with me but it won't work in bed'; Rose, 'Yes, I did expect you to call me back. I don't betray my boyfriend lightly'; Helen, 'You will ruin it by criticising my friends'; Colleen, 'Please don't give me your opinions, I'm just after your cock'. Eva's placard just read 'T.R.O.U.B.L.E.'

The thing is, although I fulfilled one of my contradictory aims of being promiscuous and finding the love of my life at university, what stays with me from most of my encounters with women is not the fun, though much of it was fun, but failure. Failure to connect, to carry things forward, to be going on that holiday together, to love and be loved.

Little destinies were swirling around the disco, but to me they were invisible, untouchable. I tried to talk to girls, but I was rooted to the spot by the weight of expectation. I was tongue-tied and my feet felt heavy. Every time I saw another man talking to an attractive woman it was as if he was robbing me, but I was powerless to prevent it. One of the songs asked me what I was going to do if I really didn't want to dance by standing on the wall. Not make an idiot of myself was my reply. I met some friends and tried to say mad things in order to convince them I was the sort of person it was worth hanging around with. It was a peculiarly muted affair. No one really seemed to meet anyone, very likely fearing the disapproving eye of Andrea Dworkin upon them. The disco finished at eleven, as they did in those days, and I clung on trying to look casual, hoping that I'd bump into a girl, hoping that one would just fall on me like I'd fallen on Sarah all those years ago. It didn't happen. I talked some more about anarchism and was expelled by a woman with a mop – the nearest I got to female company that evening. At midnight I was back in my room, lying on my bed looking up at the luminous stars I'd stuck to the roof in an occult symbol, in the hope that I could impress a girl with that. Day 7 at university, no girl, no future. Where was she, the girl I needed? I could have started by looking next door.

9 THE EXOTIC

I finally justified all my struggle at A level just before the Christmas break when, for two days of seventy, I had what I considered a girlfriend. In a small irony I had been placed in the university's Park Village halls, which were mainly for overseas and mature students. That's right, mature students. I had an American girl living next door to me, the witty and pretty Phyllis: dark hair, Bette Davis eyes and a good slice of that film star's world-weary style. I could just imagine her putting on that slightly down-mouthed look and saying 'Why am I so good at playing bitches? I think it's because I'm not a bitch. Maybe that's why Miss Crawford always plays ladies.'

Phyllis actually terrified me. She came from a rich Chicago family, had a tinder dry sense of humour and seemed terminally unimpressed by anything I had to say. I was quite used to having the last word on anything, but Phyllis knew the power of silence, how to let one of my one-liners hang in the air until it withered in the wind.

Having an American next door to me was too good an opportunity to miss. There is nothing the English wag loves more than a crack at Uncle Sam, or Auntie Samantha, and I wasted no time in piling in to Phyllis, begging her not to shoot me if I passed her on the landing, asking, when she told me her dad had bought her a Rolex, if that was some sort of expensive gun. Actually, that wasn't too much of a joke, I had no idea what a Rolex was and the thought that anyone would want a watch when there were so many public clocks around struck me as ludicrous.

I introduced her to my friends. 'Charlie, this is Phyllis,' I said, 'her dad earns a million dollars a year.' I'd been fascinated to meet someone rich and had been taking the piss ever since I'd forced her father's earnings out of her. Phyllis was American and didn't realise there is something embarrassing about money, something you need to apologise for. We are all Americans now but, back when we were British, we would rather have confessed to the clap than a six-figure bank account. The richest people I'd known before university were plumbers' sons and I found her wealth a fine target for sarcasm.

Phyllis rolled her eyes.

'I did not say that!' she said, 'I said he earned *more* than a million a year.'

Phyllis found it strange that her nationality should make her the butt of a joke but – unlike some other Americans I met who found this sort of thing gratifyingly offensive – she joined in, pretending to search through her bag for her gun when she saw me or pointing out that they execute in Texas for rooms as untidy as mine. In the kitchen when I consumed my cod roe sandwiches she'd warn others 'Don't get your hands near his mouth when he's eating!' and she'd roll her eyes when John, another American student and a much easier mark for me, went on about how much he owed God. 'Most loans you pay with interest,' she said, 'the debt to God is paid in boredom. Other people's, largely.'

She was pretty, she was very funny, she had the ability to flatten my best lines by just remaining silent for a few seconds after I'd delivered them – of course I became infatuated with her.

The difficulty with upper-class American girls, though, is

that they just don't do pubs – or at least she didn't at that stage. I had no idea what you did with a girl if you didn't take her to a pub, I had no idea what you did with anyone if you didn't take them to a pub. Girls were met in pubs, I thought, therefore my social life was overwhelmingly based in one. In fact that explains why I was not shy around strong drink, it's an accidental byproduct of my search for women. Had girls been met in table-tennis halls I would have become an expert ping-ponger.

Nowadays, of course, I know you take women out for dinner. I couldn't see the point in that when you could have cod roe sandwiches at home and save your money for beer. At that age I had a slightly resentful attitude towards food – its preparation and consumption took away time and money that could have been spent on drinking. The answer to my conundrum presented itself at the end of the first term.

'Sub-aqua club Christmas dinner,' I thought, 'Beat that, David Bloody Niven.'

I had joined the sub-aqua club because I am terrified of swimming in the sea and of deep water as a whole. In one of those conceits that young men so often come up with, I had decided to 'face my fear'. In later life I have discovered that the best thing to do with a fear is to run away from it; there's normally a pretty good reason you're scared. As it was, I didn't face my real fear – of having a sensible opinion or, more to the point, of looking at myself for what I really was.

So I'd been going up to a swimming baths with the club, flapping about underwater and keeping an eye out for sharks coming through gates at the bottom of the pool.

I don't know why the idea of romance suggested itself to me in this setting. It could have been some sort of premonition. On my way to the pool in the back of a minibus I found myself opposite a stunning auburn-haired girl with an

Art Nouveau poster look to her and a sense of humour even more relentlessly sarcastic than mine. She was, I thought, out of my class – fiercely intelligent, beautiful and with a wit that could knock your wig off. This was Ella. We wouldn't get together for three years and, after that, we'd spend a decade fucking up each other's lives.

I took Phyllis to the sub-aqua dinner where she sat gamely through in-jokes about tank filling. On the way home, I asked her for a kiss beneath one of the university bridges.

She seemed to weigh things up for a second, like someone wondering whether to go into a gallery on a sunny day or to just keep walking through the park. In the end, with a 'why the hell not?' shrug, she said 'OK.'

I spent the night with her. I thought she seemed curiously stiff when we made love. Now, of course, I can see that she wasn't that much into it. At the time, I just assumed she was too urbane to bother going through the ritual of oohing and ahhing, and that she thought my moves were predictable and petit bourgeois. There might have been something in that, I'll have to ask her one day.

One snatch of conversation stands out. I was being predictable and petit bourgeois and I was telling her about my then fetish for women in long gloves. She held up her hand.

'If you want accessories or toys, you will have to provide them,' she said. She wasn't making a joke. There was something very businesslike about her, as if she was setting out the terms of a contract right at the beginning so there would be no confusion about who was responsible for what later on. Term was about to end and we had only one more night together before she went back to the States for Christmas.

We wrote to each other over the break. I still have the letter and there's a telling line in it. After a jaunty and witty few pages she signs off 'Enjoy it while it lasts'.

Bizarrely, when it came to a crashing end at the beginning of the next term, I was bitter because I thought she'd led me on.

If I thought I'd suffered angst in the past, I was in for a rude awakening – quite literally. On our first meeting after the holiday Phyllis was keen to explain that we weren't going out together and that perhaps an arrangement might be made where we slept together occasionally, but maybe not as well. I didn't hear this. I had a girlfriend. Perhaps a new life in America would present itself. I could at least get a free holiday.

We went out to a couple of parties in the evening – this was pre-dance music and a party involved sitting around in different people's houses watching rich kids smoke dope. At one of the parties, Phyllis got talking to another boy.

I didn't see him as much in the way of competition – a public-school ponce with more than a passing resemblance to Hugh Grant and a similar slightly confused and amused style. Now what Ivy League female is going to find that sort of thing attractive?

There he was next to her, squatting like the toad close at the ear of Eve. Phyllis didn't seem so much attracted as hypnotised. Still, I thought, she was with me and wouldn't betray me. The fact that she had never made a promise that could be betrayed didn't occur to me. I showed how easy and liberated I was by giving her the space to talk to him. I even casually left the party and went home, sure that by not crowding her in she would come scuttling back.

I did try before I left.

'You don't want to come home with me?' I said.

'No,' she said, 'I find this guy really interesting.'

This was like a knife in my heart. Wasn't I the most interesting person anyone could possibly know? I certainly spent enough time trying to be.

'Interesting in what way?'

'Just interesting.'

'More than me?' This isn't a very fair question, so it begs the unfair answer: 'Yes'. Phyllis wasn't so unkind.

'Just different.'

I left.

In retrospect, I did the right thing. If someone's going to go, then they're going to go – particularly if they weren't all that there in the first place. However, there then ensued one of the most uncomfortable passages of my life. I could have borne being woken up by the sound of him giving it to her like you're meant to at four in the morning, I could have stood hearing, through the Rizla-thin walls, their painfully intense conversation about feelings and, swipe me he's on my turf, the great novels. But did I really need to write a poem about it? I did not.

The exact contents of this verse are so intensely foul that I can't even bring myself to type them out here. I have a number of awful incidents that continue to resonate with me – normally of social embarrassment – but this poem is the only thing I've ever done on my own that causes me to blush to my boots to this day. It was called . . . no I can't write it. Oh, go on, it'll be some sort of therapy, perhaps even that Holy Grail of the miserable 'Closure'. It was called 'I hear him making her laughing'.

The verse went like this. In the spirit of TS Eliot, I provide notes.

> Crepuscular, the pilferer
> Incarnadine, the dawn
> Stains the bedroom wall.
> Inviolate hearts are
> Violated.

Diminished.
Etiolated.
I hear him making her laughing
And I wear the scorned horn.

You will notice the influence of Eliot in the 'crepuscular', which I thought meant 'spotty', not 'of the twilight'. If you don't know what half the other words mean, don't worry. Neither did I, really. I thought this was proper poetry because I used scorned as scorn-ed, and made a reference to the horns betrayed husbands were said in classical literature to possess.

That's it, it's out. I don't know what depths of misery I must have sunk to in order to commit this assault on grammar and good taste. If there was a court of crimes against the language all I could hope for was that my disordered mental state would be taken into account before sentencing. The fact that other students had work such as 'As I Colour Clouds' and 'Nuclear Nightmare' published in campus magazines in no way lessens the severity of the offence.

Still, I clung to the hope that our arrangement of casual sex would hold and might one day lead to a relationship. The illusion was shattered, definitively, on a trip to London. I'd arranged this before Phyllis had met Michael (note the full use of the name. Only gay men and posh people ever say multi-syllable names in full). She didn't want to disappoint me so came along, even holding hands in London – sixty miles away from where she might bump into Mikey baby. We saw a play, went to a museum and caught the train back – at which point she announced she was nipping back to his pad.

'Why?' I said – as if she was going to come up with some other reason than 'I'd rather be with him than you.' Phyllis ummed and ahhed and in the end just told me. He was more her sort, it wasn't personal, just a matter of her peculiar taste for good-looking, polished, assured public-school boys over pretentious, spotty, working-class oafs. That's not what she said, but it was the gist.

I couldn't believe it. I hadn't seen it coming. This could have been because it wasn't coming – it was actually there and had been for more than a fortnight.

Losing Phyllis felt like more than a straight rejection, it actually felt as if I had been put in my place. I'd wanted an exotic girlfriend, but an exotic girlfriend hadn't wanted me.

10 SHE'S A FEMME FATALE

Every man dreams of meeting the one-off girl, the special one who isn't like anyone else at all, a free spirit with her own unique style, Ruby Tuesday who won't settle down with anyone – but him. We don't admit to these fantasies, of course, because they verge on the sickly sweet, but we all believe Annie Hall, Linda Fiorentino from *The Last Seduction*, Becky Sharp from *Vanity Fair* (esp as played by Natasha Little) or even the funny one off *Neighbours*, depending on your cultural preferences, might walk into our lives one day and choose us.

I had, as it turned out, several girlfriends in that first year – the beautiful hippy Helen, the serious and thoughtful Anna, with whom I spent a term sitting beneath Robert Doisneau pictures, talking about incomprehensible French philosophers and wondering how to get her into bed. When I did get her into bed it just didn't work. It didn't exactly fail either, but neither of us felt natural doing it. I can't explain why. The memory of her naked is the sort of thing that old men would recall on their deathbeds and think 'Ah, but I have lived!' She was beautiful, but there was something too self-consciously complicated between us that couldn't be reduced to the honesty of sex.

There were lesser relationships too. None of them lasted because I was too immature to be tolerated for more than a month or two, and also I wasn't enthusiastic about these girls, despite their attractiveness.

I always did something to sabotage the relationships – by being overly critical, too laid back or criticising their friends. The reason, I think, is that I wasn't looking for a beautiful girl. I wanted something much more than that. Good looks will get you laid, but they won't get you loved. To be loved you need style, you need wit, you need panache, at least if you're going to be loved by me. In fact, if you're going to be loved by me, you need to be the sort of person who has a lot better options than me and normally wouldn't go anywhere near me. Eva ticked all the boxes.

I used to long to be Mick Jagger when I was about twelve. I could take or leave his music – I was more of a Bolan and Bowie boy – but it was his girlfriends I envied. I wanted to go out with Marianne Faithful, a girl who wasn't just beautiful but seemed to represent an escape from all banality, from a life of gas bills and pebbledashing.

Eva, it seemed to me, fitted that description. She was an incredible girl with the knack of inspiring hopeless crushes in people, more remarkable for the fact that she wasn't classically goodlooking. That isn't to say she was ugly, far from it. She was tall and dark and resembled rather Morticia Addams, especially when she wore a long black dress. It was the best sort of Goth style really, one that she hadn't set out to achieve, like a good witch, half ugly and half beautiful and so much more interesting to look at than a classic belle. She was actually into heavy rock in the ironic but still engaged way that some women like Abba. Her face was very angular and you could never tell if she was laughing with you or at you, which I found enormously attractive. For all the time I spent trying to impress women then, I didn't really like the ones with whom I succeeded. I preferred Eva's 'Really, Mark?', her raised eyebrows and look of exaggerated attention followed by a deep chuckle whenever I said something particularly stupid.

Eva did like to cause a bit of trouble. At the time she was still hanging around with a couple of very nice but very girly girls who happened to live next door to her in halls. One of these girls had a stack of teddy bears and used to dress from head to foot in pink, including a bow for the hair. She is now controller of a major TV station. Eva would be more successful and, having breezed a first, would manage to avoid work almost entirely.

Eva couldn't think of a way of telling Pinky C – as I shall call this giant of the TV world – that she found her a little bit dull. So one night, as they stood on the roof of their halls of residence admiring the stars, Eva decided to start moving their relationship subtly to a close. Pinky had been fretting for weeks about a boy she was thinking of going out with and agonising that, though he'd shown signs of interest, he hadn't bought her a card for her birthday. Did he care for her? Could someone who didn't buy a birthday card really care, even if they thought they did? Had he bought her a card and she hadn't seen it? Would she make a fool of herself by putting up a notice in the kitchen asking if anyone had accidentally taken a card out of her pigeonhole? Eva couldn't work out what the problem was and, after week three, had given up trying. Her attitude was that if one man doesn't want you, there'll be another along in a minute, one being much like the next.

On the roof, Pinky C was looking up, wondering if the stars were God's daisy chain or some such penetrating question, when Eva just pushed her off. It was only a couple of storeys and her fall was cushioned by a bush, but it made me laugh for a month.

A few months later, in our second year, 'for a laugh' Eva got into bed with Pinky's rugger bugger boyfriend at a party in a room full of people. I knew nothing was going on because there's no way Eva would ever have looked at a man who wore a Harlequins rugby shirt and a jumper over his shoulders. However, it was the end of her relationship with Pinky, which was a shame because I liked them both.

I had to choose, though, and I chose Eva. I was in love with her, definitely. Through her it seemed to me that I had actually met someone from Dorothy Parker's Algonquin Hotel, though – along with Phyllis – Eva didn't need Parker's put downs; she could do a lot with silence and a raised eyebrow.

I make Eva sound like a spiteful cat, but she wasn't, really. In fact malice seemed almost entirely missing from her character. She just did these things, she didn't crow about them, she had more the attitude: 'Well, Pinky said, "Do you ever wish on a shooting star?" so I just had to give her a little push. What was a girl to do?' Eva's attempt to justify her behaviour was actually a little bit worrying. 'I'm short-sighted,' she said, 'so I had no idea how big the drop was. It could have been six inches it could have been sixty feet.'

'That makes it worse, not better,' I said.

'Oh yes,' she said, as if learning something mildly frightening about herself.

Still, I found her style tremendously alluring.

'Come to bed with me,' I said to her.

'No, Mark.'

'Why not.'

'Because for the moment I have more attractive people to go out with. If I get desperate, I'll let you know.'

'Great!' I said. 'Everyone gets desperate eventually.'

'I'll look forward to it.'

'I'll book you in around June,' I said.

There was no talking about philosophy with Eva, more discussing Motörhead and me asking her why she was denying herself the considerable pleasure of sleeping with me. It wasn't that she couldn't discuss philosophy, it's just that she didn't think I had much to say on the subject that would interest her.

There was no way I could have been so forward with the bookish Anna, even if Anna had wanted me to. It just didn't fit with my image of me and her. With Eva, though, I just couldn't restrain myself from trying to persuade her into bed. Each relationship makes its own dent in reality, a little mould into which you pour your personality. A new partner really can make you someone else, suppressing certain aspects of your psyche and bringing others to the fore.

Still, I thought she liked me more than she said, despite her avowed attraction to guitar virtuoso, druggie public schoolboy Steve, in his black leather jacket and winkle-pickers. In boxing, they talk of a fighter having a puncher's chance. This means that, though his opponent is technically more gifted and fitter, there is always the possibility that the puncher will land a blow that will knock his adversary cold. Steve might have been better looking and cooler than me but he took himself painfully seriously, so I had a joker's chance. I did make Eva laugh. This had the dual benefit of boosting my ego – women like men who can make them laugh, men like women they can make laugh – and keeping Eva interested in spending time with me.

Humour only works with women up to a point, however. Years later I remember going on a ski-ing trip as part of an article for a magazine. We were met by the two PR women from the resort. One of them was absolutely beautiful – a Nordic blonde but in the art-foundation-course rather than the porn-film style – and the other wasn't bad either. I found myself sitting next to the blonde girl in the restaurant and was very pleased that she seemed to find me funny. We spent the rest of the day and evening together and I thought she was great. She might have been being professionally polite, but I don't think so. I felt a spark, I really did.

There was one cloud with a breathable lining on the horizon. One of the other lads who had been invited on the trip was a professional snowboarder and was, I have to admit, a very good looking boy, if you go for twenty-two-year-old, 6′ 2″ muscular Robert Redford lookalikes. I've always found that style a bit obvious myself.

Back in the chalet at night he suddenly deigned to speak to the girls – he hadn't really said a word to them before because he had a girlfriend and wanted to at least try to be faithful. He'd spent most of the day smoking spliff and complaining about the snow, which seemed fine to me.

At 2.25 a.m. he awoke from his dope-induced torpor long enough to say something about half pipes. I felt her interest in me wane like a power failure at a disco. At 2.30 in the morning the Nordic girl suggested she give him a shoulder massage and I knew the game was up. At 3.00 they disappeared into the bedroom together. At 3.01 the other PR girl followed him in.

That's right, he went into the bedroom with both of them. What he did there I don't know and I prefer not to speculate, though they didn't come out before the next morning. I collared him about this the next day.

'I spend the best part of twelve hours making her laugh like she's never laughed before and you, you bastard, come along in the last five minutes and, not content with sleeping with her, have a threesome with her friend, something I've never done in my life.'

He just winked and said: 'Get used to it, Grandad.'

So that's what humour does for you. Not that much. I might not be the funniest man on earth but I was at the top of my game that evening, as was the journalist who was writing the ski-ing piece – a man with more rock 'n' roll stories than you can shake a stick at and one of the most engaging people I've ever met. We were blown out of the water by someone who hadn't managed to say anything more than 'cool', 'sick' and 'radical' all day.

Eva and I did get together in June, although I don't think she was desperate. I, however, was. In fact, it seems for much of my adult life I've been various degrees of desperate, from quite to ravenously.

Men do compete for women, but, even in the summer term of the first year when it seemed I could do no wrong, I had very low self-esteem. I assumed that if I was in competition with another man I would always lose.

I think this is because, though I was reasonably successful with women, I wasn't successful with every woman I fancied. I still felt hesitant or shy and these entirely normal feelings took on the aspect of insurmountable blocks in my head. Even the fact I was surmounting them did not shake my image of myself and I thought that, when it came to girls, I was a complete loser.

Eva, through a couple of girlfriends, knew the clique we used to refer to as The Velvet Underground – posh boys with fake heroin habits and a real addiction to sunglasses indoors. Even though I'd imagined as a boy that people like that were who I wanted to hang around with, I found them as dull as they found me. Chief among these was a painfully cool rich boy called Keith Scroop. Keith had a gratifyingly violent case of acne which gave his skin a sort of Freddy Krueger look. He had hair of the same quality as Alan Myers, he of the savage perm, and he was as thin as a racing snake. In fact, he looked a bit like an inflatable version of Myers with a puncture.

However, a testament to just how fucking cool he really was, he was very successful with girls. He went out with and then *rejected* a poshette called Natasha who was good looking, insouciant and mannered enough to cause even the super-cool Mickey to waft at his collar. Keith had no right to do this. He should have been cowering in his room, full of self-doubt, marinating in Clearasil, not picking up and chucking grade A rock chicks by the pawful.

Keith, however, had his sights set on Eva. As I said, Eva wasn't classically beautiful, but she had a real magnetism to her, an intelligence, a devilment and a sort of boredom with men that challenged them to shake her out of it. Women found her equally as attractive and she inspired several mad crushes from campus lesbians. They were wasting their time, though. She was very attracted to men – largely of the stupid and criminal sort, it seemed to me. I'm not like that, but I can occasionally do a good impression.

At a party after the summer fancy-dress barn dance – Sussex was too PC to have a rag with its sexist 'queen' – Scroop cornered her. I was dressed in a checked shirt and neckerchief, Eva had put on a flowery dress. Scroopy, of course, was too cool for that and was still clad as Bob Dylan circa 1965.

There they were at the entrance to the flat's communal area, leaning into each other in the low light, just about to kiss I thought. Actually, she told me years later, she hadn't fancied him at all and was looking for a way out. That's not how it appeared to me and I thought that in seconds he would be tickling the back of her eyeballs with his tongue. It was my worst nightmare. Again it seemed that the public-school boys were going to win. I aspired to their cool, but I was a lumpen outsider destined to watch at the window while they feasted on the fruits of the earth. I wasn't having it. I don't know if what I did next was an act of inspiration or a loutish practical joke. There was a large bowl of punch next to where they were standing. I walked up to them, picked it up and upended it over Eva's head.

'You!' she said. One of the endearing things about Eva is that she's very short-sighted and so she's always surprised to see you if she hasn't got her lenses in.

I can see the look on Scroop's face now. It bore every shade of contempt that humanity has come up with since Homo Sapiens first heard a Neanderthal describing the water features in his garden.

Eva went to smack me, but I ducked and made for the door. She ran after me screaming 'You fucking bastard, Barrowcliffe, ah, I'm soaked.' Scroop was, of course, too cool to follow.

About a hundred yards down the path, I let her catch up with me, at which point she started hitting me in that girly rabbit punching way. Now, I have never admired the style of John Wayne, as I've pointed out in some of my previous works. And, as someone who has spent his life struggling against cliché – even when it would be just easier to, say, not make your own shoes but buy them in a shop like everyone else – I'm not pleased with what I did next. I'd also like to say I didn't find it sexy – but I did. I can't even begin to consider the sexual politics of the situation but, since Eva never worried too much about that sort of thing, I don't suppose it matters too much.

I caught her wrists as she hit me and let her struggle for a couple of seconds.

'Oh, Eva,' I said, 'you're not as tough as you look.'

She called me a bastard and then suddenly stopped struggling. She looked into my eyes, I looked back and then said, 'Do you want to come back with me?'

'OK,' she said.

At the time I thought that this was a testament to my amazing powers of attraction, my disregard for the rules and willingness to take a chance. Not so. I know Eva very well now, much better than I did then, and I don't think it was all that much to do with me. She had been going to kiss the scabrous Scroop but, when a clownish oik had intervened she thought it was funny to go off and sleep with the oik. I don't think it was even that much to do with annoying Scroop, it just made her laugh to leave Lou Reed fuming at the party while she went off with Bobby Ball. This was the thing about Eva – she had a sense of humour. That didn't mean she was full of put-downs and epigrams, as I tried to be, but that she found people funny. Occasionally it felt a bit like the way a cat finds the struggles of a trapped spider funny, but well, there you go.

There was another side to her in play here too, that of a certain fecklessness and self-effacement, almost a self-negation. It was as if what she wanted didn't really matter and that the only reasonable thing to do was to abandon herself to fate. I'd only discover that later.

With Eva I thought only one thing would impress her – deviant sex. I had to show I wasn't just like all the other boys.

Eva and I slept together that night and for a couple of nights afterwards and it was great fun. I tied her up, more because I wanted to make sure the encounter stuck in her mind than out of any genuine desire to do so. I really liked her and this was my way of trying to make myself stand out from all the other boys who were vying for her attention. Sending her flowers afterwards wasn't going to work, was it?

At dawn she said she wanted to go back to her room to get some condoms and I had an anxious wait for her return.

She did come back. As I heard her knock on the door it was as if something inside me had been affirmed. I was all right, I'd made it. The coolest girl at the university had tried me, liked it and was back for more.

I wanted to bask in her approval. I ran her through my record collection, breaking from kissing to tell her about some particularly impressive lyric or where I'd first heard a particular single. After I'd hopped up and down for the fifteenth time she said, 'Do you think you could put on a long tape and then come back to bed?'

'Fair play,' I said, 'yes.'

We lay with light streaming through the curtains like it does in rubbish songs by acoustic artists. All my life I'd waited for the sensation that I was really living, that the golden days were here. That's how it felt.

I would have liked to have gone out with her, but that suggestion just didn't seem to come up. I thought I'd play it cool and then suddenly hippy Helen was on the scene and I sort of forgot that a relationship with Eva had ever been on the cards, which is fortunate because I don't think at that stage it was.

During the summer, though, I visited Eva and we went to bed together. At two in the morning Eva's sister Martha came home from a club, stuck her head round the door and said hello. She was a year younger than Eva, but her spitting image. The only physical difference between them appeared to be that Eva had dark hair and her sister was blonde. Martha was just as funny as Eva and if anything a little wilder. She shared Eva's unshockable slight distance from life and her taste in Glam/Heavy Metal outfits, in which they both managed to look good – like groupies for the Sweet rather than the hulking provincial metal women I had known as a teenager.

Martha said goodnight and I told Eva how attractive she was. I'd meant to annoy her slightly or spark her jealousy, but she just said, in that languid way of hers, 'I can ask her to come and join us if you like.'

'Are you offering me three-in-a-bed sex?' I said.

'Yes,' she said, 'we do it all the time. It's good fun.'

And, reader, I turned it down. Plrrrrr. Pfff. Hmmm. Awwwww. Nnnnnnnnnnn. This sort of exclamation could go on for pages so I'll stop it there. Once again, the central question of my life looms: what was wrong with me?

Eva may have been winding me up, particularly with her story of how she and her sister used to practise kissing each other 'to see what it would be like with a man', but she might not have.

I have grown, I have changed, I am happy and content but, for God's sake, couldn't I just have gone for it? I'm not saying I want to do it now, just that it wouldn't have been a bad memory to have.

I had two gorgeous teenage sisters, one brunette one blonde, willing to egg me on to whatever depravity I could dream and I refused. I just can't take it in. Why? Why? Why? again. And another – Why?

'She'll probably say "No",' I said.

'She won't,' said Eva.

'She might.'

'No, she won't.'

'She could.'

'She definitely won't.'

I actually had to talk her out of it, as I recall. Why? Because, for all my libertine pretensions, I was scared. This didn't attach itself to any particular outcome: I wasn't scared that I'd fail to perform or that it wouldn't be as good as I thought. I was just scared. Maybe it was the sense that, after that, everything else would be a disappointment. I had this with P.G. Wodehouse when I was nine. I read him then and have never really found much else that amusing by comparison since. We should beware of enjoying ourselves too much in the instant; it makes the long haul dull.

I've given some thought to why having sex with two women appeals so much to men. The easy answer is that there are two of them, therefore that's twice as good as one. I don't think this explains it though. If that's the case, then why not three women or four or one hundred? I'm sure there are men who have all those fantasies but two seems the magic number.

The chief appeal of two women is that it might happen. You're fantasising about something that can occur and does occur to some men. The frisson of possibility, of what might unfold on a drunken evening with your girlfriend and her mate, adds spice to the fantasy.

It's more than this, though, and brings me back to one of the central reasons men need women – personal validation. When a woman goes to bed with you it's a little tick from the world to show that you're OK. You can seduce two women, they can fall for you and they can be focused on you. Even when you're sitting back and watching them, they're performing for you. If you go to bed with three women, then you start to slide out of the picture slightly. You're not seducing people, you're at an orgy. Even if you see yourself with their hands all over you, saying 'You're so blinking great, Mark', then it's not the real you they're after.

Most of the time, when I fantasise about sex, the fantasy includes a large element of seduction. There has to be a reason we're doing what we're doing, a setting, even a historical period (WWII, strangers on a train, death at one's elbow and the emotions high, rather than knights and damsels, for the record). You can't really seduce three people, it's just sex, and sex just as sex is a little dull.

I was due to visit Eva again in a couple of weeks, but she called and cancelled me. I was going to go to Alice in Wonderland's – a psychedelic club – with her and her sister but she wasn't offering second chances, it seemed. I thought I was kicking myself that I had managed to miss out on every boy's dream but, in fact, I was kicking myself over something else. Although the sex with Eva was great, that wasn't primarily what I was interested in. I'd fallen in love with her, thought about her wherever I went, had to damp down fantasies in my head about us making a life together. It was less painful to think that I'd just missed out on another cheap thrill.

11 HOW WAS IT FOR YOU?

SEX AND THE SINGLE WOMEN

Off the cuff I can think of about a dozen women with whom I've had what you might call a one-night stand. My image of the promiscuous male when I was younger was of a roiling, broiling rake of a man searing his way through endless joyful romps. Out of a dozen or so flings I think I have roiled and broiled my way through four of them. Half of the time it's been OK, better than watching TV, and the remaining time it has been not awful but just not very good. I include a list here because I think it offers an insight into the truth of promiscuous sex.

These, then, are some of the one-night stands, the notches on my bedpost and, for better or worse, on my soul. Some of them actually lasted longer than a night, but I include them because they felt more like a series of rolling one-night stands than anything you'd call a relationship.

1. **Miss PriceSaver.** Local beauty queen who dragged me upstairs at a party. I lost my virginity properly to her in a five-minute fumble. She went home. Only went with me because seriously upset at being dumped by boyfriend, a ballroom dancing star. She was a disco diva who wanted to sleep with someone who looked as horrible as she could imagine as act of self-punishment/aggression to him. My anarcho punk, spotty self fitted the bill and I quickly volun-

teered to help. I wanted to come down the stairs and tell the world I had lost my virginity. I couldn't because I had strongly implied I'd lost it years before.

2. Punk girl at party. Bumped into her a week later and, in an attempt to spare her feelings, explained that, given our different backgrounds and aims, although I liked her, it was best not to go out with each other, although . . . She held up her hand. 'It was only a shag, Mark, and not a very good one at that.'

3. Friend of friend at Sheffield Poly. Classed as one-night stand as we had a fantastic first night together when she said she thought I was like Keats. The rest of the relationship was conducted in the sort of discomfort felt by people who have been chatting in a waiting room quite comfortably for ten minutes, but who now find themselves two hours later feeling they should carry on the conversation, but having run out of things to say. Needful, urgent sex of the sort you only have with Catholic girls who are away from home for the first time and can go on the pill without fear of discovery. I seemed struck dumb on the morning afterwards and remained tongue-tied for the rest of the relationship. She finished with me and I, stewing in self-pity, said 'You said I was like Keats.' 'I can't imagine what made me say that,' she said. More upset by blow to literary pretensions than her leaving.

4. Eileen. Catholic father's nightmare. Noticed her undressing me with her eyes at Judo, where she went in order to have more men lie on her. Met one night at club. Spoke for three seconds before she said, 'I don't really need chatting up, shall we go back to your place?' Great sex only mildly spoiled by her passing resemblance to former Soviet leader Leonid Brezhnev. One repeat performance three years later. Memorably told me that the benefit of having a reputation as a slag was that you got laid more often.

5. Tour rep on holiday in Crete (someone else's tour; my middle-class pretensions wouldn't allow me to take a package at that stage of my life). A wild night with her egging me on to go faster and faster on a hired motorbike with a huge Cretan moon over the water, she lithe and beautiful behind me. She took me down to a secret beach she knew and whispered in my ear, 'I'm not going to have sex with you.' And then, rather disappointingly, didn't. Still, spent all night in bed with her naked and kissing and somehow felt very alive so still classed as one-night stand, one of the best.

6. Friend of Keith Scroop, met at party. Beautiful Jewish girl who looked like the woman Cher had in her head when briefing the plastic surgeon. Particularly gratifying that none of her friends liked me. Joyful, wonderful sex. She asked me to call. I didn't because I was seeing Ella at the time. Not going out with Ella, 'just sleeping with her', she wanted to keep her options open. Kicked self for ten years after that, because I threw her number away.

7. Accountant at party conference. Had fantastic night of champagne-fuelled sex. Next day realised I found her very irritating and attempted to not sleep with her on second night of conference. She became furious and forced me to. Said I would have to call her because she'd had oral sex with me. Bumped into her in London (thanks God) a month later and she was incandescently angry with me.

8. Paula. A near ménage à trois experience of the wrong sort – that is, involving another man. We'd gone on a group holiday to the east coast and had all gone for a walk. It had rained heavily and we'd been stuck in the pub since about one in the afternoon. When it closed at eleven we all went down to the beach. Paula and I started kissing, while others were swimming in the sea. I had removed her bra and applied tongue to breast when I became aware of a strange smell, a sort of rancid perfume. I suddenly identified it. Aftershave. I looked up to see a pair of eyes peering at me over her other tit like a racoon popping up from behind a rock. It was my friend Ian who, seeing a spare nipple, had decided to latch on. Paula was all for this, but I'm afraid – no matter how fashionable this sort of thing might be with young footballers – I cannot countenance it and was forced to drive him off with alarums and cries. Paula didn't forgive me and, although we went to bed, she couldn't pull herself out of her sulk.

9. Phoebe. She was the sort of girl you commonly see painted on the side of American military aircraft, very often with devil horns on her head, holding a trident and giving a saucy wink. I went out with her for about three months, but include her here because our relationship was like a series of one-night stands, all mad salsa dancing, drinking and falling into bed together.

She'd been a burlesque artist in Paris, where she was MC of a semi-successful show. She could speak perfect French, but chose not to, playing up her English accent in a way that the average Gallic male finds irresistible. As the average English man, I wasn't far behind.

In addition to being physically gorgeous – 5′ 4″ of taut curves in her fishnets, 8′ 9″ in her heels – she had the added advantage of a convent education which left her with a fruity posh accent, not dissimilar to Fenella Fielding in *Carry On Screaming*.

I actually cannot recall her without imagining a kind of sizzling noise in the background. She was hot stuff.

Her style was very amusing, too – all eyelash fluttering, flappy arms and stories like 'and then the dwarf bit the llama and all hell broke loose'. I found the combination very sexy. Phoebe would look appalled if anyone tried to raise the conversation above which sequins look best close up and what you should wear in a bigger hall. I remember trying to discuss some item with her that had been in the news – I think the war in Bosnia might have been on at the time.

'Blah, blah, blah, fume, blah Bosnia, half-baked opinion, blah, sweeping statement,' I said to Phoebe, in my normal armchair revolutionary manner, 'what do you think?' She took an expression like actresses affect when the spotlight lands on them and they discover it is they who has won the Oscar – a sort of shocked 'Never in a million years did I imagine . . .' look.

'Moi?' she said. 'What do *I* think? Oh, darling, I don't think anything at all. I never do. How would I know? God!' The last part of the sentence was delivered in an appalled manner, as if she were a dowager aunt in a bath chair and I'd suggested she join in the egg and spoon.

On our first night together we went for a meal and afterwards I asked her if she wanted to go for a drink somewhere.

'Oh,' she said, looking crestfallen, 'I was rather hoping you were going to take me home and fuck me with your big dick.'

'Can I take you home and fuck you with my medium-sized dick?' I said.

'That will do nicely,' she said.

Finished with her as her 'always on it', theatrical personality became too difficult to live with. Through her had the first intimation that I had a choice in who I went out with, I didn't just have to accept anyone who ticked seven boxes out of ten.

10. Carmen. Friend of a friend. She had a strange steroid-head staying on her floor, visiting from her home town. I met her one night at a pub and she said when we got back to her flat she'd tell him he could sleep in the kitchen. I bet her £10 that he was smitten with her and would go berserk. She said 'No, he's cool.' I went back with her, she asked him to sleep in the kitchen, he attacked me and ripped my coat, then ran off crying with the words 'I'm getting the bus!' – £10 to me, or minus £90 for a new coat. It didn't concern me. Carmen was lovely and a sock round the ear and a ripped coat were a price worth paying. Carmen and I might have made a go of it – she was pretty, good fun and I found her very attractive, but she met someone else a week after we'd got it together and phoned to say she'd met the love of her life. They later got married, so I guess she was telling the truth.

11. Friend of Charlie's. Nice, affectionate girl who looked strangely like Phoebe – that is, small, dark, slim and curvy. I asked her for a kiss one night after we'd all sat up drinking and doing a Ouija board. She said no. Then she said 'Oh, OK.' We kissed at her bedroom door for a few minutes and then she said 'I've promised myself I'm not going to do this sort of thing.' I took this as a clear green light. I unbuttoned her top and unhooked her bra. 'I'm not going to have sex with you,' she said. I asked her for one last kiss before we said good night then. 'OK, but only if you promise not to take it any further.' I noticed she made no attempt at all to take my hands of her tits. 'OK', I said. We kissed and I noticed she was fiddling with something. Then her skirt fell to the floor. 'Oh, God, I shouldn't be doing this,' she said before sinking to her knees and redefining my idea of a blow job. I had imagined in the past that they were mildly pleasing, visually stimulating, things. In fact, many of them had been vaguely disappointing – tongue applied to the wrong spot, pauses for breath just as things were getting interesting, over-enthusiastic nibbling, nausea-inducing licking down top of shaft, that sort of thing. Sometimes women had gone about it so gently that I could hardly feel it at all. This girl was a revelation. She began by pushing her tongue inside my fore-skin and sandpapering it back and forth over the underside of the tip of my penis, which was certainly very pleasurable. Then she teased with her nails and teeth, running her tongue up and down the length, looking up at me with a wink as she took me in her mouth, which was expert but still in the realms of what I had experienced before. Then she plugged my penis into a light socket – or that's how it felt. She managed to exert the sort of suction that you would think might be useful to the dredging industry, combined with a rubbing of the tongue that seemed to engage every available nerve ending I had. The feeling wasn't limited to what was in her mouth, but seemed to fire off everywhere from my belly to my knees. I imagined my entire body being sucked in through my backside until I was nothing more than a sorry flag of flesh dangling off the pole of my penis. I didn't know that the human body was capable of producing such extreme sensations. I nearly fell over.

'God,' I said, 'how did you do that?'

'Like this,' she said, doing it again and causing me to collapse to the bed. It was actually on the borders of being painful, but a sort of chilli pain, where as soon as it's worn off you think you wouldn't mind a little more.

How is it done? I tried to get her secret out of her so I could pass it on to others. I have experienced this since and the consensus seems to be it just involves sucking very hard, with particular attention to making sure the maximum point of suction is applied to the underside of the tip. I think it's more than that, though I couldn't say what. I just know there appears to be an art to it, along with the science.

We saw each other five or six times – spending all day in bed together. I finished with her when she bought me a teddy bear and it became clear she was becoming serious about me. She was lovely, but not for me. She was a down to earth girl who worked in a shop and didn't really fit in with my pretentious image of myself.

12. Girl from publishers. Asked why she, 22, was sleeping with me, 35. She said 'You're a writer.' Finally all that tapping away at the keyboard came good. She was very pretty and I would have liked to have gone out with her, but I was committed to a failing relationship and couldn't see a way out.

13. Girl met through on-line dating. Warned me that photo on website was very flattering. Not conventionally attractive – built for comfort rather than speed. Told me 'You don't float my boat', then drank three bottles of wine and took me home for night and morning in bed. At first she insisted on having the lights off, I got the feeling because she wasn't confident about the way she looked. Strange because she looked OK to me. Told me to 'leave my bum alone' almost before I'd touched her. I found this odd because I had gone nowhere near her bum. I think the explanation is this: most men are horrible. They are willing to sleep with a girl they find less than attractive on a one-night stand after a few drinks. However, the self-loathing this inspires in them means they favour rough and abusive sex. A very slightly kinder reading of the situation is that, if they have no intention of calling back, then it's an excuse to try the full repertoire of circus tricks on day one.

12   ALL TOMORROW'S PARTIES

Of course, uncasual sex was what I was really after. All I wanted was the golden girl, the life partner, The One. Life without her fell into predictable rhythms. I wish some fortune teller could have filled me in, let me know how it was going to be until *she* would come along to cure me. If, at eighteen, I had gone to such a seer, this is what I would have been told:

The evening begins at home as you shower, put on your clothes and look at your hair. You look great at one angle in the mirror and rubbish at all the others. Can you make sure you approach any woman you are going to meet that night at exactly that angle? Well you can try, sliding up to them at 22.45 degrees and quickly hopping around if they should change their orientation to you.

You don't care what you look like though, do you? Men don't. Of course not. In fact you really, really, care in the way that only a man who repeatedly tells himself he doesn't care can. You can remember a day when you looked great and it haunts you. Will you ever look like that again?

The hair won't do as it's told, a spot lights up like a beacon on your face, your jowls seem to carry too much weight, you have a strangely disappointed look to you like a boxer dog who has been told he's not going on a walk. Everything is wrong. Already the anxiety is building. Will tonight be the night? Will *she* be there?

You meet at the pub. There are three of you, maybe more, and you spend the evening wisecracking and telling stories. Because you cannot bear to drink in a trendy bar you are in a pool table and lino place and there are relatively few girls there, so no real chance to meet anyone. You look around, though; you'd like to meet someone. Perhaps she will come in soon and start playing dominoes. It's not beyond the bounds of possibility. Doesn't quantum physics tell us anything is possible?

At eleven you go to a club. It's not one you've heard of, but it's nearby and someone has recommended it. It must be popular because you have to queue outside until 12.30. You pay, give in your coat and go in. It's not as full as you hoped – they were just holding you outside as advertising. It's not really your crowd either – overcool serious dance music-heads rather than the Madness and Abba party scene you'd hoped for.

The décor is brutal and minimal, the music is insufferably loud, the room is dark and you buy a pint of horrible lager in a plastic glass because you're not the sort for Sol with lime. There are girls there, but they all seem to be talking or dancing. You try not to look desperate, which has the effect of making you look more desperate. There's a girl at the bar, but she looks very different culturally to you, neat and polished and somehow you know it's just not on. Still, there's a really attractive woman on the dancefloor. Oh God, you're going to have to dance. No, she's out of your class, forget it. You put it off for an hour or two, chatting to your friends as best you can. It's nearly impossible, though, like trying to talk in a jet-testing lab.

Eventually, having repeated some crack ten times such as 'No. I said "You say what you like Vicar, my duty as an

Englishman means I'm not leaving without that baboon!" – I said "*Baboon*! Baboon, not *Balloon*.". Oh, I give up.'

You're losing the will to live so you go out onto the dancefloor. The attractive girl has gone, but you hop about gamely, fearful that you will be mistaken for a bear on a hot plate and that someone will try to kidnap you and make you perform in a Russian circus. But how do you approach anyone? Look like you're enjoying it, that's the way. That doesn't work. How could anyone enjoy this music, there aren't even any words? You catch a glimpse of yourself in a reflective surface and you have a look on your face like someone having his nails pulled out by the Gestapo, but who won't give the bastards the satisfaction of screaming. You try to convert this into a smile and slough up and dance opposite a girl. She moves off. Or she stays there. This is rave culture, remember – maybe its very beginning, maybe its middle, maybe the truly depressing days of its end. These women are dancing for the love of it, not as a mating ritual. However, just occasionally you will see her – beautiful, intelligent-looking. You catch her eye. She smiles. You restrain the urge to propose.

'You going to buy me a drink then?'

Oh no, it's some toxic blonde who is dressed for a hen night she will never be invited on because she hasn't got any friends. She's interposed herself between you and the girl of your dreams, wobbling like a blancmange in a boob tube. You're too polite to tell her to sod off and now the girl, the one you saw for the first time ten seconds ago but with whom you have already envisaged a holiday in Tuscany, has gone. Perhaps you deserve it anyway because you've rather leaped ahead of yourself and, buoyed by her imaginary love, have started wondering what sort of school she favours for the kids.

The peroxide munter is swaying in front of you, waiting for a reply.

'I'm gay,' you say, wishing it was that simple. Oh to be gay, to be able to divorce love from sex, to settle down with someone who would assemble flat packs for you, reach high shelves and never need to discuss problems. God didn't make it that easy on you, son.

Eventually, after pretending to get excited when some tune that sounds exactly like the last one comes on, you stagger off the dancefloor. You bump into the girl, the one who was in your fantasy about Tuscany.

'Hello,' you say.

'Hi,' she says, really friendly. You find an island in the torrent of sound, maybe you have to go out of the doors and into the corridor with the loos. You talk and you get on, she's pretty and engaging and nice and then her boyfriend comes over and you realise they're both off their tits. She wasn't being friendly to you, she was being friendly to everyone. Her boyfriend looks exactly the sort of bloke you'd like to be.

'Do you go clubbing a lot?' you ask.

'No, we stay in a lot of weekends now,' he says. Of course they do, the lucky, lucky, bastards. You dream of that glorious Saturday night when you will be free of your bonds. There will be wine, curry, and a French film until 10.30, sex in front of *Match of the Day*, a couple of lines of coke and then you'll sit up chatting, drinking, smoking, kissing and being in love until three. You'll fall asleep in each other's arms then up in time for a roast dinner in a pub the next day. All afternoon will be spent strolling the south bank in the sunshine, there'll be a play, a ride on the river past St Paul's, holding hands as the spray makes rainbows with the light. This is life as it was meant to be lived. This is civilisation.

But not for you, my love, not tonight my love. For you the grind, the blind toil of the dancefloor where they will try to break you like Samson upon the wheel. You wouldn't mind, if only they'd throw in a Delilah.

The loneliness grows inside you and the lager hasn't made you drunk, it's just given you a headache. Ask someone the time, you never will get a watch. It's 2.30. In another four hours the club will close and you can go home. You just can't risk going at 5.25 in case she turns up at 5.30. You're twenty-two. Never mind, there's only another eighteen years of this to go – on average twice a week, more when you're alone, less when you're with someone.

If you don't go to a club you will go to some underpopulated party and get stuck in the kitchen trying to prove to an equally desperate bloke that Van Morrison should be condemned and pulled down and that Nick Drake was rubbish. You do like a row.

There will be one very plain girl there who would spend a lot of time dancing, but you won't be able to get the energy up to talk to her so you'll just go home. The whole experience will feel like trying to start some old car. It's not the despair that will kill you but the hope.

Fortune tellers don't give readings like that do they? They prefer to be positive and to be paid. That was my life. I wanted to go away to the sea, to climb mountains and visit museums with the girl of my dreams, but the only way I could see of doing it was spending my time on the treadmill, stuck in some box of a club poisoning myself, screaming without being heard and hoping that *she* was going to walk through the door to take me away from it all.

13 PLATONIC

'If you were a *Godfather* character, which one would you most likely be?' says Vanessa, speccing over the top of some film magazine.

'Fredo,' I say. It is lunchtime and we are sitting outside the pub nearest work. The freedom of university is just a memory and the day taunts me with its sunlight. I have an hour of this before it's back to the must and the dust of the office. The yuppie thing has not yet died. In fact, in the spirit of the firework burning brightest just before it goes out, it seems we are in a thicket of yuppies, but this is yuppie manqué – lopsided shoulderpads, over-red lipstick, fake-leather Filofaxes and chinos from Next. The idea of being a self-seeking cash pig on mega-bucks has been caught by self-seeking cash pigs on mini-bucks and I am attached to this culture like some hideous fat tick, hating it and hated, yet sustained and nourished by it. I smoke my fags and drink my beer, trying to block out conversations about mortgage rates. I am a creature out of time.

It's probably three years, maybe four or five, before Noel Gallagher will change the words to 'Get It On' and explain the world from my point of view. *Loaded* magazine is not yet dreamt of. When it does come out it will describe its readers as 'fifty per cent *Guardian*, fifty per cent *Sun*'. My brain feels pulled in both directions. I don't know it but, for once in my life, I am ahead of the times. This is just a coincidence. I – and plenty like me – was like this before 'lad culture', I will be like it afterwards, but, owing to a historical accident, I am briefly at the cutting edge. It's like my friend Charlie. He has worn the same thing since he was sixteen: grey V-neck, black jeans, black shoes. He never varies. Every five years a fashion student approaches him at a party and tells him she's never seen anyone so cool. He must be in the industry, right, to be so in tune with next season's look?

Vanessa finds my disregard for advancement, my dedication to cigarettes and alcohol, combined with my knowledge of, but lack of enthusiasm for, PC intellectual theory, fascinating. I find her burning intelligence amazing. She is falling in love with me. I am falling in love with her, though neither of us know it.

'Fredo? Really, I would have thought you'd have been more like Sonny.'

'Nah, too tough for me. I'm Fredo. Fun, but don't stake your life on me,' I say.

She laughs and shakes her head.

'Which one would you be?' I say.

'The lawyer, Tom Hagen. He's got my colouring.'

True, I think, and he was bright and thoughtful, but I see an opportunity to tease the feminist Vanessa.

'You can't choose a man, that is abhorrent and against nature. What next? Shall ships sail upon the land?'

'There aren't that many female characters in it. Kay, I suppose.'

'The clever, beautiful girlfriend who realises her man isn't the person she supposed him to be?'

As it turned out that parallel was pretty much on the money. If Vanessa reminded me of any character from fiction, though, it wasn't anyone from *The Godfather* but Lisa Simpson. She was bright, funny, talented and incredibly perceptive but when it came to men, and me in particular, there was something she just didn't get.

I can remember her wondering aloud what the playwright Arthur Miller had seen in Marylin Monroe to marry her. What did they talk about? she'd asked.

'Well I expect she had difficulty speaking with her mouth full,' I said.

Vanessa and I teamed up virtually as soon as we met. I'd briefly moved out of journalism to take a well-paid job in financial PR. She was a cerebral Yorkshire woman who was a fellow PR goon in the agency where I worked in the primordial gloom of north London. She sat next to me and we immediately got on.

We made an unlikely pair. She'd spent her university years shaving her head and publishing feminist tracts. When I met her she was still part of a women's collective, whatever they do, but she was moving away from the meetings and placard-waving model of the eighties women's movement. That is, like many women at that point, she had not abandoned her feminism, but was abandoning her Puritanism. She'd come to the position that she would quite like a nice frock, and that putting make-up on wasn't a ritual defilement of her face in order to fit with masculine standards of beauty but good fun. At the beginning of the nineties there was a women's movement, by the end we had Girl Power. It was an enormous shift.

Still, I think people would have expected us to rub each other up the wrong way. Maybe this was part of our initial attraction. It surprised others that we got on so well and I think we both enjoyed that. It wasn't just show, though. Despite our apparent differences we shared a sense of humour and came from very similar backgrounds.

'How's the relationship with Ella, finished or not finished at the mo?' she says.

I turned Vanessa's wrist and looked at her watch. 'Finished, I think. Unless the watch is slow. She normally calls to say it's back on around 1.30, two to three hours after my traditional 11 a.m. answerphone apology, anyway. At five we will have a row about what we're going to do tonight. She will say "It isn't working, is it?" We will then break up and I'll be free until the evening reconciliation at around nine if you fancy a pint later.'

'You have a tidal relationship,' says Vanessa. 'Are the highs and lows particularly marked during spring and full moons?'

'No, it's pretty much always shit,' I say.

I think of Ella and a song I used to listen to pops into my head. It posed the question: can a moment of perfect pleasure be worth a lifetime of remorse?

I have the answer to that one: 'No.'

It's the nature of bills that they are given to you after your meal. Only then do you realise that the relatively inexpensive starter, the frankly cheap main course, the olives and the breadsticks and the water you had to go with your wine add up to a near fortune. If someone had given me the bill for my relationship with Ella right at the beginning, I doubt either of us would ever have gone for it. We got together the week after university finished and had our last kiss fifteen years later. In that time our proportion of civil to uncivil words to each other was about 35/65, I think.

This is how the bill would have been itemised.

Break-ups: 20 or so. *Cost: Dignity.*

Reconciliations: 19. *Cost: Weariness of friends.*

Plates (to my head): 1. *Cost. Slight cut. Luckily I still have the reactions of a panther.*

French pastries (bodged in her face): 1. *Cost: Lecture on violence against women.*

Household items (broken in rows): 30. *Cost: About £600.*

Days of unadulterated pleasure: 50 – as in a total of 1,200 hours. *Cost: Wistfulness in remembrance.*

Whole uninterrupted days of getting on: 10 – mostly at start of relationship. *Cost: Sum total of misery of rest of relationship. Attempt to recapture will sustain us in anguish for 15 years.*

Days of undiluted woe: 2,548. *Cost: Premature ageing. Weakened immune systems. Probable early death.*

Attempts to give up smoking (me): 200, final one successful. *Cost: More rows.*

Attempts to give up smoking (she): more than 200. *Cost: More rows.*

Attempts to give up drinking (me): 20 – unsuccessful during this period. *Cost: Thousands of pounds when failure sees me dive back into a sea of pints.*

Diets (me): 10. *Cost: 1 stone heavier by end.*

Diets (she): 6. *Cost: Self-esteem when collapses.*

Rows: About 8,000. *Cost. All the brilliant times we could have been having.*

Total cost: Both of our sanities.

Tip: The first time it goes wrong, get out.

There was one moment that has sustained me throughout this. We'd got together at the end of university after three years of being friends. There had been a hitch at the last minute when my friend the Lothario Terry Bate had appeared on the first night we went for a drink as prospective lovers. Luckily I'd won a pint off Ella by betting that Bate would try to chat her up by saying how an earlier betrayal by a girl had left him very wary of women and that, having spoken to Ella about it, he'd seen things in a different light and felt ready to love again. It was his standard chat-up patter and, unbelievably, it was powerfully effective. I also told her he had herpes, just to be doubly sure. Well, he did have herpes.

Bate off the scene, I'd gone up to see her in her home in the east of England when her parents were away. I remember her face, looking for me as I got off the train. She seemed so young and full of hope as we fell into each other's arms. We'd spent afternoons naked in front of the fire, drinking and smoking and talking. She looked pale and beautiful in the dying light and I'd seen she was in love with me. I was in love with her too. I was supposed to go back to work in Brighton at the weekend, but the Great Storm of 1987 had struck. South-east England was flat, nothing was moving anywhere and God had granted me another couple of days of just looking at her. It should always have been like that, I thought: no cares, no jobs, no wish to be going anywhere or to be anything that we weren't, wine and firelight and midnight conversations forever. But then we'd come back to Brighton. It had looked stripped and bare without its trees. The whole town had the air of a party room after the guests had gone. It was time to leave. We'd moved to London and work had displaced me as the centre of her life. She was still funny and beautiful, but I wasn't as important as her next promotion or her next appointment. She was still important to me, though. I had fallen in love like you might fall into a pit and now had no idea how to get out.

My life began at 5.30 p.m. She didn't want a social life,

work gave her all she needed. We had been together for three years at the point I was talking to Vanessa and would continue to go out with each other for another four, buying a house, getting engaged. Our last crack at making it work was in about 2003. At least we gave it a go.

Vanessa continues reading her film magazine and I tell her news about Ella.

'She's had all her hair cut off.' Ella had trimmed her beautiful Art Nouveau sweep of hair in an attempt to look more work-like.

'The page boy look's in.'

'Not with me. If I'd wanted to go out with a page boy I'd have joined the clergy. She's six feet tall, white as a ghost and has a crop of red hair on the top. She looks like the cartoon rooster Foghorn Leghorn.'

'You told her that didn't you?'

'Might have.'

'You did. And you said "Ah say, ah say, ah say boy"?'

'Might have.'

Vanessa shakes her head. 'You'd find it easier to keep in a mouthful of bees than hold down a joke, Barrowcliffe.'

I shrugged and raised my glass.

'I am what I am.'

'Did she go mad?'

'Of course. She said I was being brutal.'

'Which you were.'

'No, I was holding back from what I wanted to say.'

'What did you want to say?' Vanessa puts her hand on her head, bracing herself for the worst.

'You have betrayed your beauty.'

'You see, this is it with you isn't it Mark?' She laughed. 'I think you've gone as low as you can possibly go, but you can always surprise me. There are undreamt-of basements to the hell of your soul.'

She seems to find it amusing that I'm like this. It's certainly a change from her boyfriend.

'How's Seb?' I say. Seb is the heir of an industrial dynasty who is working as a model, but really wants to make it as a fine artist. There are, needless to say, a number of levels on which I don't like the sound of Seb.

'He's fine. His friends are wankers, though. Do you know what one of them said to me this weekend?'

'Relate the outrage,' I say.

'She said "Oh, hello, you're Seb's lodger aren't you?"'

'How long have you been together now?'

'Five years. We've been living together for three.'

'Did you chin her?'

'Of course I fucking chinned her.'

It is understood by both of us that she didn't in fact chin Seb's snobby Oxbridge friend, just as it's understood that she'd have liked to.

'How's the counselling going?' she says.

'Oh, a weight's been lifted from my shoulders just by paying £30 to have someone nod slowly and say "And how does that make you feel?" If she asks me three more times I think all our problems will be at an end.'

'You have to give it a chance, Mark.'

'OK,' I say, 'you judge. Here's the questionnaire we did last week.'

I hoick it out and supply our comments, for the amusement and horror of Vanessa.

'*Question. Your partner says they will make dinner.*'

Vanessa has just taken some wine, which she now snorts out down her nose.

'Bear with me,' I say. I go on reading from the question-naire.

'*Do you:*

A) Look forward to it. They know you so well, and take such care, it's bound to be something nice.

B) Laugh. You know they'll get a takeaway, but that's OK.

C) Think you have to remind them to get some ingredients or they'll forget to do it.'

Vanessa is now howling with laughter. 'You don't cook. You don't even do takeaways. In fact, takeaways would represent a substantial improvement to your diet. For most of your life, Barrowcliffe, you have eaten from newsagents. You're the only man I know who regards three packets of dry roast nuts as an entrée.'

I continue.

'Ella's answer is C. She said she had to remind me to do everything, despite the fact I will never do it. She said my solution is to ask her to stop moaning, not to do it.

'My answer is C too. Although I wouldn't dare to remind her, and I know she'll forget because something will have come up at work. And I'll approach the meal with a feeling of sinking dread that she will start offloading anxieties about work or blaming me for not being a cross between Melvyn Bragg and Keanu Reeves (artistic kudos of former, looks of latter, not other way round).'

'You're not that unlike Keanu Reeves,' says Vanessa.

'Lowest form of wit,' I say. She nods a 'thank you very much' like a grateful performer.

'*Question 2. Your partner is on a night out with friends and they are enjoying themselves. Does your partner:*

A) Leave early to snuggle up with you.

B) Invite them back to yours. Says you won't mind.

C) Phone and say they'll be back late.

'Ella's answer is: "Oh my God, not only are my problems severe, they're commonplace. I'm one of the herd. That is so depressing. *B.* He invites them back to our house despite the fact he knows I will mind. They will still be there two days later having an impromptu party that I am expected to join."

'My answer is: *A.* She leaves early to snuggle up with some project development. In fact, she doesn't go. She stays in working on "ideas".

'*Question 3. Describe all your positive feelings towards your partner.*

'She says she's not quite in that space at the moment, then has a go at the counsellor for asking a stupid question. I refuse to answer as it'll only get used as a stick to beat me.

'*Question 4. Describe all the negative things you think about your partner in less than 25 words.*

'Ella's answer is: boorish, lazy, self-satisfied (only counts as one word), drunk, self-obsessed, loud, philistine, unsupportive, unambitious, competitive in small things, quitter in the big.'

'I think drunk's unfair,' says Vanessa. 'You don't actually get drunk, which has to go down as a near miracle considering the amount you drink.'

'Boorish, lazy etc etc?'

'Oh, they were right on the nose,' she says. 'What did you say about her?'

'Trembling, aspirational twerp petrified that she will be discovered as a dirty little shop girl who hasn't yet shaken the Kettering muck from her boots.'

'Congratulations on your restraint.'

'*Question 5. Why are you together?*

'Ella's answer: "I love him."

'My answer: "I love her."'

I did love her too. There had been a bitter row on the way back from the counsellor's office when I'd said, 'You just can't laugh at yourself, can you Ella?'

'Why bother when I've got so much to go on with you?' she said. She made me laugh, as she so often did, and it had led to a brief truce in which we nipped into Claridges, had a drink and had sex in the loos. This sounds exciting, but these tempestuous relationships are draining and you move through your days with a mild pressure headache.

'That's almost beautiful,' says Vanessa, as I finished the story. 'Time to go back to work.'

'To fulfil my life's vocation. "What do you want to be when you grow up, little Mark?", "Why I'd like to be in financial PR and spend my days making money for people I hate,"' I say.

'Follow me, my ray of sunshine,' she says.

I really loved Vanessa. She was like no other girl I'd met. She was my soul mate: same culture, same sense of humour, different enough to make me think, similar enough for us to click. At this stage of our relationship we never tired of each other, no matter how long we spent in each other's company. She had a depth to her intelligence that you very rarely encounter and an emotional perceptiveness that was sometimes stunning.

For instance, I had an argument with Mickey about the attendance of another friend, Tom, at my birthday party.

'He can come as long as he promises not to condescend to me,' I said.

Mickey erupted, accusing me of always being nasty for the sake of it, of seeing the worst in people and never giving anyone a chance. I found this surprising because Tom is famously condescending. He's an upper-middle-class boy from west London and he's in the Hip Hop fashion industry. The prosecution rests, m'lud.

Vanessa intervened, established that Tom had just lost a parent and, not only that, had just been diagnosed as seriously ill himself. She said it was understandable that Mickey felt defensive towards his friend, but the argument wasn't really about Tom at all. The terms of my relationship with Mickey had shifted in the last year or so and I was seeing less of him. I felt that Mickey had only liked me at university as some sort of comedy Midlander and was now reverting to his cool metropolitan friends. No wonder I was scathing about them; I thought they were taking Mickey away from me. It wasn't an expression of discontent with Tom but of affection for Mickey.

She finished speaking and Mickey and I looked at each other.

'Er, yes,' I said.

'You're not a therapist are you?' said Mickey, 'because I think you probably should be.' She'd hit it bang on and told us something that we'd not even realised ourselves.

Vanessa and I clicked completely. We didn't need to say that to us Woody Allen, Half Man Half Biscuit, Bowie, Morrissey and Jane Austen were heroes, nor that Noel Edmunds, Kilroy and all Radio One DJs of the time apart from John Peel – I'd ditched the offensive badge years before – were villains. Suddenly I had someone who understood exactly where I was coming from, that if you liked football you weren't a moron and if you liked books you weren't a snob. You could do both and be OK. We discovered ourselves in each other.

Best of all, we were free to be friends. There was no expectation that we'd finish up in bed together. It was like having a smart, brilliant sister. If Vanessa liked me, I must be OK. I might even have hidden depths. I was tremendously proud of her friendship, which I considered as a sort of badge of my worth as a human being.

Then one day Vanessa was in the office in a terrible state. Her eyes were puffy and, in the middle of a conversation, she suddenly left the room. Even I, who was in a different sort of terrible state, being typically hungover, noticed. I thought a near relative must have died, but it wasn't that. She and Seb had split up; she never told me the exact details, but she had left him. Her attitude was that it had gone and now she was moving on. No, they would not be friends.

I wonder in retrospect if it was to do with me. I don't say that Vanessa was lining me up before she risked parting from Seb; that sort of behaviour is more my style. It's just that one of the things that prevents many people splitting with unsuitable partners is that they feel they have a lack of options. They know they'll get someone one day, but they can't face the lonely months, the parties and the nightclubs, Christmas at the parents on their own. Having someone at least on the horizon gives courage. I doubt this was the case with Vanessa, really. She was very strong minded and has something of a 'no pain, no gain' attitude to life that rather contrasts with my 'no pain, no problem' approach.

Our relationship continued as before; I ran her through my vicissitudes with Ella and she talked about Seb, a bit. I think she realised what I realised; I was unlikely to come up with anything she hadn't thought of herself. In fact, asking me to give advice on matters of the heart is rather like inviting one of those people who says stuff like 'have you looked in your coat pockets?' and 'Where did you last see them?' to help you find your keys. I'm not going to add anything to the equation.

Still, like Fredo from *The Godfather*, I was there to take her out to cinema, to pub and to party. Even in my times away from Ella, it never occurred to me that Vanessa and I might go out with each other. I don't know why not. She was pretty, she was funny, she was my best friend. There was no real thought involved in it. Men are creatures of habit and I simply hadn't started off considering her as a girlfriend, so I didn't when she left Seb. In some ways she got 'friended out'. This had happened to me countless times. Your relationship has a pattern and a rhythm which kisses would disrupt.

Beyond this there was always the spectre of Ella, calling me back for one last go to see if we could get it right, to see if the destiny I'd expected to embark on when I went to university was going to come to fruition. I don't think I considered taking things further with Vanessa until about four seconds before I actually did. It would have been better for all if maybe I had.

14 CUPID AND PSYCHE

There were clear warning signs if I had been able to pay them heed. Vanessa is a tactile person and sometimes punctuates her conversation with taps on the arm, affectionate cuffs and hugs. I was very uncomfortable with this. At the time I assumed it was just because that was how I was brought up. My family are not huggers, nor handshakers, nor peckers on the cheek. I think the only time I've touched my father since I haven't needed carrying is when helping him out of a seat. So my uncomfortable shifting away from Vanessa's chummy pats signalled nothing to me beyond my normal dislike of casual physical contact. In fact, I think it was a subconscious reluctance to take things any further.

I have always disliked the word 'empowering', but I have to admit that Vanessa's friendship empowered me. I had someone to give me all the companionship and stability of an ongoing relationship that I was seeking. This took the heat off my search for another woman. I didn't have to look for Miss Right, I could just go with Miss There and Available without worrying that she thought Big Audio Dynamite were better than The Clash. Vanessa gave me all the confidence of going out with a girl without the dashed inconvenience of actually having to do so. The result was that the smell of failure that might have clung to me after Ella's departure was blown away and I could approach women in the manner of Bond flicking a casino chip onto 13 black rather than a washed-up punter putting his last fiver on the 3.15.

The male ego's preferred food is the regard of an intelligent woman. I'm not sure this was a good thing for me. Rejected by Ella for a longer period than a lunchtime – we split for around three months – perhaps I would have re-evaluated who I was, modified my approach to life. Vanessa, though, loved my laddy, over-ironic, under-focused character and helped me feel proud of it all over again. Ella had been the idiot for finishing with me, not me for driving her away, I thought.

So when Catriona appeared in my life, I was ready to act in the cool and carefree manner necessary to represent myself as the smooth hound at large. In other moods I might have wilted in front of Catriona, found myself stumbling over my words or trying too hard to be liked. Propped up by Vanessa's friendship, though, I felt ready for anything.

From the second I saw Catriona she entered my fantasy life, in fact she fitted in so well with my passions and tastes that it seemed for a while almost that she'd been created by them.

I was downstairs in production, sorting out the line-up for the company football team the first time I saw her, and I'm afraid to say it was like something from a *Carry On* film.

'Right, Bob, we'll play 4, 4, 2, you up front with Leroy; Dave, Al, Sean and Knobhead in midfield, back four of . . . and who is this charming creature?'

Catriona wouldn't be everyone's cup of tea but, to me, she seemed to have walked out of my 'design your own woman' store. She was about twenty-three, had long, straight, black hair, pale skin, a face like a rather spiteful elf and a slim but curvy figure. A few years later, when I saw Christina Ricci in *Buffalo 66* I thought that she looked rather like her.

She had a rock-chick air, blood-red lips and nails, and

dramatic eyeshadow to go with her eyes of unholy green. Her clothes weren't exactly office standard either – a floaty blouse and sailor-style trousers that tied at the top. On other people this might have looked earth mothery, but on her it managed to convey unconventionality, as well as a bit of decadence, without being *that* tarty. It was a fine balancing act and she pulled it off perfectly.

I didn't actually say 'and who is this charming creature?' Instead I gave her my best chat-up line.

'Hello,' I said, looking directly at her. You could, and should, never do this to most women, because it would rightly be seen as sexual harassment. How do you know the ones who will like it, though? You don't, but, when they look like Catriona, you can take a good guess.

'Hello,' she said back, holding full eye contact. She was doing one of the most responsible jobs in the department, was paid much more than me and was on the fast track to the top, but she had an accent straight off the Mersey docks.

'Can I help?' said Bob.

'Just borrowing a rubber,' said Catriona, with heavy emphasis on the 'rubber'. She was chewing gum as she spoke and didn't stop looking straight into my eyes.

'Right,' said Bob, 'er, the team.'

Catriona said 'See ya!' and was gone, although as she left her eyes did a sort of sly catty slide and seemed to stay behind slightly longer than the rest of her.

'I see trouble ahead,' sang Bob under his breath after she'd gone.

'Fingers crossed,' I said.

I was delighted when, at a gig at the Underworld in Camden the next week, part of a Death Metal movement I wanted a laugh at, I saw her. This time she was much more rocky looking, sort of Gothy, but without being that obvious.

She dressed like a female version of Ian Astbury from the Cult – Red Indian meets Siouxsie Sioux meets someone a bit more glam. It looks better on a girl.

It turned out she'd come on her own to the gig. Her boyfriend couldn't make it and she really wanted to see Bolt Thrower who, I think I'm right, were on with Pestilence and Autopsy, although it could have been Nocturnus. What impressed me was that she did actually want to see them. She hadn't come to chat to anyone, or even – annoyingly – to pick anyone up. She'd come to see the band. Girls don't often do that.

It was a good gig if you like that sort of thing – which I did – and we spoke at the end and immediately set up a sort of teasing banter, which was great. I was determined that, if she liked me, I wouldn't get friended out. I'd learned a bit in the preceding years and wanted to make my intentions absolutely clear. We kind of went into a *Saturday Night, Sunday Morning* routine that was, I suppose, our heritage.

'Have you got a boyfriend?' I said.

'Oh yeah.' Her eyes flicked from me, up and down, as if to signal 'Go on then, impress me.'

'How long have you been going out?'

'A year.' She tilted her head from side to side.

'Christ, you must be bored with him by now. Get rid of him.'

'You're a cheeky fucker aren't you?' She laughed.

'I'm just trying to help you. A girl like you needs a bit of variety.'

'I know the sort of variety you've got in mind,' she said. 'I've seen you at work, you reckon you're the dog's bollocks, don't you?'

'That's just what they made me have on my office door. Inside I'm a deeply sensitive bundle of nerves.'

'Yes, I can see.' She tapped me on the chest with one of her dark fingernails, 'Get us a drink.'

'You get me one. You wanted the equality.' In casting off the PC shackles of Sussex University, I rather went the other way for a bit.

'I'm not like that.'

'What are you like?'

'Get us a drink and you might find out.'

'I'll get you a big drink for that. Would you like it in a bucket?'

'I think I'll get the drinks,' she said. 'What do you want?'

'Everything,' I said in a faux cockney accent. And she knew, it was a quote from *The Italian Job* – the proper version, with Michael Caine. Things couldn't have been better.

'You'll make do with a lager for now.'

'OK, I will. For now.'

I have rarely been in such a sexually charged conversation. As I spoke I moved nearer and nearer to her and she didn't back off, just inclining her head to keep focused on my eyes. It was like something from the 1970s and we both knew we were playing roles, but it just seemed very natural. I immediately sensed the sort of thing she liked. Girls who follow bands like Bolt Thrower go for slightly ridiculous, overstated men. I am quite like that anyway and it was fun to play up that side of myself.

On the Wednesday we had a Labour Party disco bash, which I attended with Vanessa. This was my kind of political activism – a subsidised bar, roast spud buffet and Hot Chocolate on the turntable.

Vanessa and I had the most incredible conversation. I had been finished with Ella for three or four months or so and it was maybe six months after Vanessa had split with Seb. It was as if we laid our lives open to each other, not in a miserable way, but all our hopes and fears were out on the table. I had the feeling there was a rare honesty between us.

I've said before that fantasy plays as strong a part in the male mind as reality. There was an almost palpable tenderness between us, like that moment in the movies just before the heroine and hero kiss, a kiss that comes as a reward for struggles and hard-won respect. It was as if a declaration of love was what the situation called for, the line that turns the second act of the play and sends you helter-skeltering towards the end. This sounds strange, but it was almost an artistic requirement of the rare feeling we had summoned that we should kiss. The beauty of the moment destroyed all context. I didn't see that we were about to wreck everything we had ever valued between us.

'I'm glad you finished with Seb,' I said, leaning close to her.

'I wanted to thank you,' she said, 'you've been very good.'

'What do you mean?'

'You haven't tried to take things forward between us. A lot of men would have leaped in as soon as Seb was off the scene.'

There was an idea. Why hadn't I made a play for her? I couldn't work it out. She was the best female friend I'd ever had, she was pretty, stylish, fun. What had been wrong with me?

We sat at the corner of the rope-lighted disco very close to each other. Then something occurred to me about our friendship which hadn't occurred to me before.

'I love you,' I said.

'I know,' she said, 'I love you too.'

We kissed and I expected to feel that my whole life had been made worthwhile. I expected a supernova. Instead, there was a strange feeling of anti-climax, like the one that must sweep mission control when the announcer cries 'Lift off!', a little puff of smoke emerges, and the rocket stays where it is. It was like with Anna at university. I'd mooned after her for ages and then known it wasn't going to work the second I'd kissed her.

In a flash I realised I had held back not because I wanted to give Vanessa time but because I liked our relationship just the way it was. I would have liked her to have met some man, like me but not me, for me to have got together with Catriona, and for us all to have gone out on the town together, shared a chalet on holiday, babysat for each other.

All the confidences, the admissions, the honesties that I'd had with Vanessa were now compromised. She had moved from being my confessor to the subject of my confessions. We had been walking a path together, side by side. Now we would have to take turns carrying each other, be responsible for each other, answerable, even. I could never be as honest with her again because now, if I said I was afraid or lonely or even if I just fancied someone, those things would cost her. I had never had a proper friendship with a woman before. Was I going to throw that away, bury it beneath a load of arguments about the washing-up?

My head was swimming and not just with alcohol as we got into a taxi and went back to her house. I was having second thoughts on the way through the front door. I immediately knew that we should have stayed as just friends, but I also felt that I really did love her. I did love her, it was genuine and it was confusing.

We went to bed, but I couldn't concentrate because I was gripped by the overwhelming feeling of having crossed a line we shouldn't have crossed. Why couldn't I have stopped it, just have said 'No, we've made a mistake' as we got back to her house? Because I didn't want to upset her. Better to drag things out for several years and inflict some genuine psychic harm than risk some short-term discomfort.

Sex, really great sex, is all in the eyes, I think. There are understandings between you, what someone enjoys, what they would like to do and to have done to them, and it's all communicated in glances. There are glances of complicity as she undoes your belt or you put your hand beneath her bra strap, narrowings of the eyes as she approaches something she really likes to do, widenings of pleasure as you surprise her or are surprised. I couldn't look at Vanessa while we were doing it.

Our complicities were those of conversation. It felt very wrong – like trying to catch the twinkle in someone's gaze while you were both strangling a puppy. I didn't feel as if I was making love to her, I felt as if I was destroying it.

I don't think Vanessa enjoyed it much, and did actually ask me if I was OK at one point. The next day I was hungover, in need of a shower, wearing yesterday's shirt and my tie felt like an old poultice, too tight no matter how I loosened it. It was not a good feeling.

My mind was disordered and I couldn't decide whether I was the happiest man alive or just a complete bastard, to myself as much as Vanessa. Why hadn't it worked between us? Was there any chance we could go back to what we'd had before, a good and precious friendship?

I couldn't look at Vanessa all day and, as the second hand swung on to 5.29 and fifty-nine seconds, I stood to make my way through the door. Vanessa fixed me with a glare.

'You,' she said, 'I want to talk to you.'

I do believe, to an extent, in national stereotypes. The Dutch are literal-minded and rude, the Germans rule-bound and rude, the Americans rule-bound, naïve and very polite.

I know these aren't really true – Dorothy Parker was not rule-bound, naïve nor noted for her politeness and Van Gogh wasn't all that literal-minded – but they are little prejudices I carry in my head. I'll say this, when it comes to bone-chilling anger the women of Yorkshire set the standard.

'What is your problem?' she said, catching me halfway down the stairs. She seemed to be vibrating slightly in her rage.

'I'm just hungover.'

'You haven't looked at me all day.'

She'd been trying to catch my eye, to give me a knowing smile or a cheeky wink. I'd just kept my head below the barricade of my typewriter.

'If you think it's a mistake then you just need to say,' she said.

'It's not that,' I said. 'I just feel really ill.'

Why didn't I say 'Yes, it was a mistake, but I would like you as my dear friend for the rest of my life'? Politeness. Warped politeness. And also arrogance. I just didn't think she could take the information that I didn't want to go out with her. Then there was cowardice: I was afraid she'd be angry with me. On top of all this, I wasn't at all sure I didn't want to go out with her. Perhaps it was such a momentous step that I was just getting temporary cold feet. It was certainly possible. That had happened with Anna. I'd regretted not forming a relationship with her for years afterwards.

Vanessa asked me to come for a drink, but I said I needed to go home. I hit the sack early. The next day was a Friday and, as I recall, Vanessa had booked it off to visit her parents.

Her absence lifted my spirits because I didn't want to have to think about where we were going from there just at that second. I clattered on through the day at my typewriter, smoking roll-ups and drinking too much coffee. I'd come to the conclusion that the best way to make the hours fly was to work hard, rather than sit staring at the wall and, as a result, was enjoying work more.

It was 5.30 and I was at a loose end. This wasn't unusual, we very rarely gathered the troops until the last minute in those days. It was taken for granted that I'd meet up with Frank and Callum each weekend evening, there was no need to book. I was about to start phoning my friends when Bob from production stuck his head around the door and asked if I wanted to come to the pub. When I got out into the hall, who should be waiting but Catriona.

'Well, look who's here,' I said.

'You do not mind if I tag along do you?' she said, clacking away on her gum.

'Obviously not,' I said.

We'd evolved this sort of chiming way of speaking, enunciating every syllable almost as if singing in a style vaguely reminiscent of Malcolm MacDowell in *A Clockwork Orange*: 'You – do – not – mind'; 'Ob-vi-ous–ily not'. Already there was an understanding between us, we had an in joke. It did occur to me to turn to Bob and say, 'Told you I was in here.' I know I could have got away with it and it might even have got her to give me a thwack and a 'You cheeky bugger', but I thought it would just be showboating.

Bob left at about 9.30 and I carried on drinking with Catriona until closing time. She was the genuine article rock-chick, sipping Jack Daniels and Coke and looking directly at you as she lit her cigarettes, her pale, slightly stubby, long-nailed fingers curling around her Zippo. I found her almost dizzying to look at, a tight tingle gripping me from throat to knees as she gave me that side-of-the-eye evaluating glance that certain Siamese cats reserve for goldfish.

We had that favourite rock-ist conversation – who is the maddest person you've ever known. Mine was a friend of a friend who had a large scar up the middle of his forehead where he'd put his head into a circular saw at work for a bet. She could better it.

'My friend Whaley makes up his own subtitles for foreign films on the telly. They'll say "Où est la gare?" and he'll say something funny instead of the right translation.'

'Well that makes my bandsaw bloke look pretty tame,' I said.

We looked at each other for a couple of beats and just started laughing, more with the fun of being together than at anything funny either of us had said.

We went out into the street to call her a cab.

'Where's your boyfriend tonight?'

'He's away,' she said, in a sort of rising intonation that seemed to say 'fancy that'.

She was standing right up against me, hands by her side and I could feel her breasts brush my chest. I looked at her, she looked at me, three heartbeats and we crossed the diehard inch between us to kiss.

'I'd like to say that was a surprise,' she said when we broke to flag down a cab. 'You don't disappoint, do you?'

'Sounds like a challenge,' I said. 'I bet I can disappoint you.'

'We'll see,' she said. 'Get in the cab, you're paying.'

'And what's your side of the bargain?'

'I'm cooking breakfast.'

15 THE PRICE OF LOVE

I was infatuated with Catriona, absolutely smitten. That's not the same as being in love but, to an idiot, it feels the same. She was everything I'd ever dreamed of. Her room was a proper rock 'n' roll junk yard, like something out of *Performance*, the Nick Roeg film that features Mick Jagger and some actors. There was a massive Buddha in one corner – in those days they weren't available in Habitat – a wall papered in gig flyers and a large stuffed bear with a pork-pie hat on in the corner. Actually the bear may be my memory playing tricks on me, but there should have been such a bear. An electric bass she was learning to play was propped against a table and a bloke's leather jacket lay over the back of a chair. She had a dresser overflowing with nail varnishes, mascara, brushes and potions. The place looked like a set designed by Peter Blake, the chap who did the *Sgt Pepper* cover.

The sex was incredible and I had that feeling of wanting to start it again before I'd finished the first time. She had a way of kissing that seemed to almost deny me breath. With other women I would have found this repulsive, with her I found it fascinating and addictive. I remember her as a series of colours: pale skin, dark lipstick, her dark hair hanging over my face. The next morning, she came good on her promise of a fry-up and we had some more fantastic sex. What does this actually mean? It's difficult to say, other than we seemed to take delight in each other. It felt exhilarating to surprise and please her and to be pleased and surprised in return. All those glances that had been missing between me and Vanessa were there with her, a slightly spiteful look as she broke from kissing me, a steady evaluating gaze as I kissed her. There was nowhere in the world I would rather be; no one I would rather be with, nothing I would rather be doing.

We lay in bed in her room and I had that delicious feeling: a new girl, a new day and nothing to do but be with each other. Already, though, the forty-five or so hours separating me from work on Monday morning seemed injudiciously fragile things.

'What are we going to do now?' I said.

'I don't know about you, but I'm going down the pub,' she said.

I was in wonderland, but my attraction to her was much more than the fact she was a lad's wet dream, though she was.

There was something really artistic about Catriona, 1960s artistic. I lay on the bed and watched her get ready to go out, putting on her make-up in the bright morning light, her silk Chinese robe, open at the front, offering glimpses of her small, pale, perfect tits as she transformed herself from a beautiful girl into a bird of paradise. I could have sat there looking at her forever. I had a lot of cheesy but enjoyable thoughts. I imagined her as an Egyptian temple priestess preparing herself for some strange rites, a Sultan's houri readying herself to charm some visiting ambassador, a faerie anointing herself in pungent oils to seduce some wood-land traveller to his doom. As I said earlier, I did a lot of Dungeons and Dragons as a kid; I think that explains it.

The smell of her was incredible too, cigarettes: cheap musk, alcohol, conditioner and the lightest sweat blending to form something that could have plucked me off the pavement and dragged me down the street in her wake. If you bottled it and had me sniff it in a blind tasting I'd identify it in one word: 'Girl'. I'd probably say that in a low growl as well, something like 'Girrrrrrrrrrl.' And then I might add a 'woof'.

She tasted of smoke and lipstick, which entranced me, as did her smooth white skin. While I am on this banal trawl through the five senses, even the way she sounded did it for me. Her Scouse accent was like the chilli in the curry, the blue streak in the cheese. It just made her perfect.

This is what turns men on about women. There's so much more to it than just naked bodies; there are a million and one tiny signs of femininity, from the way the cloth of a blouse hangs from a breast to the way of holding an expression or a body position, the curve of a calf, a style of smoking. When someone gets them all just right – or right as we like them – there is very little we can do to resist.

I had the strangest feeling when I looked at her, a combination of pre-driving test nerves and 'you have passed' euphoria. It was like approaching the really big dip on a roller coaster, an incredibly edgy excitement.

Ten minutes after she was ready we were in a cab back to my house so I could get changed out of my work clothes. I wouldn't have let most other girls in, but Catriona was one of us, Catriona would understand. I was living at that moment in a big Victorian house in Stoke Newington. There were mushrooms in the shower and the cooker didn't work – something I only discovered after six months of living there when a mate of mine tried to do some hot knives.

My room was tiny – scarcely bigger than a single bed. That's not an exaggeration. In the end I had become sick of crawling around tripping over the mattress and just thrown it away. I was sleeping in a sleeping bag on the floor, getting up in the morning and going to press conferences at The Treasury. I'd even brought one girl back there – an opera singer called Sally. She hadn't seemed that bothered by it.

There was something almost monastic about my approach to life back then; I think it's possible I may have been a Zen master without even knowing it. My field of Zen expertise wasn't calligraphy or sword play, it was the pursuit of women. That's different to the capture of women or the forming a meaningful relationship with women, just the pursuit. I was not absorbed in the task, the task had absorbed me. I was the pursuit of women. Everything extraneous to going out and meeting girls had been stripped from my life. I had no TV, I had no fridge, I had no bed, no stereo and no records – they'd all been stolen from the back of my friend's car when I'd moved house and I'd accidentally gone to the pub halfway through unpacking. My suit hung on a peg and all my other clothes were in dustbin bags. All my money was spent on what used to be called 'nightlife'. It was all I thought about and all I did.

I didn't want anything other than a girlfriend – not a car, not a house, not a holiday, nothing. Even my drinking had evolved because pubs and clubs were where I perceived girls to be, so to pubs and clubs I went.

When Vanessa had dropped round to my house she had been horrified by what she'd seen. She'd insisted I should get a bed, she'd bought me some pillows to replace the leather jacket I'd been using for that purpose and said there was no way anyone should be using a sleeping bag on the floor as their permanent bed. Vanessa wanted to look after me, but I didn't want looking after. Catriona actually seemed impressed by my living arrangements.

We went into Camden and spent the day in the Good

Mixer pub, which was still fit to drink in, in the days before Blur started using it. Nothing against Blur, but it just altered the balance of the pub from minor criminal with a few trendies to a lot of trendies with a few minor criminals. For anyone who doesn't know it, it's an old man's pub, pool table, bare lino and, in a glass cabinet, a cheese sandwich that has been there since 1963. The roll-up smoke was thick and the clientele thicker. Catriona loved it.

I've very rarely had the experience of wanting to run out and tell the world that I'm with a girl, but I really did. There was only the problem of Vanessa on the Monday morning. Vanessa who I loved but, as countless numbers of the divorced would attest, love loses out to infatuation every time.

Catriona and I stayed together all day, went back to her flat in the evening and went out to the pub again the next day. At eleven on the Sunday night I went home. I didn't even ask her if she was going to finish with her boyfriend, though I wanted to. I felt sure she would, anyway. For her I had presented myself as a super-confident working-class hero so I tried to believe that myself.

Monday dawned and I bumped into Catriona getting a pre-work coffee in the sandwich bar. Lots of other people from work were in there.

'Good weekend?' I said.

'So, so,' she said, 'I've met a new bloke.'

'What's he like?'

'Not bad, if you like that sort of thing.'

'And do you?'

'I don't know yet,' she said, tapping me on the chest with her finger, 'depends if he plays his cards right. Early signs are promising. Ta ra.' She took her coffee and left. I closed my eyes and felt a shiver go through me. I had to see her, that night, earlier if possible. It left me wondering if it was practical for us to nip into one of the meeting rooms and go for it at lunchtime. No, was the answer I rather reluctantly came to.

'I think she fancies you,' said Dave, one of my fellow PR-ists, waiting for a sandwich.

'Nah,' I said, 'she's like that with everyone.'

'Wish she'd be like it with me,' he said, and thumped the door frame with his newspaper, revealing a hitherto unsuspected darkness in his character.

I couldn't see her that lunchtime because instinctively neither of us wanted to feed office gossips. Also, I spent every lunch with Vanessa. I'd need an explanation if I wanted to see someone else. What happened next is going to sound unbelievable to anyone who, well, who has a brain really.

I hadn't actually connected in my head the event of sleeping with Vanessa and that of sleeping with Catriona. How could I not? I honestly don't know. There were physical signs that something was wrong. My legs started tapping at work that day, to the annoyance of other staff. I'd always done that a little bit, but that day it was as if a giant woodpecker had got loose beneath the desk. This restless-leg behaviour is quite common among men and I often wondered why I did it and why, when I became a full-time writer, it stopped. Then I read an explanation in the health pages one day – it's a sign that you want to escape; your legs are trying to run away.

I also felt mildly sick when I contemplated telling Vanessa that it was no go between us. How I would come up with an explanation, I didn't know. I'm not sure there even was an explanation. It was just that being with Catriona had made it clear to me that I wanted to stay only as Vanessa's friend. I couldn't tell her that, could I? She had a sharp nose for bullshit, and though my main aim was not to hurt her feelings, what could I say that she would believe?

I didn't speak to Vanessa properly until that evening. It was a Monday and the busiest day in the office so we didn't get lunch. After work, though, she insisted on going to the pub with me, which was OK because I wanted to play it a bit cool with Catriona. 'Treat 'em mean to keep 'em keen,' was the advice a friend's dad had once given me. Mind you, his wife had left him. There was, however, something to be gained from a certain restraint.

Naturally, Vanessa wanted to discuss what had happened between us. We went to the pub and sat opposite each other. She looked worried, understanding, ready to talk.

As often happened in my relationship with Vanessa, she thought she was prepared for the worst. Imagination had failed her, however, in foreseeing exactly what the worst might be.

I explained that I felt it was all a bit rushed and that I didn't feel ready to enter another serious relationship after Ella. Vanessa was a very, very perceptive woman, but even she had a blind spot for this sort of thing. She said she understood and that we could still be friends as we were. Who knows, maybe something would come of it, maybe it wouldn't.

We kissed on the cheek and sat back to enjoy a few pints. The riotous atmosphere we normally had between us was slightly dampened but, that aside, everything was as it had been. That left me free to tell her about Catriona, just as I would have done the week before when she would have demanded to know all the juicy details. Oh twit of twits who dwells in twitdom, how shalst thou ever untwit thyself?

'You'll never guess who I got off with on Friday,' I said. She stiffened.

'Who?'

'Catriona.'

'Who?' It came out more like a cry of pain than a question. I didn't register it properly at the time. I don't think I had truly understood love before that second when, in Vanessa's voice, I heard it wounded.

'From production.'

The frightening thing about Vanessa's rage was not that she let it out, far from it. It was that she tried to suppress it. Her whole body shook.

'I would never have guessed you would be attracted to her,' she said in the tone of a rupturing pressure cooker.

I don't know what she thought I was attracted to. I mean, I really liked Anna Nichole Smith's look. And I fancy Paris Hilton. I don't *just* fancy girls like that, but I do fancy them.

'Why not?' Even I could see that something was wrong.

'She's so. I don't know. She so *obvious*.'

I disagreed on that one. I thought Catriona had a style all of her own. It didn't seem wise to argue, though. I just shrugged.

The initial shock faded and Vanessa regained her considerable wits. The problem wasn't that I'd made an error in taste, it was that I'd taken everything she, and I, thought we had together and ground it into the dust over someone she considered to be a Scouse floozy. Catriona was irrelevant, really. I had revealed myself to be someone else.

For her I would be different, she thought, but the leopard whose fur had looked so stripy in the light of late-night conversations, when it seemed too dangerous to touch in case we disturbed the rare understanding we had between us, showed himself to be covered in spots after all.

All the shared confidences, all the resonances from our

past and present, the similar tastes and, much more, the feeling that of all the people on the planet, this was the one who suited you best, had that been a lie?

Despite all my stories of infidelities, fuck-ups and gape-making stupidities, she'd thought that, for her, I would change. And, this is what made me so dangerous at that time: I thought so too. She could improve me. I genuinely thought that. I wasn't leading her on. I couldn't have. I'm not bright enough to pull a fast one on Vanessa. No wilful deceiver could have done it. Sometimes, though, stupidity can prevail where intelligence fails.

'How could you?' she said, 'how could you?'

The answer is simple, though I didn't say it. Vanessa felt like my soul mate, but what's that when I found Catriona so attractive it was almost as if she had her own personal gravity, pulling me out of my normal orbit to crush myself against her?

'Sorry,' I said, 'I didn't think it was all that much. I'm not going out with her officially.' I'm afraid to say Vanessa saw this as something of a technicality.

'That's so fucking irrelevant,' she said.

I can't remember what was said next, but it wasn't 'Never mind and jolly good luck old chum.' Maybe the reason for my lapse in memory is not that she tore a strip off me, but that she made me feel how it was for her. She was good at that. I don't know whether she said it then or later, but I do recall her saying 'I loved you so much. So much.' The passion in her voice told me what a fool I'd been without her having to say anything more. For all her strong minded-ness, I had dealt a hurtful blow to her. I had rejected her, not because I loved Catriona more, but because I fancied her more. In Vanessa's mind I had balanced her hard-won love and respect, commodities she didn't give easily and which any man should value more than his life, against some make-up and fishnet tights and gone for the latter.

Shame descended on me, hot as a hangover, and I sat staring miserably into my pint. Synapses in my head were bridged and the connection I'd failed to make between sleeping with Vanessa and sleeping with Catriona suddenly came on-line. I could see it all, and feel it all, just how terribly I had treated Vanessa.

I can look back now and see how right she was. If only I had just gone home instead of getting the cab with Catriona, I might still be friends with Vanessa to this day. I think our relationship could have survived sleeping together once if it had not been followed so quickly by an infidelity.

Of course, technically, it wasn't an infidelity. How many times do you have to sleep with someone before you are going out with them? Betrayal loves a definition. It would be great if I could let myself off with that, to say that we had not yet achieved the requisite numbers to be considered boyfriend and girlfriend. It was an infidelity and it would probably have been an infidelity even if I hadn't slept with Vanessa. I hadn't seen that I had pledged myself to her simply because of the depth of the friendship we had achieved.

There are no strong platonic friendships, not really, between a single man and a single woman of the same age. Sex is always there in the background, even if it's only a slight reluctance to discuss why it's not happening. From that position, even considering taking a lover, while not infidelity, is a betrayal and a rejection. No matter how much I wanted to, I couldn't make sleeping with Vanessa the same as picking someone up at a party. She had rights to me until I was willing to make it clear that she hadn't.

If I could go back and change time, though, I wouldn't.

To be loved by someone like Vanessa is a rare and incredible thing, but it pales into insignificance next to what I felt for Catriona. Every time I looked at her I felt like my bones were made of Alka-Seltzer and that the only thing that could stop the fizzing in my head was to touch her. That feeling bypassed my brain entirely, and if I'd died that morning in that room with the gig posters, the flyers and the imaginary stuffed bear while I watched Catriona put her make-up on, I wouldn't have minded. I didn't see how life could get much better. Of course, the depressing thing is that, for years, it couldn't.

16 MARK-ISM

Vanessa was an immensely popular person at work and my office was nearly entirely female. On top of this, it was a cut-throat competitive environment and some people used what had happened as an excuse to vent their considerable spleen on me. Those who were angry with me for competing with them had a green light to abuse me to my face. All knew my stain and took the opportunity to be sanctimonious about it, or good friends to Vanessa depending on your point of view.

Managers looking for team-building exercises should forgo hikes over dangerous terrain in the Lake District and just nominate one person for everyone to pick on. Bullying brings people together much better than learning how to get over a river using a barrel and some rope. Through me, the team bonded splendidly.

I became a pariah, ignored by most, virtually spat at by some and simply hated by Vanessa. Everything I said would be met by cold stares; I could neither make anyone a cup of coffee nor receive one myself; lunchtimes were spent alone – Catriona was normally busy and kept her work and social life very separate. I had nothing to do but work, ever harder. I couldn't chat so I had to put the calls in. This meant my clients' stories were everywhere. It did nothing to dilute the venom of those who were trying to shove me off the ladder on their way to the top.

I did feel lonely and, as someone who has always been desperate to be liked, I found it hard going. I remember one meeting when I made some sort of joke with the boss – a straightforward blokey ex-journo who I don't think had any idea of what was going on until that point.

'God, I hate him so much!' Vanessa burst out, virtually wringing her hands.

I can see the boss's face now. The average Englishman is about as comfortable with naked expressions of emotion as he is with the presence of funnel web spiders in the room. He reminded me of a vicar delivering a speech to the WI while manfully rising above the explosions of a Tourette's sufferer.

'Right,' he said, with a light cough, 'trade press, how are we doing there?'

I knew how to handle all this, though. I'd seen Pat, my Northern Irish friend, being lambasted by Jackie, his girl-friend. Pat had a habit of going out on a Friday night and only turning up at home on a Sunday evening, by which time the dinner had been through the dog, deposited in a local park and placed in an appropriate bin. Jackie was a Scottish girl who was as tough as they come and could box good ear. She was also very good in bed, as I discovered a few years later after she and Pat had broken up. I was interested in seeing her again, but she didn't want to see me. I'd always been the uncool one in that gang and I think she couldn't shake that perception from her mind.

Jackie would occasionally find Pat in a pub and come in to stamp on his head. Pat never said a word, never replied, never criticised her, never did anything. Eventually she'd just realise she was looking stupid and sit down for a Spritzer. Pat would act as though nothing had happened. Even after she went home he never once mentioned to his friends that an extremely glamorous Glaswegian had spent half an hour banging his head off the table. It's a form of sexism, really, the view that women are strange creatures, almost child-like, and you just let them have their tantrum and ignore them. This was my tactic. For once in my life I simply shut up.

Vanessa, who sat less than six feet away from me, could hiss, she could denounce me, she could insult me or just snarl, which she sometimes seemed to do, but I would not respond. If anyone was going to make an idiot of themselves in public it wasn't going to be me. And, being fair, I thought she did make an idiot of herself. She was sophisticated in virtually every sphere of her life, but she handled rejection poorly. If someone had done that to me I wouldn't have flattered their ego by showing my anger. I would have been polite, pleasant and gone from their lives.

I pitied the boss. He was a nice bloke and a very good manager, but this definitely was not favourite ground for him. I have no idea if he overcame his bone deep reluctance to acknowledge the presence of emotions in his office and asked her to can it during work hours, but eventually the open hostility . . . hmm, I was going to say ceased, but I think it's more accurate to say that it took on a different quality. It was as if the office had invented a new category of prejudice just for me, a Mark-ism, that was as intangible as it was corrosive. It still made me miserable but, then again, I was seeing Catriona. In some ways I was really happy.

Catriona had the misfortune to endure a couple of very unpleasant lift rides with Vanessa. The lift in that company was like an upright coffin and poor Catriona was stuck opposite the bubbling and blaspheming Vanessa from floors one to five.

'Get that mad moo away from me,' she phoned me to say.

'*You* couldn't get her away from me could you?' I said.

Vanessa was consumed by anger and not thinking straight. Had that been the case she might have seen that by acting aggressively to me and Catriona, she was cementing our relationship.

There were compensations. Women love a drama and being at the centre of one brought me to the attention of some of the account-handler girls who regarded Vanessa as something of a po-faced lefty. I became a bit of a star around the rest of the building and women who had never spoken to me before suddenly took an interest. I think they were fascinated by the unfolding soap opera and one of them, on the day I eventually left that company, took the trouble to find out whether I'd been worth the fuss.

Also, I discovered for the first time that I quite like isolation. I didn't miss the life of the office at all and was pleased to go through the days in my own pod, relieved of banter and gossip.

I've always been wary of the idea of 'life lessons'. It seems to me that most people repeat the same mistakes time and time again. One of the reasons we're drawn to stories is that they show people developing through them – the Luke Skywalker of *Return of the Jedi* is a very different person to the Luke who bought the droids. In real life this doesn't happen quite as neatly. Some people get stuck and are essentially the same at sixty as they were at sixteen. Others, like me, actually regress. I'd behaved terribly and brought social exclusion on myself. The lesson I drew was that I quite enjoy being socially excluded. I didn't like most people I met at work all that much and was quite glad to have the burden of their company lifted from me. It certainly didn't encourage me to be any more thoughtful in future. I wish it had.

Surprisingly I didn't get seduced by the theatre of the proceedings. It's absolutely in my character to feel good about being in the middle of a cat fight, but I didn't. I felt really sorry for Vanessa. She was my friend and I hated to have to watch her suffer for eight hours a day, even if she did take it out on me.

Catriona and I did split up and very quickly thanks entirely to my stupid behaviour. Like I say, I was smitten with her, really smitten. I imagined myself moving in with her, making it in a band, touring the world with her and she and I being just perfect together. We'd be partners in paradise. The trouble with living in the Garden of Eden, though, is that you have to watch out for snakes.

I am not a jealous person. I'm too arrogant for that. My girlfriend can spend all evening chatting to another man and, be he never so goodlooking and accomplished, it will never occur to me that she could possibly leave me for him. This has been the case even when she has left me for him. I assume some sort of mistake has occurred, that reality will shortly readjust and she'll realise that I'm by far the best catch.

For reasons only known to God and my therapist I decided to treat Catriona to the one serious fit of jealousy I've had in my life. The problem was that she hung around with bands. I have spoken to her since we split up and I do believe her when she says there was nothing between them, but when you hear that you can't stay at her flat that night because the bassist from the Ugly Sods is kipping down there then the bile begins to rise. I know musicians, I have been in many bands. Bassists from touring bands do not kip on the floor of rock goddesses' pads without making a very serious attempt to get into bed with them. In fact, he wouldn't attempt. He'd just get in and then it would be up to her to fight him off all night, if she had the energy and the inclination.

The conversation between us would go like this.

'Yeah, I've got passes to see this new metal band.'

'Oh, what are they called?'

'Girlfriend Defiler. Anyway, we'll watch them, go to the aftershow and then I've said the lead singer Shagger and Bonker the drummer can crash at mine, so you'll have to go home tonight.'

'Why can't they sleep in the kitchen and I'll stay with you?'

'It's a lino floor in there, they'll be uncomfortable.'

'They'll be a lot more uncomfortable if I have to hunt them down and kill them.'

My anxiety was not relaxed by the muso-fucking antics of her friend Rose.

'Oh yeah,' said Catriona, 'she slept with Dave Knobalot out of We're After Your Woman the other week.'

'Oh yes,' I'd say, aware that this very Knobalot could, but for the grace of God, have saved his B&B costs by sleeping with my girlfriend.

'They didn't have anywhere to go so she shagged him in a skip.'

'In a skip?' I don't have high standards of accommodation but, you know, a line has to be drawn somewhere.

'It was a nice skip. It had a roof on and everything.'

That is a word for word quote. This was the company she was keeping.

I wasn't being unreasonable, but, in another way, I was. I'd only just started seeing her and it was up to her who she wanted to stay and, really, up to her if she wanted to sleep with them. The ironic thing is that I don't think she did. I think for a few weeks she was pretty serious about me, she'd finished with her last boyfriend to go out with me after all. It was just her way of being and I should have gone with it.

Sexual jealousy would have been enough to make me behave like I did, but there was more at work. I was jealous of these sort-of-successful bands with their transit-van tours and small pics in *NME*. That's what I wanted to be doing, not shuffling paper in a PR firm. I was trying, but music industry complacency, and my own severe lack of talent, kept holding me back.

There was another problem. On certain nights, even if we'd been out together, she preferred to sleep alone. I think she just wanted her sleep – she was serious about work – but I took it as an enormous rejection. Still, for the first part, we had a great time. We went to the party conferences together, which were always occasions of great sexual tension anyway. Something to do with mixing alcohol, boredom, arguments and – the key ingredient – opportunity.

The year before, I'd slept with an Indian girl at the Tory conference. She was an accountant. We had one female Indian member of staff at our firm who was also an accountant and the rumour spread that I'd slept with her. It seems that, when it comes down to it, the PC right-on Medja crew thought that if I'd been to bed with one Asian, I'd been to bed with the lot.

The break-up with Catriona came one night when we went out with my friend Callum. We met in a pub near her house. I had all my things in an overnight bag and was proud to introduce her to my friend for the first time. At the end of the evening she said she didn't want me to come back to the house. I don't think she was finishing with me, she just had to get up for work, which meant more to her than it did to me.

I took it very badly. I felt humiliated in front of my friend and angry that I had to get the bus home and spend the night on the floor in a sleeping bag rather than in the bower of bliss with Catriona. When I got home there was a note on my door. Ella had called. The next day I called her and the day after that we were going back out with each other again. Three weeks later we weren't, but my ties with Catriona had been severed.

I didn't even consider what I might have lost with Catriona. A certain and easy future presented itself and I wasn't ready to struggle to make the harder one work. It was over between us. I never called her again and I later heard that Catriona thought I was the most difficult man she'd ever been out with. In a way, considering her taste was in rockers, I should take that as a compliment. I didn't though. I was crazy about her and, because I was crazy about her, I'd blown it.

17 A DAMN GOOD THRASHING

You may be reading about my behaviour so far and thinking that I needed horsewhipping. It may, then, reassure you to know that it was during this period that I was actually horsewhipped. Well, technically that's not true. It was a riding crop which is a *horse* whip but not a horsewhip, which is a longer thing. It still bloody hurt, though. I have a new respect for Desert Orchid, I'll say that much.

I do believe in the idea of zeitgeist – that times have a spirit to them. Sex, like anything else, has its fashions and, for a period, I couldn't meet anyone who didn't want to thrash or be thrashed. S&M was in. The fashion seemed to end in about 2002, when an internet-inspired bottom-sex fad came in. In the nineties, though, few women wanted to give the greatest gift a woman can give without preceding it with a little common assault.

I do remember one girl who asked me to tie her up and wee on her. I wanted to ask: 'What happened to blow jobs, what happened to fucking, what happened to plain old, British-as-a-boiled-egg buggery? Why does it all have to be whips and knots? If I'd wanted that I'd have joined the navy. I'm no good at knots and I don't want to learn. I don't want to have the sort of sex that requires you to go to night school first. I don't like vending machine coffee.'

A work-experience girl, Selina, had started with us. She was twenty-two, straight out of college and, though she did her best to knock the south-London council estate out of her vowels she had clearly come from a tough background. Still, she was pretty, extravagantly breasted and lively. She had no alliance with Vanessa because she worked in a different department. I was surprised, and delighted, when I bumped into her in the sandwich shop and she asked me if I wanted to go for a drink with her.

Catriona was a memory, Ella and I had split up again, so I said 'Yes.'

'Good,' she said, 'I'll meet you tonight at X Bar in Clapham – 8.30, don't be late.'

X Bar is one of those places I would normally only enter if it was raining molten lead outside. Even then I'd have a think as to whether it was better to be fried in boiling metal than sit in the moulded plastic interior on a designer-fucked seat while a DJ achieved the considerable feat of making the pebble-in-a-washing machine Drum 'n' Bass even more unlistenable by ranting inanities over the top of it. Still, she liked it, so I thought I'd go along with it as a loss leader until I could manoeuvre her into somewhere proper with 'Rose', 'Crown' or 'King' in its title, lino on the floor and a juke box that hadn't changed its singles since 1979 when they used to record this old-fashioned stuff called 'music'.

We arrived at 8.30. Luckily it operated as a bad restaurant and cocktail bar until ten when the rubbish started, so we at least got to talk to each other. I say 'luckily'. Perhaps the evening would have turned out a lot better if we had just listened to DJ Pants saying stuff like 'Let me see you now!', 'Rinsin' it,' and 'It's all about the Benjamins' over and over again.

We were served some drinks. I had a beer and there was some kerfuffle when I insisted on having it in a glass like an Englishman in full possession of his dignity, rather than direct from the bottle like a GI in a Saigon knocking shop.

We sat down at an over-low table, ordered some food and chatted pleasantly. So far so good. We talked about work, about what she planned to do when her work experience was over, about her university life and where she lived – not a street away. She was at her sister's flat and her sister was away. I was very pleased to receive that piece of information, with all its implied promise.

We finished the food and the atmosphere suddenly changed. She was looking at me with a face of exaggerated anger, like a bulldog who had just heard the rights to the bulldog brand had been bought by a cat.

'You make a lot of small talk, don't you?' she said.

'Er, sorry?' I said, 'were you expecting a critique of Michael Ignatieff's views on the nature of nationalism? What did you think I'd talk about?'

'Sex!' she said, as if I was a moron.

'Right,' I said, 'in the abstract or the specifi—'

'Shut up!' she said, holding up her hands, 'you look in need of a right spanking to me. I'm going to take you back home, put you across my knee and tan your fucking arse for you.'

'Er, no,' I said, 'you're not.' Surrendering control in sex has never been my thing, not so much that I could finish up with a rump like a Grand National winner's after a close finish but that she might tickle my neck with a feather. I think I'd be sick.

'Yes I am,' she said. 'What were you expecting – that I'd want to lie back, open my legs and let you fuck me like a good little girl? I've worked hard to get to where I am today, I've really had to struggle. Do you think I'm going to let someone like you take it away from me?'

I obviously heard the final two sentences of that paragraph

because I can recall them, but I didn't register them, or understand them for the babble of madness that they clearly were. I knew the ground we were on, I thought – slightly risqué talk designed to titillate before a return to her house for a meat and two veg bonk, maybe with the trimmings of a domination fantasy thrown in. Perhaps she was trying to goad me into some sort of response and wanted me to tie her up. I hoped that, if that was the case, she had some handcuffs. As I say, I'm useless at knots and, when I'd done that sort of thing before, had either made them so puny the girl came out of them in a couple of seconds or so secure we'd had to cut them with a bread knife. That was particularly embarrassing with one girl when I'd lashed her up with the cord from her dad's dressing gown and we'd had to shred it to set her free.

'We'll continue this conversation at my flat,' she said.

Now I am a liberal man. I am open to new experiences. So, on the way across the road I decided that if tying me up was her thing then I'd let her do it. I was fairly certain I wouldn't like it, but who knows? Life's rich tapestry and all that, what?

There then looms the question of how to go about being a submissive. What do you say, what do you do? You wouldn't want to do something to make the dominatrix angry. Or perhaps you would.

I decided the best thing to do was to adopt the air of an officer and a gentleman subjecting himself to an intrusive but necessary medical exam.

'In here?' I said, as we came into the flat, gesturing to the living room. The flat was a split-level affair – living room on the ground floor, bedroom upstairs.

'Not until we've seen you with your clothes off,' she said.

'We?' I said, rather fearing that some steroid-swollen

boyfriend called Horst was going to suddenly leap from the Habitat canvas cupboard sporting an erection like the World Cup sideways.

'The royal we,' she said. 'Take off your clothes.'

'Any chance of a glass of wine first?' I said.

'No,' she said, coming up to me and pulling at my belt.

In for a penny, in for a pound, I allowed her to undress me. I suppose it was quite sexy in a way, although I couldn't quite get rid of the nagging doubt that some of Vanessa's henchwomen had set this whole thing up in order to humiliate me.

As I took off my clothes she grasped my penis and stroked it back and forth, her lips against my cheek. She had to stand on tiptoe to do this, as she was only about 5′ 2″.

'You thought you were going to get to stick this inside me did you?' she said. 'I bet you've been looking at my tits and thinking about sticking your dirty knob up me haven't you?'

'It did cross my mind, I have to confess,' I said, 'although it is not a dirty knob. I actually have my knob cleanliness badge from cubs. I am, it has to be said, a noted knob polisher.'

'God, you talk like a twat,' she said. I didn't let this put me off because I was, after all, getting quite turned on. She really did have lovely tits, I thought, and a curiosity to see them rose in my mind. I made to open her blouse, but she pulled back from me.

'Don't even think about it,' she said. 'You'll get to see those in good time, but first we have to make sure you're fully under control.'

She pulled back from me and rummaged in her handbag from where she produced a coil of white braided rope. I have to say that doubt entered my mind at this point.

'Is she,' I thought, 'a serial killer?'

Probably not, was the conclusion I came to because, for all she knew, I had mentioned that I was seeing her to someone and, should my head kick up in a rubbish bag somewhere, they would doubtless mention that to the police.

'Put your hands behind your back,' she said.

I did as I was told.

'Through the stair rail, twat,' she said.

'Enough with the "twat",' I said, although I put my hands through.

She shot behind me and got to work, reaching through to stroke my neck as she did so. I am very ticklish so I started to laugh and move my head to stop her doing it. This seemed to make her even more angry and she pulled the cords quite tight about my wrists.

'Careful, you'll cut my circulation off,' I said.

'I'll do what I fucking like,' she said. 'I see you looking at my tits at work, you fucking pervert. You know what I do to perverts?'

'Fuck them?' I said, rather hopefully.

'You'll see,' she said, giving the rope a last pull. She'd obviously had some sort of practice at this sort of thing because I was totally stuck there. Still, I tried to concentrate on what was coming next. Nails dragged over the body, I thought. Maybe she'd grasp the banister and come up with some way of climbing on top of me. Whatever happened it was going to be interesting. I was right there. The next thing I knew, she'd produced a blindfold of the sort you get on aircraft and had put it over my eyes. I can't say I liked this and had visions of chainsaws being sparked up or, worse, of the door opening and everyone from work filing in.

'That's better,' she said, 'now I've got you where I want you.'

'No weeing on me,' I said.

'You should have thought of that before I tied you up,' she said.

'No wee,' I said, 'or anything else.'

I heard her come round the front of me and then there was some rummaging about.

'Here's your glass of wine,' she said as I felt something splash over my face.

I let out a sigh and tentatively tasted to see it wasn't piss. It wasn't, thank God.

'Thankyou,' I said, 'a naïve, domestic Burgundy but I am amused by its presumption.' I found the whole thing a bit depressing. All I'd wanted, ever, was a girlfriend. Is this what I had to go through to get one? They say you have to kiss a lot of frogs, but do you have to let the frogs tie you to their lily pads and smack you up with their webby feet?

'What?'

'I wanted Chardonnay, really.'

'You want my tits more than that, don't you?'

Actually, I was quite thirsty so I wouldn't have minded the Chardonnay and then her tits, or even the Chardonnay on her tits. I had the feeling that this sort of answer wouldn't do me any good, so I just said 'Yes.'

'Here you are then, darling,' she said.

She was close to me and her hand took me behind the head and forced it into her breast. I was surprised to find they were naked and she pushed a nipple into my mouth.

'Do you like that?'

'Yes.'

'Do you like it?'

'Yes.'

'You dirty fucker!' Suddenly the nipple was gone and a burning pain shot across my shoulder and chest. She'd hit me with something, something like a whip, really hard.

'Steady on!' I said, 'that really, ow!'

Another blow ripped into me. I'd had enough at that point.

'Right, untie me!' I said.

'Yeah, right,' she said, whacking me again.

These blows weren't agony, but they were certainly very uncomfortable and unpleasant.

'Game over,' I said, 'ow, stop it!'

'You think you can get one over on me?' she said. 'You think I'd let you put your dirty dick inside me?'

'Once and for all, it's not dirty,' I said, 'and ow! Fucking stop it, I'm serious. Untie me or I'll break this stair rail.'

'No one's managed it yet,' she said, in a low chuckle.

Great, I'm with a psycho, I thought, they'll be digging bits of me out of the drains in about fourteen years' time when a Dyno Rod bloke stumbles upon my foot by accident. People will point to her road and say 'That's where that Selina X did all those murders.' As a final indignity it will be she who hands her name to posterity, not me. None of this, I thought, was good.

We were just about within the bounds of conventionality still. I wasn't actually going to break the stair rail as, well, I don't go round smashing up girls' flats. Also, she was on work experience. What was I going to say if they asked me my impressions of her for a reference? Hard working, reliable, intelligent sadistic pervert?

She was bound to let me go, wasn't she?

'If you hit me once more . . .' I said.

'You'll what?' she said. 'Tell your mum on me?'

'You'll see,' I said.

At first I thought that she'd been put off by my firmness. No. There was a buzzing sound near to my ear. Then she whipped my blindfold off and thrust something into my face.

It was a twelve-inch dildo, thick as your arm and bright green – though the colour wasn't my immediate concern. My eyes popped out of my head as she said, 'Well, you seem to think it's OK to go around penetrating people, let's see how you like it yourself.' She did actually look quite sexy – tight skirt, breasts exposed, wielding a dildo. This is what I mean when I say sex is all about context. If she was intending to use the dildo on herself I'd have pulled up a chair and some popcorn and enjoyed the view. Knowing her intent, however, I couldn't quite take the same erotic charge from the scene. It's not even that I'd be immediately opposed to allowing a girl to perform a bit of prostate massage on me. I'll give anything a go three or four times, you know. It's just that I didn't feel like being introduced to that particular world of forbidden pleasure by a lunatic wielding a false cock the size of a rolled-up telephone directory. I'd have ended up with piles like I'd sat in a bag of sultanas.

I broke the stair rail. In fact, I broke about three of them. Her previous captives clearly had not thought laterally. If pulling doesn't work, what comes next? Pushing. I smashed into them with my back about three times and was free. She'd used some sort of knot that incorporated the rod and, with it broken, my hands were untied. As they came out they seemed to make shapes in the air, first to mime strangling her, then to float towards my boxers, then to point at the leather riding whip that was on the floor. I shook away the remaining debris of rope and wood.

'What have you done?' she said, 'it was only a bit of fun. That's going to cost a fortune to repair, my sister'll go mad. She's a nutter and all.'

'Genetic, then, obviously,' I thought.

'A bit of fun?' I said, 'I've got weals, woman, weals!' Still, she did have her incredible breasts poking out of the top of her bra. I didn't really know what to say. Nothing prepares you for this sort of thing. I should have left but, once things get moving in a certain direction they have a sort of momentum.

'Where are we on the having sex front?' I said.

'I don't really fancy you,' she said, 'your head's too big for your body. You look like a big pink beered-up tadpole.'

'Oh,' I said. I looked around the hall. For some reason I noticed the woodchip wallpaper had been put on strangely. One roll had bigger chips than all the rest. Clearly a mistake in Do-It-All, I thought. I looked at her. She was very pretty, small, with those enormous tits still spilling out of the top of her bra, the one nipple I'd sucked to erection pointing at me like Lesley Crowther's finger saying 'Come on down.'

'What were you doing bringing me back?'

'You don't have to fancy someone to have fun with them.'

'You call this fun?'

'Yes,' she said.

'Right.'

Time seemed to slow down. What to do? What to say? Rain beat at the window. I tried to console myself by thinking 'somewhere, someone is dying and therefore worse off than you'. It didn't work. Downstairs someone was playing REM's 'Shiny Happy People'. I breathed in like someone who has just decided the minimum period has elapsed that would allow him to end his visit to an elderly relative's house without causing too much offence.

'Well, I'll get a cab, then.'

'Yeah, I should.'

I looked outside. It was pouring.

'Can I get one from here?'

She had taken on a dark and brooding expression, staring at the broken rails.

'You're not going to kill me, are you?' I said.

'The phone's there.'

So I called a cab and it came – twenty-five minutes later. I tried to fill in the time.

'Weather's crap,' I said.

She just looked at the rails.

'I don't feel conversation is appropriate,' she said.

'Nah, you're probably right,' I said.

The cab rang and I went.

'Well it's been an enchanting evening darling and . . .'

'Just go,' she said.

'A good night?' said the cabbie as we drove home.

'Awful, but I expect I'll have worse,' I said.

And do you know what? I was right.

18 BACK TO THE SCENE OF THE CRIME

I saw a review of a novel once that said it was scarcely credible a man was still mourning the loss of a girl after three years. Three years is nothing. Three years is a blink. Men can carry a torch for a woman for decades. Seven years after one girlfriend, Francesca, dumped me I still used to think I saw her on average about four times a day. I'd see a Spanish–looking girl across the street, just getting onto a bus maybe, and I'd run to the next stop just to see if it was her. She'd appear to me in passing cars and in crowd scenes on TV. Once, bizarrely, I thought I glimpsed her in a 'Where's Wally?' picture. It was only when I met someone that I felt more for that she faded from my mind. If that hadn't happened I'd still be thinking I saw her five check-outs down in Tesco's. This is a common experience for men.

A friend of mine, Sara, has an ex-boyfriend who calls her roughly every three years. Her husband is less sanguine than me about his partner seeing her exes and objects strongly to her ever meeting him.

The conversations have gone something like this (historical notes are provided for context):

1989. *English footballer Theo Walcott born. Tiananmen Square Massacre. George Bush Snr takes over from Ronald Reagan. Sony Play Station SNES CD-ROM System development cancelled.*

Ex-Boyf: Yeah, goodbye. I'm better off without you. Seen my new girlfriend? Pretty cool eh? Oh, you're seeing someone too. Come back to me, I can't live without you.

1992. *Michael Schumacher wins first Grand Prix. Boutros Boutros-Ghali becomes secretary general of the UN. Bill Clinton receives Democratic nomination to run for president.*

Ex-Boyf: Still with Harry? Great, ah, it's great that you two are getting along so well, considering what he's like. Fancy a drink? Oh well, never mind.

1995: *Barings Bank collapses. Christopher Reeve paralysed in horse-riding accident, Srebrenica massacre and Oklahoma bombing. Unabomber kills lobbyist Gilbert Murray in Sacramento.*

Ex-Boyf: You are *still* with Harry? That's brilliant! I never thought it would last. He's a lucky, lucky . . . man. Fancy a drink? Oh well, never mind.

1998. *Bill Clinton impeached in Lewinsky affair. Osama Bin Laden publishes a fatwa, declaring jihad against all Jews and Crusaders. Unabomber Theodore Kaczynski pleads guilty, and accepts a sentence of life without the possibility of parole. US Congress passes the 'Iraq Liberation Act', which states that the US wants to remove Saddam Hussein from power and replace the government with a democratic institution*

Ex-Boyf: I've been through such a terrible time. I just need someone who understands me to talk to. Fancy a drink? Oh, Harry says 'No' does he? Ahhh, never mind.

2001. *Tony Blair elected, promising an 'end to sleaze'. George W. Bush inaugurated. Timothy McVeigh executed for Oklahoma bombing. World Trade Center attack.*

Ex-Boyf: I'm having such a brilliant time. I need someone to go out and celebrate with! *Still* with Harry, despite the millennium and the need for forward thinking? Oh, never mind.

2004. *Michael Schumacher wins record seventh world championship. Madrid bombings. Thousands throng in Hong Kong to mark fifteenth anniversary of Tiananmen Square massacre. Ronald Reagan dies. Trial of Saddam Hussein commences. George W. Bush re-elected.*

    Ex-Boyf: You moved without telling me. How could you? I'm really, er, how would you like me to be? Still with . . . Oh, never mind.

2007. *Theo Walcott scores first goal for Arsenal. Tony Blair questioned in 'cash for honours' affair. Playstation 3 launched. Ban Ki Moon succeeds Kofi Annan as secretary general of United Nations. Virginia Tech Massacre. Boris Yeltsin dies.*

    Ex-Boyf: You married him? That's great! Let's go out to have a drink to celebrate. Harry says 'No'? Oh, never mind. What's the average length of time till divorce? Eight years? I'll talk to you in 2015, then.

History has whirled, nations have risen and fallen in the last eighteen years, only this chap's devotion has remained constant. She confidently expects a call sometime around 2040 along the lines of 'You're going to be buried next to him? Are you sure? I have a lovely plot in Stevenage. Oh, never mind, I'll try you in the next life.'

    This man is suffering from something that most men suffer from at some point with some woman. He imagines that only he really understood her, that he meant as much to her as she means to him. Only a sense of misguided loyalty to her unsuitable husband keeps her from throwing herself into his arms and reliving those days when life seemed kind all over again.

This seems like the behaviour of a loser but, if a man was marooned on a desert island, we'd honour him for keeping a love alive for twenty years. It's a form of romanticism, really, of hope against reality. And exclusion orders.

You can see, then, that it wasn't unusual Ella was still on my mind, even though we'd been finished for months. I had glimpsed romance with her and thought that we might be able to resurrect it. Also, I was lonely. I wanted the one for me right there and then, not in a week, a month or a year. Ella had been the nearest thing to that, so of course I wanted her back.

We met for a drink in Notting Hill. Her hair was longer and she had regained her *fin-de-siècle* beauty. We made some small talk and at about 8.30 went to her place to go to bed. We were on again and, this time, it seemed, she was prepared to love me back. She'd tried a number of other boyfriends and found that, among the collection of egotists, whiners, show-offs and perverts that make up modern manhood, I came off quite well. She'd just traded one kind of idiot for another.

One had been a gym-bunny and would never eat in restaurants 'but didn't mind watching her eat'; another, who had been basically gay – though trying to hide it from himself – wanted to choose her clothes and didn't sleep with her; and another, the worst, had been a miser whose treasures lay in unsunned heaps. There is no bigger turn-off for a woman, I have found, than penny pinching, even if it doesn't grow on trees and you are only being careful. I was fascinated to hear her stories and glad they reflected well on me. Ella moved in with me, in a house with six other lads in Shepherd's Bush, which showed willing, and then into a flat with just us two together on the edge of the White City estate.

She and I still argued, all the time, but we did a few things together, even having a memorable party where she relaxed and it felt like when we were first going out. One of the chief attractions of going out with Ella, although I wouldn't have seen it at the time, was that she was a link to the golden past, that time at university when I'd been doing what I wanted to do with people I wanted to do it with, and the last point at which I'd had an ambition I had half a chance of fulfilling.

Then our love grew even deeper. I felt closer to her than ever before and she felt closer to me, largely because she went away for six months. We were much more comfortable with each other as fantasies in our heads without having the real human being popping along and spoiling things.

She was organising some major TV event in the Arctic, living my life, in my opinion, while I was still being nice to accountants' leaders. Do accountants really have leaders? That's what they call themselves – the heads of their trade bodies anyway. However, hearing her voice crackling down the satellite phone and wishing she was back brought me a strange sort of peace. I even felt the lure of domesticity briefly and started staying in occasionally. Once I even cooked a meal for myself – a curry, not even from a can, slicing the chillis and everything.

When Ella returned from the pole I proposed to her, doing it the old-fashioned way by asking her dad first. He said Yes and so did she.

It was time for our parents to meet. This, as it turned out, was a mistake.

My mum and dad had met a variety of my girlfriends over the years. I think my mum secretly wished I had married Sarah. She was certainly the sort of girl she admired: kind – i.e., she said 'ahhh!' when she saw a baby and remembered when people's birthdays were – honest, hard-working and down to earth. What my mother didn't admire was an argumentative, arty farty, over-clever wannabe sophisticate with a posh voice and arch sense of humour that could easily be taken for evidence of condescension, i.e., Ella. Ella wasn't really like this but, nervous with my parents, she wanted to make a good impression. To her that meant showing she was witty and irreverent. What goes down well in Bar Italia Soho, though, tends to bomb a little in Coventry.

Things had gone badly on Ella's visits to my house. The first thing had been an argument between her and my middle brother. We had been discussing film and, as boys do at aged eighteen, my brother had thought that which movies or bands were good and which bad was a matter of objective fact, rather than opinion. The best band in the world were Queen, the best motorbike an RD350LC, leather jackets were best brown and pre-faded and no one, but no one, played guitar better than Brian May of Queen. Brian wasn't just a brilliant guitarist but an all round great bloke. He built his own guitar from a fireplace and studied astronomy at university, so beat that Johnny Marr. Oh, and Freddy Mercury isn't gay. No way. It would have come out in the papers if he was.

When the topic of film arose, then, Ella was under the impression that my brother was inviting debate. He was under the impression that she was asking for his verdict in order that she might adjust her viewing accordingly.

'I love *Jules Et Jim*,' said Ella, 'and, oh Mark, what's that film we went to see? *Tirez Sur Le Pianiste*. It's not classic Truffaut, but it's got a tremendous sense of fun to it.'

There was already some air of antagonism and I think Ella was – knowingly or not – playing up to an arty farty stereotype that wasn't really her.

As she spoke, my brother was shaking his head with a knowing smile, like a master carpenter looking down at the misguided bodgings of an apprentice.

'No,' he said.

'No what?'

'You'll kick yourself when I tell you, but easily the best film ever made is Dudley Moore's *10*,' he said.

There was a pause.

'It is easily the funniest thing ever,' he went on, 'and it's got a great-looking girl in it.'

There was another pause while my brother waited for the signs of sudden enlightenment to sweep over our faces.

'It's sexist crap,' said Ella, who was in a more relaxed mood now and didn't realise that my brother didn't take well to disagreement, particularly from posh girls.

'What do you mean sexist?' he said.

'It treats a woman as nothing more than a masturbation fantasy,' she said. My mother's ironing fluttered as the 'masturbation' whizzed by, and my dad's comb-over lifted. Ella's upbringing was more middle-class than mine, such words could be used in the living room. Not in my house.

'Oh, God,' said my brother, getting instantly angry, 'everything's sexist nowadays isn't it? You just say that about anything you don't like.'

To be fair to my brother, I think many men of his class and background had a very hard time understanding exactly what was meant by sexism. To a lot of them it just meant that you weren't allowed to fancy a girl, or be sarcastic about one, and that you had to take orders from women, as well as never saying anything funny in case it offended them.

'*10* is infantile, drooling rubbish,' said Ella, 'it's not far removed from Benny Hill.'

'So Benny Hill is sexist now, is he? What next? What next? Frank Zappa?'

Back then, when my brother was crossed, he would sort of work himself up into a fearful tizz designed to bludgeon down opposition.

Ella called him on this.

'What are you going to do?' she giggled, 'hit me?'

At eighteen my brother did not cope well with being laughed at by a woman and he flew into a blue fit. Strangely, my mother – who had been on the receiving end of many of these fits herself – viewed this as Ella's fault, rather than seeing it for what it was, a culture clash between two immature people.

So, when the day of Ella's parents' visit arrived, my mother wasn't really in the best mood to give them a good reception. Ella had made mum feel she (Ella) was looking down her nose at her (Mum's) family, which may have been partly true, and so my mum went on to hyper alert for any signs of such arrogance from Ella's mum and dad.

The central problem between my parents and Ella's was that they were virtually identical people. Both our fathers are affable, practical men with a taste for slightly ridiculous humour. So far so good. Both our mothers are intelligent women who always imagined – probably quite rightly – that they could have done more fulfilling jobs had they had more opportunity. Both also had active brains that, lacking drama or interest from the direction of work, sought it out in their private lives. They always had a worry, a concern, some nagging dissatisfaction with the day-to-day that, at its best, gave them something to think about but, at its worst, made them miserable.

Neither, however, was at all comfortable with this aspect of themselves and certainly wouldn't have recognised it. My own mum aspired to an ideal of battling through, no matter what your problems, summed up in her phrase: 'They don't have psychotherapists in the Rhondda.' They do, actually, along with a sizeable number of prescriptions for anti-depressants.

So when my mother started to suspect – through conversations with Ella – that Ella's mum might not be the sort of happy-go-lucky, grafting, mentally unassailable figure she wanted to be herself, she was not in the best frame of mind to receive her. Ella had doubtless related to her mother – as she related everything to her mother – the story of her run-in with my brother and unwittingly prepared her to confront a family of uncultured hooligans.

Accordingly there was a tense atmosphere at the meeting where everyone seemed to end up playing caricatures of themselves.

A key difference between the couples, for instance, is that Ella's parents are *Daily Mail*-reading Conservative voters who think the country is going to the dogs. My parents are *Daily Mail*-reading Labour voters who think the country has gone to the dogs already. Still, there is a cultural split and it was perhaps unfortunate that my mother answered the door holding my baby nephew Jake, who was wearing a red hammer-and-sickle hat and waving the former Soviet flag. There was a straightforward explanation. The child had been given these items by some Russian space scientists who my mum was boarding at the time while they worked at Warwick University.

However, it did immediately move the conversation on to politics, an area in which my family have rather strong views. Ella's parents are more reticent and won't out and out disagree with someone, but neither will they go along with statements such as 'The bosses have sponged off the workers for years', particularly when her dad's own factory had gone broke due to industrial unrest. What they will do is smile weakly and try to move the conversation on. To my family this is a lot worse than someone shouting 'Rubbish!' and calling them idiots to their faces. It implies condescension, something that cannot be borne.

The other thing is, my parents don't actually think things like 'The bosses have sponged off the workers for years'. But someone said it.

The meal was like a vision of hell. My family start the second the food hits their plates, which meant my dad had finished his before the peas had reached Ella's mum. My mum asked if anyone minded if she smoked. 'Not if my wife can fart,' said Ella's dad, who was also propelled to saying things he would never normally say just by the tension of the situation.

The whole visit was over in an hour and a half. Ella's mum has a number of qualities that my family would very much admire. She's bright – my family later complained she was opinionated, which is rich coming from us; she's kind – my family said she was soppy; she loves her daughter – my family complained she was mauling Ella by holding her hand when sitting next to each other; she's open – my family said she seemed a nervous wreck. On the nerves side, she was simply willing to express the very anxieties that my own mother felt. No one could see all that, though. I was incredibly frustrated and felt like screaming 'You're the same people, can't you see? You'd really like each other if you met at work.'

Still, we didn't let this disaster worry us, not when we could knock one up of our own. We bought a house in Fulham together – our one act of compromise as it was near the football ground for me, aspirational for her. It was a run-down wreck of a place that was almost designed to put a stress on our relationship. It didn't matter at first because Ella had to go away for a long period with work again, so there was no one to argue with. Typically, though, when she returned the stakes were raised. Ella moves at light speed, I am more glacial in my approach. Again, my immaturity came to the fore. She wanted to stay in at the weekends and do DIY. This should have been the time of my life: a shared project, a girl I loved and even her tremendously affable builder dad (sorry, former factory owner) to help us. I, however, saw no reason I should compromise my lifestyle a jot. Now I just had a bigger space in which to party when the clubs closed.

I was occasionally unfaithful to Ella and I think she might have been unfaithful to me. It didn't really matter at the time because the infidelities weren't serious and neither of us knew. It's strange how attitudes to this can change according to the partner. If Eva had slept with someone else, I would have just asked her what it was like and told her I was going to get my own back on her by doing that myself. If Catriona had slept with someone else, I'd probably have killed us both.

With Ella I would have been jealous if I'd thought the person was a serious rival, a bit annoyed if he wasn't but, if I'd found out a year after the event, I wouldn't really have minded. I'd have probably kicked up a squall to get some collateral against future misbehaviours of my own, but that's about it. I might be wrong but I can't believe that having spent six months working with a bunch of TV guys battling the elements, all pulling together for a common cause, that there wasn't at least one late night hoo-ha. I know TV men and, at the bottom line, they're all inwardly apologising for not being builders and over-compensating with the macho behaviour.

My infidelities were, I thought at the time, nothing for her to get worried about: one girl at the Madstock festival who pounced on me and with whom I found a secluded nook behind a caravan, and one friend who moaned on her birthday that she hadn't had sex for two years, so I was really only being gallant.

What had never sunk in, and what wouldn't sink in for another eight years, is how corrosive infidelity is and, in the end, how boring. Even the small ones leave you a degree less committed, a tiny bit further away than you were before. In the back of your mind you have options. If you love someone, then you don't want options. It's also tedious to live a life covering things up.

I had no sense that infidelity was morally wrong, though. What are morals anyway? To treat others as you would wish to be treated yourself? I didn't mind if Ella very, very occasionally slept with other people, as long as I didn't find out about it. There's another view, though, that morals are codes which have evolved over the centuries in order to allow human beings to live with a minimum of trouble amongst themselves and within themselves. I saw no difference between sleeping with a girl and doing anything else enjoyable on a night out. I'd have a drink, maybe occasionally take some drugs, and even more rarely go to bed with someone.

What I didn't realise is that infidelity is always a sign there's something awry. I didn't want to be unfaithful to Francesca and I wasn't once; I wouldn't have wanted to be unfaithful to Catriona; I was unfaithful to Eva because for years it never coalesced into anything you could call a relationship. If she'd have been more into me I would have been more into her. The reason I was unfaithful to Ella was that I was preparing ways out, or at least testing to see that I was attractive in case it came crashing down. That's not how I would have thought about it at the time. I would have thought I was having fun.

Still, there are infidelities and infidelities. I was about to be on the receiving end of a big one.

19 THE MAN I'D LIKE TO BE

Xavier Viana was a phenomenon. He was Colombian, educated at Eton and Oxford, and at twenty-six he was already
the darling documentary maker of a major independent TV
company. He'd done a number of award-winning documentaries including an absolute belter on Fidel Castro. No one
from the West had interviewed El Commandante for years.
Xavier had brought home the bacon. A piece he wrote for a
magazine typified his swashbuckling style: '3 a.m. The phone
rang. Blearily I reached over and took it. "Viana." It was the
producer with the news I'd been waiting for. "You've done
it. Castro. We have him." "I'm on my way," I said.'

Ella was full of stories about what he'd done and what
he'd said. 'He's an exotic,' she said, like a Roman adolescent
describing some piece of hunky slave flesh at a market. She'd
been working hard with him on a film and, unusually, staying
out late at Bar Italia in order to 'discuss projects'. Normally
she was in from work at around ten and, a cigarette and a
shower later, was in bed by 10.30.

I met him for the first time when Ella invited me to a
restaurant in Charlotte Street in the middle of Medja London.
I've said I'm not the jealous sort and I'm not. However, when
I enter a restaurant to find a snake-hipped handsome central-
American in, I kid you not, leather trousers, leaning across
the table to clasp the pale hand of m'lady with only a rose
and a bottle of champagne between them, my suspicions are
raised. At this stage of my life I didn't mind the occasional

infidelity, but my relationship with Ella was too fragile to stand the intervention of a force like Xavier. I marked his card the second I saw him.

As I came in Xavier gave me a warm welcome, stretching out his arm to put it around my shoulder. He was in command, was the little lesson I took from that. I was wary of him from the second I met him. He was interested in finding out about me, only to draw attention to his own accomplishments. That was my trick, he should have left it alone.

'What do you like to do to relax, Mark?'

'I play football.'

He tapped his chest in the manner of Napoleon. 'I play at Wembley Stadium. What do you think of that?' It turned out he'd pitched up for Oxford in a Varsity game. I was, it has to be said, mildly impressed, but not in a way that made me like him.

Xavier had very much the style of Jose Mourinho, the football manager, but without his humour or likeability – at least from where I was sitting. In fact, when Jose first appeared on the scene, for a second I thought it was Xavier, he looked a little like him. I wouldn't have put it past him to land the Chelsea job.

Then we had the descriptions of the youth in the big house in Colombia, but how he chose to spend his days among the poor of the barrios, learning what they had to teach, always watching, always taking notes. I really hate it when authors try to convey the style of non-native English speakers by changing the words to reflect their style of speech, all 'I looove eeeet' and stuff like that, but with Xavier there is no way around it, largely because I suspect he put on his style of speech for effect.

'This impress you. When I was boy, I train as bullfighter.'

'Sorry, did you say bull*fighter*?' I said. He got the slight. Xavier was a lot of things, but thick wasn't one of them. I wasn't finished with him, though.

'I see the bull got his revenge!' I said pointing at the leather trousers. It was laying it on thick, but, well, that's just me. Even though I was plainly losing a woman I was meant to be engaged to, it was important to cram as many leather-trouser jokes into the following hours as possible. The humour was useless and even served to emphasise my desperation. He was taking my girl. He didn't need jokes.

Ella shot me a dark look. This was her boss, after all. I often felt threatened by TV types, basically because I envied them. Xavier was doing a documentary on Maradona ('a personal friend of mine,' he said). I was working on *Actuary Cash Pig* magazine, or something like it. I did envy him.

He was better looking than me, better educated and said he was an aristocrat, which Ella lapped up. He'd been spectacularly successful and, if rumour was true, it was all certain people at Ella's company could do to stop themselves de-cowing him and bending him over the desk. Otherwise heterosexual men openly speculated what it would be like to have an affair with him, and senior management's attitude to him was said to resemble love. I described my friend Pat as a charmer. Xavier was a seducer, a powerfully magnetic character who could have charmed the birds from the trees.

There is a category of posh English person that buys this sort of style as fast as people like Xavier can sell it. There is another category of not-so-posh English lad to whom it is anathema. We're brought up to take the piss out of ourselves and to be very wary of anyone who doesn't.

Xavier wasn't one to take a slight lying down. I had besmirched his pants and he wanted revenge.

'Oh God!' he said, 'I've just remembered, we have to get

those rushes off tonight, we're going to have to go back to the office for a bit Ella.'

'Tonight?' said Ella, 'I thought it was Monday.'

'No, I had a call and I forgot, sorry.'

'Oh, yeah, right, tonight, oh yeah. I see,' said Ella.

They swigged back their champagne and were gone, leaving me with a 'but, what, eh, you can't!' on my lips.

'He's after her!' I said to my friend Charlie who had come with me.

'Don't be an idiot,' he said, 'he's really nice. Ella wouldn't do something like that. You're being paranoid.'

I looked out of the window to see them going into the office opposite, he kindly shepherding her in with an arm across her back. I'd seen a programme that said that when you leave the house, the dog is never sure if you've just gone to the shops or if you've left him forever. I knew how the dog felt.

They were an age in there – forty-five minutes or so – and his message was clear: any time I want her, she's mine. In fact, I'm probably having her now while you sit like a big fat cuckolded neuter praying she's going to come home. Eventually they returned and he suggested we go on to a media club in town.

The idea of sitting around like the plain girl at the princess's party while he was glad-handed by the shiterati of the TV world was about as appealing as breakfasting on my own eyeballs.

'Great!' said Ella. For once it was me who wanted to go home.

'I really don't want to,' I said.

'Why not?' said Ella.

'I just don't.'

I stamped my feet and eventually we left, going to the car – my exotic Lancia Fulvia, a symbol of the life I wasn't living.

'You're just threatened by him aren't you?'

'I am not threatened by a man in literally the back end of a pantomime cow,' I said.

'I think you'll find he's more used to playing the lead. It's you whose content to bend over and swish your tail,' she said.

'He's a wanker,' I said.

'No, Mark,' said Ella, 'I'll tell you who he is. He's the man you think you are.'

She was right, I knew. At least he appeared that way. I wasn't having it, though.

'I can just see straight through him. He's a fantasist. "I used to be a bullfighter", shiter, more like.'

'I got the joke the first time you used it,' she said, 'where's the fantasy? He's incredibly successful, very gifted and very well rewarded for those gifts. If there's a fantasist here it's you.'

I couldn't reply. I just sat grasping the steering wheel and wishing I had an argument to come back with. I didn't.

Ella spoke: 'This isn't working is it?'

'What isn't working.'

'Us.'

The dead syllable, like the thud of the headsman's axe.

I felt utterly useless, weary, almost as if I might fall out of the car. We had struggled for so long only for it to come to this.

'Ella,' I said. When I was a kid I'd read a book about wizards that said that if you knew something's true name, a rock, a bird, a flower, then you could make it do your will. That was how I spoke to her then. I was trying to reach down into her soul, to make her realise how much I cared for her and what she was doing to me.

'What?' she said.

'Just nothing,' I said.

Two weekends later, Ella went home to her mum's. I called her on the Sunday to see how she was and I could hear a huge tremble in her voice. She didn't have to tell me what had happened. She'd decided it was over. Not 'over' as it had been before but properly finished. There would be no coming back because finally she had somewhere she wanted to go.

She came to our house for the last time on the Monday morning early, to pick up things for work. I didn't suspect that she'd spent the Friday and Saturday with him, but I quizzed her about him anyway.

'You like him more than you like me, don't you?' I said.

'Well, he is very attractive,' she said. She was, as always, hurrying to get out, to get into the office. She was actually too busy to finish with me, 'Oh God, I really have to find these files,' she said.

And then I just saw it, as plain as day.

'You've been with him this weekend, haven't you? You only went up to your mum's on Sunday because you knew I'd call and you wanted an alibi.'

She couldn't deny it, just looked glum and scared. Sometimes thoughts have a momentum of their own. Ever since I'd pushed a pain au chocolat in her face she'd been convinced I was on the road to giving her a beating. She had been chewing my ear off about some task I hadn't completed correctly, not even looking up from her paper as she did so.

'So bloody lazy, blah, friends more important than setting up home, blah, munch, my friends' partners do things for them, munch, ah!'

I'd gone past her to get to the kettle and, as I did so, just bodged the pastry she was eating into her face, not hard, but just enough to make her mistime her munching and have to cough a bit out. She accused me of violence against women, which I suppose it was from one angle. I found that incredibly depressing. There are people who would argue that I had crossed a line and it would only get worse. My answer is 'It was only a cake in the face and I immediately regretted doing it. Do clowns go on to commit homicide?' And did not her plate to my head count for anything? Probably not, is the answer. Still, I had to accept the fact, Ella was frightened of me. After nearly seven years together, did she not know me better than that?

There's a strange thing that happens when someone takes a strong dim view of me. It creates a sort of self-loathing attitude where I do everything I can to prove them right. I'd known this union chap at work, a very articulate, interesting, inspirational leader, if a bit in love with himself. He plainly thought I was a loud-mouthed berk. Every time I saw him I wanted to prove him wrong, and every time I saw him I acted more like a loud-mouthed berk. Once I even used the phrase 'we on the left' to him, as if claiming some equivalence between his fifteen years of solid campaigning and my occasional shouting at the television – and the fact that, as I once noted of my granddad, I am a socialist in everything but my views. That is, I say I'm a socialist, I like the hats socialists wear, I attend festivals for socialist causes and listen to songs by the Clash, but, when it comes down to it, you couldn't get much of a wedge between me and David Cameron on most things.

It was similar with Ella. She thought I was cruel and potentially violent, so I played up to it, without wanting to. Obviously I didn't hit her, but I just went very quiet and cold. After a few seconds staring at her I said: 'Don't bother coming back tonight. And make sure you come for your things when I'm out.' I didn't openly physically threaten her but, in that situation, I knew that letting her feel my anger in a few beats of quiet would really disconcert her. It was the shameful behaviour of a true coward, but it was all I had left in my locker. The thing is, I didn't even feel angry. I was just exhausted, not even able to take in the misery of the situation. It was as if I'd studied for years for an exam and had just learned that I'd failed on my ninth retake. In some ways the feeling wasn't as bad as I'd anticipated, and in some ways the encroaching numbness in my head was worse. In one of those weird coincidences my eye fell on one of her self-help books that was lying on the table. 'Ready or not, the rest of your life is starting NOW!' said the cover. It was the sort of thing that's too cheesy to put into a novel, but it happened to me.

I went upstairs and she gathered her work things to leave. There would be no begging this time, no emotional blackmail. They say an Englishman never knows when he is beaten. This one does. Just as Catriona had been my 'design your own woman', Xavier was Ella's 'design your own man'.

I couldn't stay upstairs, though. I came down again and watched her go, remembering in a lamentably sentimental way the look of optimism and love on her face when she'd picked me up from the station in Kettering all those years ago. She had her hand on the door and she gave me a sad smile. I gave her one back, and then the very weirdest feeling of my entire life overtook me.

All the jealousies I had, the resentments, the feeling of being short-changed on an interesting life, the self-hatred for not doing something about it, the fact that I knew in my bones that Xavier was a fake and that I was being cast into the pit of loneliness by a phoney, all coalesced into the most putrid emotion I've ever felt. I tried to hold it in, but I couldn't and the words burst as if from a tumour in my throat. At the time it felt like a curse, of the magical variety, as if I had something so powerful inside me that I feared to let it out.

'He will do you harm,' I said.

And boy, was I right.

20   FINAL REEL

I drove out to Dorking where I was working in numbness, which is not a county but felt like one. As I came into the outskirts and past the station I saw the sign for some sort of science park. It was the final straw, I burst into tears. I don't know why it set me off, just that I've always found science parks very depressing. It's something about the ornamental water features.

I was crying and thumping the steering wheel as I drove, and then I heard another sound. I couldn't identify it at first but then I did. It was laughter. I was laughing.

'Yes! Fucking yes!' I shouted. I even punched the air, which is something I'd no more normally do than high-five, that is at gunpoint or to humour a backwards child. A bright child should simply be informed that if it continues to act like an American it will be required to go and live there, where it will be shot.

I pulled up at work, glad that I'd had such a narrow escape, though still feeling rejected, inferior, cheated and stupid for wasting so much time in my life.

I needed a period of reflection, some time to myself to assess where I wanted to go, to reflect on my mistakes and to achieve some inner calm. I had that on my way across the carpark and, by the time I sat at my desk, I was ready for another girlfriend. Steps needed to be taken. First was that I gave up drinking. I wasn't going to drink at work, but I gave up the idea of going out for a drink. Then I phoned a gym and arranged to join it. Then I threw my BLT in the bin. Rocky was getting back in the ring and needed to be in trim to do so.

What I needed was a clean break from the past – but first, I thought I'd just call Vanessa. When you've finally rid yourself of one Freddy Krueger of a relationship – every time you think it's dead, its face looms up at the window and the horror just gets worse – the best thing to do is to go stirring up another. If my life was a horror film, calling Vanessa was the equivalent of saying 'Oh, the car's broken down, why don't we see if there's a phone over there in that deserted house with the ghostly child in the window?'

It wasn't actually a cynical move. After the emotional stripping I'd received from my relationship with Ella, I just wanted to know there was a woman somewhere who I respected and who thought I was OK. Despite all that had gone on between us, despite her hating me, I hoped Vanessa was still fond of me.

We met up again at a little Belgian mussel bar in east London, all checked table cloths and low light. I got to the restaurant first because I knew my habit of being late annoyed her. I also wanted to have some time to work out what I was going to say. I didn't get very far. 'Hi' was the work of half an hour.

I had been battered and bruised and was grieving, but there was no agenda to my meeting with Vanessa. All I wanted to do was see her. I didn't even want to cry on her shoulder, I think I just wanted to know there were women who liked me out there in the world. Look in the dictionary and you will see that the above is the definition of 'on the rebound'.

Vanessa came into the bar, impeccably neat and stylish in her smart and fashionable rain coat. Her hair was longer than

I remembered, she looked like someone from a film: *All About Eve*, maybe or *Separate Tables*, the bright ingénue emerging from the wet day to greet . . . well, my role in the picture was as yet up for grabs. Mind you, I wasn't in one of the slick pictures Vanessa would have inhabited. I'd have been more likely to be part of some grim social realism flick about thick men and pregnant women, or maybe just in *On the Buses*, not the series, but the trying-too-hard transition to film.

Vanessa was an ingénue in some ways. She was hugely perceptive when it came to other people and had a great understanding of herself. I was her one blind spot, it seemed. The explanation for that is easy. I had no view of myself, I didn't know where I was coming from, so how could she? What did I think of her? I really didn't know and it changed from day to day. I did try to work it out briefly. The nearest I got was 'I love her, but.'

She took off her coat and sat next to me. A few questions about what we'd been doing, who we'd been seeing, a few drinks and we were back in the old routine.

I realised that, no matter the hurt I had caused her, Vanessa still really cared for me. I felt very sorry for what I'd done. I'm not sure if this was a good thing. Maybe I was deep in self-pity and, when I saw someone who had been foully mistreated, the good emotions of care I felt for her were actually the ones I was feeling for myself. 'There's someone miserable, just like me, boo hoo.' I hope this wasn't the case. There were plenty of fine reasons for falling for Vanessa again that evening, but there were bad ones too. There would be no painful period of loneliness, no slowly building a relationship and risking investing six months or a year and finding out I didn't like someone. I could just exchange one permanent, serious girlfriend for another. When she invited me back to her house for coffee, I went.

We never got as far as the coffee. The door of the flat opened and suddenly we were kissing, going for it with urgency and it worked. It was great sex, the sort *Cosmopolitan* aspires to and that you see in those films. Now I come to think of it, the film that best represents the style of what went on is *Fatal Attraction*, the early scene in the lift between Douglas and Close. It wasn't perhaps the best omen.

The next morning I was happy. I couldn't believe that we'd finally clicked physically. Again, I'm drawn to comparisons with film. It was like the bit where you think everything must be lost and then something amazing happens and it's all OK. We had used the Force; we had been shot but fallen on the detonator on the River Kwai. It was like a dream come true. So I became Vanessa's partner, for how long I can't remember – maybe a year, maybe less. There was too much latent anger in the relationship, though. I don't think she ever really forgave me for the betrayal with Catriona.

We were never far from an argument. I became uncertain I had done the right thing and Vanessa, with her usual perceptiveness, picked up on it immediately. We'd go out, have a nice time, although resentments and complications were boiling in both of us, and then, some gesture of affection not welcomed, some glance not returned, Vanessa would blow into anger. It was taking its toll on me and I felt thoroughly miserable.

I understood her point of view. She'd had faith in me, tolerated my indecision and weakness, and now it was time we started the rest of our lives as proper, committed lovers. When that didn't happen her fury rose and we were into the classic vicious circle – me not loving her quite enough, she becoming angry and so me loving her slightly less, she loving me slightly less . . .

It probably didn't help that I managed to turn myself into

Eddie Large. Frustrated by the nearly nature of our relationship, I started drinking quite heavily and, by the second month of us being together, a rumour started at work that I was on steroids for cancer, so much had I swollen. Vanessa certainly mentioned that she found a chap we used to work with much better looking than me so, even if she was attracted to me, I wasn't exactly her dream come true.

I have to admit that I was looking particularly rough at this period. It will sound as if I'm making the next bit up, but I'm really not. I wish I was. I'd taken my nephew to Madame Tussauds, and, uninterested in celebrity, I had found it a very dull experience. The final horror was the chamber of horrors, which was monstrously dull. Still, Jake seemed to enjoy it and, while he inspected the various murderers, I stood staring into space, daydreaming. I came back to reality to see a man in a 'Good boys go to heaven, bad boys go to London' T-shirt examining me with his face about two inches from mine.

'Get away from me!' I said.

He nearly leapt out of his skin. He'd thought I was an exhibit.

This is funny, I suppose, but the fact that my skin was of such a pallor that I could be mistaken for a waxwork psychopath couldn't have made me that attractive to Vanessa.

The relationship didn't really have a chance anyway. Vanessa never forgave me all the many pains I had caused her. She might have thought she had, but she was always on a short fuse with me. The quality of her anger was different from that of Ella's. There was nothing threatened about it, no sense she was having to fight for her psychic life. It was just that I had been a twat, and needed it pointing out, in clear and unambiguous terms, exactly why I was such a twat.

Any intimacy between us had gone. There was no truth

between us any more. When the best friend you've ever had asks you 'What's wrong?' how do you reply 'You'?

I discovered she was becoming increasingly desperate as she sought for clues to my interior motivations when I arrived at her house in my car one day.

'What were you doing in there?' she said. She'd heard me pull up and was watching from the window.

'What do you mean?'

'You sat in there on your own just staring into space and laughing for ten minutes.'

I'd been listening to the end of a Harry Hill show on the radio, but she thought she might have finally unearthed evidence I was a dangerous nutter.

Unlike with Ella, I always saw Vanessa's point of view, but I didn't have to let it sink in because there was a power imbalance between us. I was in between my abject relationship with Ella and my positively prostrate one that followed with Francesca, but there I was on top. Vanessa was fully prepared to walk away from me, more prepared than I was to leave her, but we both knew it would hurt her more. She would need strength, I could go in a moment of weakness or stupidity or anger when I forgot exactly what I had with her. I'd do the crying six months later when I finally realised what I'd lost.

Of all the difficulties between us it seemed odd that we should finally split up rowing over a toilet seat. No one will believe that I had never heard that women prefer the loo seat left down. My mum wasn't bothered about it and I grew up with only brothers. I went to an all-boys school. I lived with men as flatmates. Hand on heart, I had no idea that women don't like to have to touch the seat. I know now that it's a cliché, but I didn't then.

'I don't want to have to touch that when I go to the loo,' she said.

'Well, if you put it down, I have to touch it to lift it up,' I said. 'Fair's fair.'

She thought I was being wilfully annoying and the closet of both of our resentments spilled open. We were still at it on the way into the cinema – an arty dive serving flapjacks, rather than a flecky-carpeted multiplex.

We sat next to each other, quietly simmering. It was a French film, the sort that features gorgeous looking actresses, puffing on Gitanes, laughing and pouting and living, the sort of girl who makes your blood rush to look at and, crucially, doesn't forensically deconstruct your ample sack of shortcomings at every possible opportunity. I can't remember who the girl was, but I can remember what I thought: 'I want one of those.'

And suddenly I had the courage to try for one. This, in the end, is what the famous inability to commit comes down to – the feeling that you could get someone better fighting against the fear that you couldn't. That's why he doesn't feel ready to marry you quite yet, but why he doesn't want to finish with you.

I realised that what Vanessa and I had in common wasn't enough any more. Our friendship had been fatally wounded from the second I'd slept with Catriona. What was left? Two people who argued a lot. We'd been sustained through nostalgia for a period when we were best friends, but the magic wasn't going to come back.

By the time the film was over I'd made up my mind.

'I'm collecting my things,' I said.

'OK,' she said.

We walked back in silence and I loaded a couple of tapes and shirts into a plastic bag.

'Goodbye,' I said.

'Goodbye,' she said.

And that was it for me and my soul mate.

21 WHAT WOMEN REALLY WANT

I don't think it's possible to break your own heart. It is, however, possible to put it on the floor and invite someone to stamp on it.

On the surface there was so much right between me and Francesca that it's amazing it ever went wrong. In fact there was nothing right in our relationship. I didn't see it, but all we had on our side was timing. We were the right people for each other at that stage in our lives and that was it. The thing was, I've only really been in one stage since I was seventeen, so, for me, she could have come along at any point in a twenty-five-year period. Francesca had been other places before, and she had other places to go though she did a very good job of disguising it.

Why would you have wanted to be anywhere else anyway? London was buzzing and had been for years. I went for a night out in Camden in about 1990 and didn't really come home for a decade. Ella's obsession with work had finally seen her base her love life there. Vanessa and I had spent months in mental turmoil. The next person I went out with, I prayed, would want to have some more fun. When the gods wish to punish us, they answer our prayers.

Francesca was very pretty in an olive-skinned, dishevelled, pouting sort of way. Her father was Spanish and her mother was Italian, though she'd been convent educated in Britain since she was fourteen. She looked like the sort of girl who is designed to breakfast on cigarettes and coffee while wearing only her boyfriend's shirt. She was a shop-soiled Spanish rose, a glorious, corrupt sexy cliché who you could quite easily imagine blinking in the paparazzi's flashbulbs as she peered from the door of the young Mick Jagger's hotel room. A friend of mine said she had a 'just fucked' look to her and I think he was on the money there, largely because – for most of the time I knew her – Francesca had actually just been fucked.

Naturally, after our first date, I immediately forgot her completely for six months.

This wasn't strictly my fault. Francesca was, in the terminology of the time, 'a binner'. This meant that she liked to party hard. I've been on about eight stag weekends in my life and none of them have ever come close in terms of alcohol consumption, drug taking or staying power to the average night out with the petite and dainty Francesca.

We'd met through mutual friends one Saturday night. Francesca was in the process of breaking up from her long-term boyfriend. She was still living with him, but had made it clear that she needed a period to think about things. This always means only one thing: 'I haven't the courage to finish with you outright, but I think that if I behave ludicrously unreasonably over the coming weeks you will have no choice but to end it yourself. I cannot even admit to myself that this is what I am doing.' This was where I came in.

I immediately liked her. She spoke English in a posh voice with a trace of Andalucia thrown in and had a laugh not unlike The Penguin from *Batman*, and I could see she liked boys. That is, she wasn't looking for some emotionally sorted, well-balanced *man*, some listening, understanding potential father for her children. In fact, she had one of those in her boyfriend Scott. I knew him vaguely and he was a genuinely pleasant, quietly humorous, good-looking guy who no one ever said a bad word against. Her parents loved him, her brothers regarded him as a best mate and he would have died for her.

She didn't want Scott. She wanted a partner in crime, some overconfident gobshite to take the piss with through 48-hour sessions in pub and club. My CV fitted the advertisement, I'm sorry to say.

We talked about Scott for a while and it was clear that she loved him, just as it was clear that she didn't want to be with him. There was a kind of distant look in her eye. Her attitude to him was more like he'd died, or that they'd been parted by war or blind mischance, than that she was taking a decision to leave him. She reminded me of a character from a play, nursing some fatal flaw that she couldn't reveal to the world. It turned out I was right, but not in the way that I thought.

That first night she wanted – as she always did – to go on to a nightclub. I was the only one who was willing to go with her. Everyone else, I think, sensed there was something between us and tactfully butted out. My aim, from the second we got into the taxi together, was to get her back home and into bed.

This had little to do with lust, though lust came into it. It was simply a matter of finding out where I stood. Francesca was pretty, funny and shared my love of partying. Of course I wanted her for my girlfriend. Despite how I sound, I'm a romantic. I've very rarely ever gone into a relationship without hoping that this could be the one. In our immediate rapport, our teasing, slightly sarcastic repartee, our love of music, books and good times we were really well suited. I was fairly smitten right from the start and needed to know if she at least returned some of that feeling. However, I couldn't tell her that. It's as if we're in the reverse position of the one couples in the nineteenth century used to find themselves in. Then the only honourable way was to declare your love. In the late twentieth century that would have been immediate poison. The acceptable way forward, the one she was culturally primed to accept, was for me to try to get her into bed. Choosing the moment to ask, though, proved difficult.

She scored some ecstasy at the nightclub for us. This was nerve-racking because I'd immediately sensed that the drug dealers were exactly the sort of men she was drawn to and, with her air of stained innocence and blonde good looks, they were definitely interested in her. Still, I played it cool and she returned.

'I could only get two each,' she said, 'maybe we'll be able to get more later.'

'Wouldn't want to risk an underdose, would you?' I said. Most people I knew took drugs – though weirdly very few of my girlfriends. Vanessa and Ella hated that sort of thing. However, underneath it all, I've always been a beer monster. I used to like E and cocaine when I was offered them, but I wouldn't go out of my way. I even regard drinking beer out of bottles as a bit wilfully corrupt when there's a perfectly good pint to be had. So two Es was precisely one and a half more than I'd ever taken.

'Tally ho!' said Francesca, downing them in full view of the bar. Whatever, I did the same. I had the feeling I was with one of the most exciting people I'd ever met. The evening had gone mad after that. We'd been thrown out of the club at eight in the morning and I asked her if she wanted to come back to my house.

'No,' she said, 'I just want to stay out.'

'Well, we could just go back to my house for a bit,' I said.

'I'm not going to sleep with you,' she said.

'Nothing was further from my mind,' I said. 'I'd envisaged

heavy petting. Just enough to get us thrown out of a swim-ming pool, that sort of thing.'

She laughed and gave me a nudge with her shoulder. I wanted to put my arm around her, but I knew that would spoil things. She was entirely in control and I had to like it or leave it.

'Shall we find somewhere for a drink?' she said.

'Of course,' I said, feigning disgust that she even had to ask.

There wasn't anywhere, so we wandered around Soho for a couple of hours.

I felt bizarrely privileged to be in her company. It was as if the early Sunday shoppers were all living in black and white, that only me and Francesca were in colour and knew what was going on, as if we were immortals strolling through the ordinary world. I think I would have had that feeling without the ecstasy.

The day was cold and so I stopped to buy a sweater, a thin V-neck item from Benetton, the sort of thing I still wear to this day. Choosing it together felt like an act of intimacy, like our first step on the road to coupledom. I've never invested very much of my personality in the car I drive, the house I live in or the job I do. My self-esteem, however, has always depended on my girlfriend – what she looks like, how engaging is her personality, even the clothes she wears (jeans and a T-shirt worn with panache beating Bond Street every time). Buying my pullover, I thought there was no man in the world who wouldn't want to change places with me.

Francesca phoned her boyfriend to tell him she was out enjoying herself and wasn't coming home until later that evening, and I stood at a respectful distance from the phone box. She emerged crying and then we found a hotel bar that was open.

It may sound strange, or even repulsive, to those who haven't grown up in a drinking culture – those who didn't have their first beers at fifteen and then spent their pocket money, their grants or loans and eventually their wages solely on going out – but we carried on shifting the beers until the pubs closed that evening. You don't come to this sort of endurance overnight and both Francesca and I had put in the hard hours building up to it. Neither of us were in love with the drugs or the drink, we were in love with the world that came with them – of friendship and fun and dancing. Well, she was in love with the dancing, I was more just for the friendship and fun.

We even rang the people we'd been with the night before and met up with them again. There comes a time, particularly when drinking cooking lager, that your rate of consumption falls to about two pints an hour, maybe less. Then you're getting rid of the beer at roughly the same rate that you're putting it in. Add this to the effects of some cocaine purchased from a bloke in a pub – Francesca could always spot dealers a mile away and they always felt confident to sell to her because few policewomen are that pretty or that exotic-looking – and it meant that we could carry on drinking almost indefinitely without becoming slavering drunk.

This was excess nineties style, that is to say we weren't caning it like previous generations did, as a statement about who we were or to shock or even to expand our conscious-ness. This was simply a lifestyle choice, and a very common one at that, particularly back then, reflected in the music of the day. Songs like 'Cigarettes and Alcohol' and 'Rock and Roll Star' by Oasis sprang out of the life we were living. We might have been financial advisers and salespeople in the week but, come the weekend, the suits came off, the glad rags were put on and we were 48-hour Gallagher brothers, going out and on one. There were a lot of people who felt that way – one in twenty Britons applied for tickets to see Oasis at Knebworth. I would have gone, but I needed the money for cigarettes and alcohol.

Actually, perhaps it wasn't a lifestyle choice for me. I didn't know what other options were available. I had no idea how anyone filled a weekend without spending most of it in a pub or a nightclub.

I talked about everything with Francesca – films, books, bands – and, although I thought her taste a bit questionable (she liked *Captain Corelli's Mandolin*), it was great to have someone who shared my passions without taking the whole thing too seriously.

I trotted out all my stories, all my favourite quotes and anecdotes, and she did the same. You either like this sort of thing or you don't. That is, she found it interesting when I told her that my favourite rock quote was when John Peel once commented on David Bowie's hilarious performance of Brecht's 'Baal' with the words 'David Bowie, there, who began his career sounding like Anthony Newley and seems determined to end it the same way,' and I found it interesting when she told me that her favourite was when a reporter asked John Lennon 'Is Ringo Starr the best drummer in the world?' and Lennon replied 'Ringo Starr isn't the best drummer in The Beatles.' This was our world, where it's important to talk about what pop stars and authors say and think and it's a basic assumption that Sting is rubbish and M People should be shot.

I knew that we were going to get it together when she was clearly treating me to some set-piece jokes. 'All the most successful people in life take a lot of hallucinogens,' she said.

'Really?' I said, 'I thought it was more the domain of hippy losers.'

'Well, it depends on your definition of success,' she said, 'if you're talking about stuff like having lots of money, a nice house, a steady relationship and all that sort of stuff, maybe not. If you judge it by how many elves you know, then it's a very different picture.'

I thought this was funny and, better than that, it showed she wanted to impress me.

At the time I genuinely thought this was the best part of a relationship – right at the beginning, hovering on the edge of a kiss, beyond tiredness, beyond drunkenness, in a little cocoon where no one in the rest of the world mattered and the only dark cloud on the horizon was Monday morning. I felt alive, almost blessed, really. This has always been the thing about drink and drugs to me – it's not about getting off your head, it's about spending a long time in someone else's company and achieving a level of intimacy that you couldn't achieve in any other way. This isn't because the intoxicants loosen your tongue, it's because they stave off boredom. After twenty-four solid hours with the same person, just sitting as if in a waiting room, things can be said and feelings felt that you'd never have the endurance to get to if you were straight. It's not unlike that experience of pulling together when you have to work through the night on something.

We said goodbye at Piccadilly Circus.

'I suppose a kiss is out of the question,' I said.

''Fraid so,' she said with that distant look in her eye again.

She gave me her business card – she worked in a company that managed property, a job I had no idea actually existed – and she disappeared down the steps into the tube.

I caught a cab and slept for the next twenty-four hours – only waking up to ring in to tell work I was ill. Actually, this was true. At that age I felt considerably more sick with a hangover than I had through any cold, flu, food poisoning or headache in my life. Obviously I thought of Francesca and what I wished we were doing together and that got me off to sleep.

But then, I don't know why, I completely forgot about her. One of our mutual friends told me she was just going through a blip with Scott and that they were made for each other. She didn't so much fade from my mind as disappear in a puff of smoke. By the next weekend I couldn't remember her name. I don't think she even intruded on my fantasies, despite the fact that I definitely found her madly attractive.

Six months later my need for a girlfriend was getting desperate, I could tell. Like most men, I have virtually no interior life, so I can normally only get clues to my emotional state by observing my behaviour closely. In this case there were two main indicators – I was on a diet and I was buying unusual trousers. Checked ones. Sorry.

I'd been on a sort of tour of London's satellite towns at that point in my career – Dorking, Guildford, even Staines. I'd somehow ended up in Egham. It was a well-paid job but dull. I'd bought myself an old Porsche (clue number three) to make the journey from my home in Fulham more bearable. Only on one morning out of three did I have a serious urge to steer it headlong into the oncoming traffic. The other hungover mornings I just felt like pulling into a layby and waiting for the council to tow me to a landfill.

When I say I needed a girlfriend, that's exactly what I mean – someone to hold hands with, to take on picnics and to the cinema and restaurants. Propelled by the dullness of my situation, I was actually having sex, but I didn't want that. Or rather, I didn't want just that. I wanted someone to buy flowers for.

I'd accidentally become involved with a woman at work and couldn't think of a way out of it. I was on the copy-writing side of things, she was in sales. This meant that we had to have regular meetings together, very often with clients. We were allied to the building industry, which still had a culture of long boozy lunches.

Laura was about my age, quite goodlooking in a blonde, over-manicured sort of way – a typical half-bright salesgirl with a Sloaney look consisting of turned-up collars, pearls, and pullovers worn draped across the shoulders. Her icon was Princess Diana and she didn't look dissimilar in a skinny, big-beaked, Hermès-scarfed way. I've never liked this look and, as a confirmed lefty son of Indie, I had very little in common with her culturally. However, the place we were working was full of provincial nutcases.

The people there seemed much more limited than London-ers and also quite weird. On my first day on the job I was sitting on the loo when one of the print staff knocked on the door.

'Yes?' I said.

'There's a phone call for you,' he said.

'Well I'm rather indisposed,' I said.

'Oh,' he said, genuinely nonplussed, 'well, what do you want me to do?'

'Take a message?' I said. I'd spent most of my career in central London and this was like landing on planet Zog.

Laura too was more used to the West End than she was the provinces, and so we sort of hit it off. I think her being married was what might have made her attractive to me. At least, I thought, we could have a one-night stand and then forget about it. Actually, all this talk of 'think' and 'thought' is wrong. I didn't think anything on any of the four occasions we went to bed. I didn't even want to do it once really but, despite my best efforts, didn't manage to get out of it until the fourth time.

The problem was the drink. And the drugs. Drink and drugs get mentioned a lot at this point in the story, but it's only because that was what was going around at the time. This is the amount that someone who could take or leave narcotics consumed. Imagine what the enthusiasts were up to. London was disappearing under drifts of cocaine. Don't look for the city today, all you'll find is the top of Big Ben poking out from under a mound of white powder.

Still, it was quite surprising when Laura asked me if I wanted a line. We'd been out with the world's most boring client – a man with whom we had demolished six bottles of wine while listening to his tales of his son's ski-ing prowess. His son, twenty-one years old, ski-ed twice a year on holiday so he was a reasonably keen amateur by UK standards. We had three hours as his dad ran us through virtually every mogul he'd ever negotiated.

At the end of the lunch – about 4.30 – we retired to a pub to hoot about how dull the client had been. She did a very good impression of him and she made me laugh by saying stuff like, 'Oh, you should see how my son buys sprouts, it's like watching a young gazelle break cover on the Serengeti,' in the man's John Major-like accent.

We carried on drinking until about 8.30 and then she rang her husband. He said he'd come and pick her up at 10.30 when he was finished in a meeting he was having about twenty miles away. He was an accountant and, she said, a workaholic.

This was the point at which I noticed the atmosphere change. If I'd thought about it I would have immediately seen why. I have no idea if Laura ever drove drunk but, in my experience, it was very common for salespeople in that industry to drive about entirely plastered. In fact, between wine-soaked client lunches and hungover mornings, a lot of them never drove sober. So why did she need to get her husband to come out of the way? She could have got a cab, even, and charged it to expenses seeing as she'd been out with a client.

Still, she'd steered the conversation around to drugs and asked me if I ever took cocaine. I still didn't know her that well and was aware of her potential for using weaknesses against you, so I just shrugged.

'Would you like a line?' she said, tapping her clutch bag. You could have knocked me down with a feather. I said I would, and she said she didn't trust me with it on my own, so we'd have to go back to the office and take it. I didn't find this insulting. I'd trusted someone to go to the loo with sixty-quid's-worth of biff once and he'd done the lot and eaten the wrapper.

We bought another bottle of wine and went back. She took great delight in slicing up the coke on the boss's desk. He was an Alpha-programmed Christian, a family man who restored furniture for a hobby. He was an all round normal, nice, if a bit boring, guy and I think that added to the appeal of doing drugs in his office for her.

We had a couple of lines each, sitting on the floor and drinking wine between them. I felt a charge in the air but I'm a good boy, her husband was on his way for God's sake.

She was talking about the women in the office and asking me who I'd like to fuck. To annoy her I mentioned one of the local girls who was pretty, but too soppy for me. Laura chopped out another line, this time on a book between us and, while she did, said that I'd annoyed her by saying that. We snorted the line and she put back her head, fixed me with a look and just dived at me, pushing her tongue deep into my mouth. I returned her kiss, but now it was me who felt annoyed. I'd enjoyed flirting with her, I'd even enjoyed feeling angry with her, but I felt threatened by the fact her husband was going to be there in under an hour.

Her taste too was disquietingly unfamiliar to me. I'd been used to more or less arty girls and, usually, poor ones at that. Cigarettes and musk was my normal thing. This was cigarettes and Chanel No 5 and it was exciting but mildly disconcerting.

My eyes slid to the window.

'Your husband is coming, help, I'm scared,' I felt like saying. I couldn't concentrate on what I was doing for the fear that some huge rugger buggering accountant was going to come crashing through the windows at any minute and skin me alive. In fact, physical violence would be a relief from having to face the pure embarrassment of the situation.

She broke from kissing me and, unbelievably, chopped out another line. She seemed very fond of it indeed.

'Well,' she said, as we polished off a fourth, 'I'm going to make that provincial little bitch's life hell from now on. I don't want to think of you getting hard for anyone else around here.' She leaned over and squeezed my crotch, which, as she had rightly assumed, was hard.

Then she went for it again, kissing me deeply, telling me that the girl's punishment was going to be all my fault and instructing me what to do, to take off my belt and lay it on the desk, then keep my hands by my sides. The memory of the lashing I'd taken at the hands of Selina came back to me. Plus, I'm just not one of life's natural subs. I don't like being told what to do, and neither do I like people biting my tongue. She sank her fangs in and it really hurt. I have almost never bitten my own tongue in any situation, even when I

240

should have, so I don't see why someone else should do it for me. So when she bit me it focused my mind on the fact I didn't like her very much, no matter that I found her funny and irreverent.

'Ouch,' I said, which I don't think you're meant to say in sado-masochistic encounters, 'that fucking hurt.' Actually, I think I said something more like 'Outsch, at ucking urt,' my tongue being rather numb.

'You haven't been hurt,' she said, 'I'm going to show you fucking hurt.' She then picked up my belt. I was annoyed, turned on, coked up, drunk and I also felt protective towards the poor local girl, who, though thick and soppy, had no harm in her. I'd had the beans beaten out of my behind for the last time, I decided.

'No you're fucking not,' I said.

There then ensued a sort of circumspect wrestling match. I was attempting the rather difficult feat of lifting up her skirt, getting her across my knee and spanking her arse blue without disordering her clothes so much that her husband would notice when he came to pick her up. She fought like a tiger and not one of these relatively peaceful jungle tigers either, a big football hooligan tattooed tiger to whom violence is a hobby as well as a profession.

However, she suddenly had the same thought as me.

'Wait,' she said, 'I don't want to mess up my suit.'

I was seething with anger by this stage. She'd not only bitten my tongue raw, she'd ripped my shirt and scratched my chest as well as pulling my hair really badly. I'd pulled her hair in return and this had got her into a position face down across the boss's desk with her skirt in the air. It did, of course, occur to me to fuck her like that, but I didn't want to give her the pleasure, even though I wanted that pleasure myself. I don't know how these full-time sadists manage because, it seemed to me, you need at least three hands in this position – one to keep hold of her hair so she'll stay still, one to pull her knickers aside, one to unholster the old chap and guide it home. It gave me a new respect for dominant males who, I concluded, must have the dexterity of octopi.

Once again I found myself wondering why I didn't seem to attract the sort of girl that expects you to seduce her with champagne and chocolates before a slow unfolding of intimacies on a sheepskin rug in front of a roaring fire. Who had slipped the tapper magnet into my back pocket? And what was this sado-masochism thing that seemed to stalk me? Do I look like a sadist? Do I look like a masochist? Is it just that this sort of thing is much more common than we suppose and everyone is called upon to wield or cower before the whip eventually.

I let her go because I couldn't think of what else to do and was genuinely concerned we might start fighting properly if it went any further. She stood up and looked me up and down. Then, staring directly at me, she took off all her clothes down to her – by now rather predictable – black stockings and suspenders. I found it a bit of a hackneyed touch. Once you knew she was a would-be dominatrix with a coke problem, then she was bound to be wearing stockings and suspenders to work, wasn't she? Still, perhaps I'm being picky.

Typically, she spent a while folding up her clothes just so, and this made me even more annoyed.

Then, just as I was ready for seconds out, round two, she went to the desk. Obviously, she cut out another line of coke, which had by now become a bit boring, but she did so leaning across the desk with her arse towards me.

Women, on the whole, have shocked me. What they want and how they act in private is often so different to how they present themselves in public. There was nothing shocking about Laura so far, in fact she was a bit of a cliché, but what she did next certainly caused me to raise a brow.

'I can't believe I'm going to let you do this,' she said, as she chopped, 'but if you want to spank me then go on.'

'Er, OK,' I said.

How does one go about this though? Like they used to on the deck of the Victory, like Basil Fawlty hit his car, like a 1970s salesman hurrying his secretary through the door? What's the protocol. What's the form? I've always had a strange attitude to sado-masochism. I find the idea of it – in its milder forms – very attractive and have often fantasised about it. It's just the practice that I find risible.

But, like I've said before, I'll give anything a go, so I picked up the belt and gave her behind a minor thwack. It was a sort of 'snap out of it' slap, more as if I was trying to revive her bottom after it had fallen asleep drunk than punish it, but it was still harder than I'd meant to.

'Oh, God, I'm sorry,' I said.

'Oh, puh-lease,' she said, looking back at me with contempt, 'believe me, I wouldn't be so nice if I was doing it to you.'

I was a bit nonplussed here. I hit her again. I only managed the sort of whack Dick Emery used to give to people while saying 'Oh, you are awful!'

'Harder!' she said.

'Er, won't it hurt?' I said.

'That's the point!' she said, 'hit me.'

Then, thank God, the phone rang.

'Yes, I'm just finishing something off,' she said, 'I'll be down in a minute. Wait in the car.' Then she mouthed 'Hit me.' I shrugged and mouthed 'He'll hear.' She just pointed at her arse so I gave her another whack, slightly harder. She let out a yelp and told her husband, for it was he, that she'd knocked over a coffee. He then clearly asked if he should come up because she told him to stay exactly where he was.

Every bone in my body but one wanted to get out of there, but there was nowhere to go. I then realised. The next time she took off her clothes in front of him he was going to see that her arse had a belt mark on it. There it was. It wasn't substantial but it was, undeniably, the print of a belt. I think this is meant to be a turn-on. I felt more like getting the first-aid kit.

She put down the phone and I sat back on the floor, nearly ducking beneath the window to avoid crossing her husband's line of sight. She walked towards me, bent down and began pulling off my trousers.

'Your husband is downstairs,' I said with the strong implication that it was game over.

'Yes,' she said.

Then she took one big suck on my cock and climbed up on top of me.

I felt like a three-year-old boy being held down to have the back of his ears scrubbed. Her husband was not fifty yards away, for God's sake. Some men would find this sexy, but I found it hideous. I don't like to introduce even the idea of another man into my sex life. I'm not quite comfortable that there are other men on the planet while I'm having sex, let alone outside listening to Classic Gold.

'For God's sake,' I felt like saying, 'he'll guess what's going on.' Mind you, I was experiencing a contradictory enjoyment, caused by having her small tits thrust into my face as she bounced up and down on my cock. I had to put my hand over her mouth at one point because she was being so loud. I was vacillating between extreme embarrassment and lust, wanting to go and wanting to come. The problem was that, with the coke, I wasn't going to come for a long time. We must have been at if for about an hour before I finally managed it.

It was only when it was over and she proposed yet another line of coke that I realised the truth. There was no need to hide from her husband. He knew. This might have turned some men on, but it made me feel slightly used, which I suppose was the point.

She left and I called a cab. There was a ring at the door. I looked out of the window to check it was the cabbie – just in case I'd been wrong about her husband's knowledge of what was going on. It was the cabbie but I couldn't help noticing the only car in the carpark – a large BMW. It was a still summer night and, even from where I was, I could see the windows were steamed up.

'I've got a bad leg,' I said to the cabbie on the intercom, 'would you mind bringing the car right up to the doors.'

So he did and I shot into the cab with my jacket over my head like Paul McCartney in *A Hard Day's Night*. I glanced across as we pulled away. If I'd been in any doubt, I wasn't when the cabbie said: 'At it like badgers in there.'

'Yes,' I said.

'You move quick for a bloke with a bad leg.'

'It's bad as in disobedient,' I said, 'keeps running off on me.'

We didn't speak much after that.

I couldn't get rid of Laura from then on. The next morning I was sitting at my desk in my office, peering from behind a stack of papers like a GI from a fox hole, when she came in, closed the door and said in a too loud voice, 'I made him lick your spunk out of me.'

I was nearly sick in a rather complicated fit of nausea. A priori, as the philosophers would say, the idea of my spunk in another man's mouth is just a non-starter. I imagined her husband with a beard and this did not improve the picture. People say that sexuality is a continuum, that none of us is entirely gay or entirely straight. Do you know who these people are? Hopeful homosexuals who like to think they have a chance with straight men. I am not on a continuum, my sexuality is not floating up and down some line. My sexuality can be represented by a dot and does not gravitate towards enjoying jizzy beards.

It was as if the mad revels of the night before were intruding on the office. It was just all too complicated. There was a hangover in the mix, plus that slightly edgy feeling you get when you've been taking drugs the night before. It all mingled in. She was part of that dirty, poisoned itch I had that morning, I was still not clean after an hour in the shower. The smell of her perfume had an effect like being offered another glass of Pernod the night after you've polished off a couple of bottles of the stuff.

'Laura,' I said, 'I think you should go back to your work.'

'Yes, Sir,' she said.

It seemed I had become a dominator, or whatever they call the cable engineers and actuaries who indulge in that sort of thing, without wanting to. I objected to this on a number of levels. I don't mind a bit of slap and tickle, but I find S&M just a lame cliché. The people who are doms are invariably the sort who wouldn't say boo to a goose in real life. Second, I didn't like Laura – and this was the addictive bit. If I heard her being unpleasant to her staff, for instance making one of them a dunce's cap, I was in a position to actually punish her. So, ironically, I was being made to enjoy something I didn't enjoy. On top of this, me ignoring her just made her think I was playing the game.

It took me three more goes in order to make her go away. She said a lot about how she normally liked to be in charge but with me it was different.

'Go away, leave me alone, you skinny witch,' I said.

'Cor!' she said, taking it that I was trying to turn her on.

She kept engineering appointments with clients for us and I kept drinking and taking drugs and sleeping with her.

The final straw came the week after my first meeting with Francesca. Even though I hadn't got it together with her, and seemingly had no prospect of doing so, even though I had virtually forgotten her, I think I was rehearsing being monogamous in my head. It might not have been in the front of my brain but, in the deeper recesses of the grey matter, cogs were whirring.

Although I've found promiscuity very alluring momentarily, it's not what I'm after in the long term. The idea of a girl in whom I would be genuinely interested, rather than some batty, fuck-hungry Sloane, was enough to make me want to clear the decks.

We went out on another of those client meetings, this time at Henley Regatta. I didn't drink, which annoyed Laura, and I avoided her during the day, despite the fact I was supposed to be driving her home to the suburbs.

She became horribly, properly drunk and publicly sexually forward with me. I like drinking and I like sexually forward women, but with restraint. I don't like people who get drunk and I don't like being groped in front of a bunch of building industry jelly moulds I have to deal with on Monday morning. I finally managed to bundle her into the car.

She put her hand over my crotch again and I removed it.

'I don't want to do this any more,' I said.

'Why not?'

'I've got a girlfriend.'

'Well I've got a husband. Come on, take me back and fuck me.'

'I'd rather not.'

She seemed to regard this as some sort of negotiating position.

'You can fuck me in the arse,' she said. She, in an uncharacteristic fit of sensitivity to pain, didn't like anal sex and so I'd been insisting that was all I was interested in, in order to put her off.

'I'll just take you home.'

'You can fuck me in the arse while I put a vibrator up me.'

'Er . . .'

'It'll make your cock go numb!' she said like Eddie Pontin urging people to book early.

I said nothing. The really annoying thing was that I was getting an erection and I did quite want to try these things, just not with her. However, I'd begun to find her hugely irritating and the idea of taking it out on her did have its appeal. She continued her offers all the way to her house.

'I'll lick your arsehole out and stick my fingers up it.' I eyed the talons she had for nails. 'I'll fuck you with a strap on. I'll invite my friend Tina round and I'll hold her down while you fuck her.'

'I don't want to rape anyone, Laura.'

'It won't be rape,' she said. 'We'll get her pissed, shove an E down her and she'll be up for anything.'

'It's just that I prefer to limit my sexual behaviour to stuff that doesn't require a legal opinion before getting stuck in,' I said.

Finally, just before she started prostituting her household pets and asking me if I wanted to deflower her dishcloths, or offered to tie me to the washing line while her trained monkey batted tennis balls up my bum, I got her home.

'Come in,' she said, 'I've got a surprise for you.'

'The only thing you could do to surprise me is invite me in for an evening's Scrabble,' I said.

She was momentarily annoyed and then employed the final card in the deck. She got out of the car and flopped to the ground as if too drunk to walk. I had to carry her up her suburban driveway. She recovered, as I had suspected she might, at the top. While she fumbled for the keys, the door opened. It was her husband.

He was nothing like I'd imagined him. He was a weedy bookish sort with wire-rimmed glasses on and a collarless granddad shirt.

'Oh, hello,' he said, 'you must be Mark. I've heard a lot about you.' He had a look in his eye that I have tried to forget but, without doing a few grand on therapy, am unlikely to in a hurry. It was almost as if he was my fan, wanting my autograph.

We all stood looking at each other for what seemed enough time for suns to cool and die.

'This is the surprise,' said Laura.

'What, exactly?' I said.

I looked at him, he looked at me and I suddenly got an inkling of what might be on the agenda.

'I'm sorry,' I said, 'I'm going to have to flee.' And flee I did.

Weirdly, although Laura periodically pestered me, she had finally got the message and things calmed down at work, particularly as my invented girlfriend took over more and more of my life. I used some of my clout with her to make her nicer to her staff, though, and the 'provincial little bitch' got promoted. This was good in one way, as it lifted her from under the awful cloud of Laura's sarcasm, but bad in another because she was pretty incompetent.

I wondered what made Laura and her husband like that. I concluded it was boredom. Their lives, our lives, were going nowhere. They had their big house, they had their posh car, they'd said what they had to say to each other and they didn't want kids. What now? I know, I'll sort you with the food mixer while the bloke from accounts wazzes on my tits. It was boredom that had drawn us together, but us being together was only a temporary suspension of ambition for me. She had given up on love. I was still hopeful it might happen.

Terminating my friendship with Laura meant that I found myself more and more pacing the high street at lunchtime, buying books I wouldn't read, clothes that didn't suit me and looking in shops that contained nothing I wanted to buy. Then one day I was on my way to the dry cleaners with a pair of my latest clown trousers. As I searched the pockets for secreted fivers I came across a business card – Francesca X, Estates Manager. I couldn't for the life of me think who she was. What had I been doing dealing with someone from a property company? I had no idea.

I went out on the Friday night and, in one of those weird synchronicities that sometimes happen, I bumped into her in a pub neither of us had ever been to in our lives before. You just don't bump into people in London; you can go years living a street away from someone you know really well and never see them by chance. Suddenly I remembered her and the unfinished business of six months before. It felt like fate and, if something feels like fate, you can make it fate.

It could have been a rerun of our previous meeting – she wanted to go to a club, of course, but this time other people wanted to go with us. We went to one of those places in

High Street Kensington that are more old-fashioned disco-theque than club and Francesca and I chatted at the bar.

She'd moved out from the house she shared with her boyfriend into a tiny flat in east London. I asked her what had been wrong between them and she said nothing. Again, she seemed distant, like a woman of a previous generation thinking of those blue remembered hills.

'I love him, but he's just not what I'm looking for,' she said. 'He never has been.'

'What are you looking for?' I said.

She seemed almost not to hear the question.

'All I want at the moment,' she said, 'is casual sex. I want someone to have that with.'

'Funnily enough,' I said, 'that's exactly the sort of thing I'm very good at; you really couldn't have come to a better person. I'll get a cab, shall I?'

She just snorted her little snort. 'Not tonight,' she said, 'it's too soon.'

'A pity,' I said. The word 'soon' sounded interesting, carrying with it the promise of 'eventually'.

'I need to go.' She said goodbye to me and to Daphne, my flatmate, and she left.

In the cab on the way back I asked Daphne if she thought I had a chance with Francesca.

'None at all,' she said, 'she's told me she doesn't fancy you.'

This didn't dent me as much as you might suppose. I'd been out with quite a few girls by this stage and I knew women well enough to read the signs of attraction. She definitely fancied me. There was a lot of body contact when she spoke to me – pats on the arm, on the leg, she directed most of her attention to me, she seemed to find me very funny. I knew when a woman liked me and she liked me. She might have told Daphne she wasn't interested, but I took that as a sign that she might be really, really interested – so interested that she couldn't risk another huge emotional entanglement just after she'd finished an eight-year relationship. Silly me.

We got home at about two in the morning – early for us in those days. Daphne and I sat chatting, me more and more insistent that Francesca did like me, Daphne more and more insistent that she didn't.

Then the phone rang. Daphne answered.

'Oh, hello Francesca,' she said. Then her eyes widened.

'It's for you,' she said.

I picked up the phone. Part of me thought she was going to ask me if I could remember if she'd left her handbag in the club or something.

'It's me,' she said, 'I've been thinking, do you want to come over?'

'Yes, I'd love to,' I said, 'when?'

'Now.'

'OK.'

All Daphne saw was a blur in the air where I used to be.

Like many things that are keenly anticipated, the sex turned out to be a disaster.

I arrived at her flat at about 3.30 in the morning and she, wearing only pyjamas, took me straight to her bedroom. That was the first time I'd noticed the sort of clothes she wore. Thinking back, it was normally some sort of top with jeans and often a long coat. Her pyjamas, however, stick in my mind – red tartan ones.

There's no set way to begin this sort of thing, no protocol to follow that can spare you any embarrassment, or something you have to say to observe a social nicety. The only way to begin is to begin. As soon as we got into the bedroom, as much to avoid difficult silences as anything, I took her in my arms and kissed her.

I can't explain why I did what I did next. It was obvious what the girl wanted – I gave her the reverse. I told her I'd been waiting a long time to do this and I really went to town on stroking her and caressing her and making sure I took things gently and slowly. She didn't want to go down on me, turning away from my cock with an expression on her face like a poodle confronted with a worming pill, so I went down on her, for about four weeks. She seemed curiously rigid and uninterested. Finally, all metaphor aside, after about an hour she looked down and said 'Can you just stop that and fuck me.'

Naturally I obliged. After it was over I tried to hold her in my arms as we went to sleep in her single bed. At about eight I woke up to find her sleeping on the floor. She awoke, looked at me coldly and said 'I'll make breakfast.' It was clear that she considered our physical relationship over.

Suddenly I became me again. The problem was, I saw, that I had progressed by the textbook despite clear feedback that the textbook was, in this case, useless. I think it was the 'I'll make breakfast' that gave me the clue, however subconsciously. Modern, assertive, feminist women don't offer to make you breakfast. They might ask you if you want to go out for it, or if you'd like to help make it, but they don't invite you over, sleep with you and then fill you full of bacon and eggs like well-brought-up little future housewives.

'No you won't,' I said, 'not until I've fucked you again.'

She suddenly looked at me with more interest.

'I'm sorry,' I said, 'I made a big mistake with you last night, it's something I've never done before. For some reason I considered what you wanted. I'm afraid this one's for me.'

I took her by the sleeve, pulled her up on to the bed and

tried to be as sexually selfish as possible. My logic was simple. She'd clearly hated it when I tried to please her. This time I'd do my best to make sure I did nothing to her that most women would enjoy. We were a long way from the shy glance across the church aisle, the perfumed note in the book of Browning. Was everyone I was destined to meet some sort of submissive? Women gave it large, talking about 'having it all', taking on the men at their own game. They exuded confidence and efficiency in the boardroom and at the negotiating table, they talked about 'fulfilling relationships' and achievements. All the time, though, they really wanted to be put across your knee and have their arses tanned. I knew it wasn't true and that I was just going through a blip – no submissives for years and then five at once – but I still couldn't understand them. I wanted a companion and a soul mate, not a whipping post. Still, this sort of thing did turn me on and, I thought, until I could find that soul mate I may as well go along with it.

I liked Francesca very much, so trying to fulfil her sexual desires – even by pretending to do the exact opposite – was OK by me. I was indirectly pleasing her. This might have been on the same locus of S&M that Laura had been on, but it was an edgy, psychological, subtle thing rather than resembling a downmarket version of WWF wrestling.

The problem I've found with submissive girls is that you have to sort out what they say they don't want from what they actually don't want. I grew up in the political ferment of the 1980s and had always firmly believed 'No means No'. With Francesca though it was 'Sometimes No means No, and sometimes No means "Oh, yes please"'. I'm aware that's a politically very uncomfortable idea but, unfortunately, human sexuality doesn't always follow the party line. Still, it is best to err on the side of caution. Also, I had the memory of

Laura. I wanted a relationship of sane equals, not a rerun of the Velvet Underground's darker moments.

That evening we drank wine and watched TV and then went back to bed again. I thought she was fantastic and I stole glances away from *Inspector Morse* just to look at how pretty she was.

'I didn't expect this,' she said. 'If it had gone on like the first time, then I wouldn't have wanted to see you again.'

I felt my heart skip.

'So you do want to see me again?' I said.

Her face darkened.

'Yes, but like I said, not as boyfriend and girlfriend. I'm not looking for a relationship.'

'Suits me,' I said, lying.

I left the next morning, painfully early because I had to get up, get back to Fulham and go to work.

'When shall we see each other again?' I said.

'Whenever,' she said, 'I've got your number. Maybe I'll call you.'

'OK,' I said.

I spent the entire day at work with a knot in my stomach. I couldn't believe she'd been so lukewarm. At five my phone rang. It was her. She asked me how I was. I was fine. Then she asked if I wanted to come over, that night. It was my boxing class but, given the choice between being repeatedly hit in the face by some jobless teenager and acting out my wildest sexual fantasies with a beautiful, half-crazy rock-chick, it wasn't a tough decision. In fact, I wasn't even acting out my sexual fantasies. I was having to come up with a few new ones.

I didn't know it at the time, but this was to be the pattern of our future relationship. We very rarely made long-term plans to see each other. If I asked her what she was doing at the weekend she would always say that she didn't know and maybe she would call me, maybe she wouldn't. Then would come the last-minute call.

We did all the things you're meant to do – we went on holiday together, walks in the country, we held hands watching sunsets and we made love by the fire. And, like the fire, it was an illusion. This wasn't a real log blaze of a romance, just a plastic imitation thing with a fan moving over a bulb doing a bad impression of genuine flames.

For weeks we'd just not mention the status of our relationship and I'd be able to kid myself that she'd changed her mind, that there was a future for us. Then, whenever the subject came up, she'd blow that fantasy to pieces.

Francesca was always absolutely firm with me: I remember taking her photo on the Cobb at Lyme Regis. It was one of those days you dream about, windy but not cold with a high, dramatic sea and the waves breaking about us. She even, strangely, had a long, baggy woollen coat with a hood on it, like something straight out of *The French Lieutenant's Woman*. For those of you who haven't seen the film or read the book, let me tell you: that wasn't a good omen.

'Now, my wild beauty,' I said as I snapped, 'I shall capture you for eternity.'

'I'm not going to be with you for eternity,' she said.

'Then why am I doing this?' I said.

'What?'

'Preserving this memory. All it's ever going to be is a token of loss.'

'Because you'll be able to show it to your grandkids and say "I had a mad weekend by the sea with her at the end of the last century."'

'Great,' I said.

I did love her, or at least I was on the borders of it, but I tried to hold back because there was nothing coming the other way. It didn't work. I was mad for her. When I say nothing was coming back, she acted as if she returned the feeling, she snuggled up to me at night, she kissed me when she woke up in the morning, she took me into the country to meet her family, she bought me books and records and said she missed me whenever we were apart.

I remember when a Greater London Radio newsreader said someone had 'misled the jury'. The reader pronounced it 'mysled the jury'. For weeks after, we asked each other 'Are you mysling me? Have I been mysled?' These in jokes made me feel we were sharing something. But I was mysling myself. Francesca let me know exactly where I stood, which was nowhere, even though what she did entirely contradicted what she said. She acted like we were going out, she just told me that we weren't. In the year that I was going out with her – or not going out with her, according to her – I was with her something like 350 days out of 365 – always responding to last-minute invitations, but always invited. She still got angry, though, if I referred to her as my girlfriend.

It wasn't her fault, though, that I convinced myself. Francesca had some inner pain. If I could identify it, maybe I could take it away and we could be happy together.

I was even faithful to her, like an idiot, the first time I ever did that deliberately. I'd been faithful to girls before, I think, but only because the opportunity to be unfaithful hadn't presented itself while I was with them. I had never seen the point of fidelity before, had no understanding of what it was for. Suddenly I grasped what I'd been missing. If you're with the right person, then the idea of being unfaithful would never cross your mind. One evening my flatmate's friend, a sexy Norwegian girl, had visited. We'd all gone for a meal and I'd stayed up chatting to the girl after my flatmate had gone to bed. She'd asked me if she could sleep in my bed, on the other side and I'd said yes. Despite the fact she took off all her clothes once she was under the covers, and despite the fact she was really attractive, I told her I had a girlfriend. I was Francesca's. Except I wasn't.

The relationship went through an arc. At its start we were always going out, always at clubs or parties. As we got to know each other better we actually started staying in – something I had never done in my adult life. The boxing classes and the exercise classes stopped for me and were replaced by evenings of wine and pistachios. Then, about two months before we finally split, we started going out more again.

Francesca was struck by a mania for clubbing, whereas before she'd just been very keen. I could never bear dance music, but I kicked along anyway. The clearest memory I have of it is being in some hideous cavern in King's Cross from ten until six, watching the genetic inheritors of the Anglo-Saxon peasantry, people designed to trudge behind a plough through the sucking earth, as they plodded the dance floor like they were still following the ox. If God had meant us to dance, he wouldn't have made us English. We'd be Brazilian and I, for one, would be proud of it. The English frame is designed to pogo, mosh and stand unflinching before French cavalry charges – you only have to look at the thighs to see that. There's no point fighting it, it's in our DNA. I'd been bored from about twelve and had been trying to suggest the possibility of leaving.

'You go,' she said, 'I'll be OK here.'

I didn't want to go without her, did I? Where would she end up and with whom? Suddenly I was threatened with being in the position Scott had been in nearly two years before, alone at home and wondering where she was, what she was doing and coming to no good conclusions. I felt utterly desperate, at the end of my endurance for staying up listening to bleep bleep bollocks and for being treated like that.

At six she came back from the dance floor to where I was alone and palely loitering by the bouncy castle. I didn't want to be fresh for work, but I would rather have been in bed with my non-girlfriend or, in fact, just in bed.

'It's OK,' she said, 'I've scored some more E. We can go to Sunday Sunday and chill out.'

The idea of chilling out at a nightclub appalled me. By this stage I hated clubbers. I despised their blissed-out conversations, their idiot grins, their 'Nice one!' expressions – and that was while I was on Ecstasy myself. Had I not taken a drug designed to induce feelings of goodwill in even the most stony breast, I fear I might have killed someone.

She was hanging around at the time with a bunch of people from her work who seemed willing to go out on Friday night and not come in until Monday morning. Never once in this time did the conversation rise above work gossip or just drugged-up expressions of good will to each other. I was sentenced to spending endless hours with people I found incredibly dull. A Saturday's fishing followed by Sunday in Homebase started to seem attractive by comparison.

'Please,' I said, 'come home.'

She shrugged. 'You don't own me,' she said.

I knew then it was over, although it limped on for another few weeks.

The end came, appropriately enough, following a Valentine's Day meal, delayed until the weekend. It was a Friday night and we went out to a bar over the road. We'd planned to eat and then to spend the rest of the evening in bed. Naturally, we decided this experience would be a lot more enjoyable with some inhibition-lowering, fantasy-inspiring, stamina-enhancing drugs. So we went into town to get some and 'bumped into' her work crew.

Twenty hours later we were in one of their houses, still talking shit. In previous generations people took drugs and then looked for the secrets of the universe. This lot seemed satisfied with saying 'innit' repeatedly, blowing raspberries and falling about laughing – for the equivalent of two and a half working days. Then Francesca and I dropped some acid. It was only mild stuff, but it focused my mind. I didn't want to be there. I whined and mewled and begged and insisted and finally she came home. It felt like my last throw of the dice and it was.

We went to bed. She was crying and, whenever I closed my eyes, I saw her face fragmented like a Picasso. How did I get there, I wondered. Wasn't I the kid who had wanted the special girl, the one for him, the life-defining romance? How had I ended up lying immersed in drugs and sex and sadness, watching her face and my life fall apart? Easy, I was so desperate for the big relationship that I was willing to take anything that even looked like it and convince myself I had the real thing. Why couldn't I have felt how I felt for Francesca about Vanessa? Vanessa was brighter, more fun, better looking. There was no why. I just didn't. God doesn't like to make things that easy on us.

'I don't want to be with you any more,' she said.

'I know,' I said.

I told her there had always been a problem between us and I wanted to know what it was. She said some stuff about me being a lot stronger when we first met – my sedentary life, with her as its focus, had submerged my boxer's body beneath a carapace of fat – she said the sex had been more exciting. This was true. I'd retreated from our coke-fuelled Bacchanalias – or cut them down to one a week – and had been treating sex as something that happens between two people who care for each other. Silly me, again.

Then, she put the final nail in the coffin. Actually, what she said convinced me that I am psychologically reasonably stable. A less solid man would never have recovered, I think. Woody Allen might have got a decade's worth of films out of it. I was about to discover her inner pain.

'I went out with this bloke Nat years ago for about three weeks,' she said, 'and I've never forgotten him. That's what came between me and Scott. All the time I was with him I knew that I'd rather have been with Nat, and it's the same with you.'

'What was it about him?' I said.

'He's really cool,' she said, an expression I've always hated, 'he's a DJ and everything.'

'Isn't that a bit shallow?' I said.

'It's more than that,' she said. She looked at the window, with that far-away air again.

'What?' I said, 'you can tell me.'

She drew in breath. 'He's got a really enormous dick,' she said.

'Right,' I said. For a second I thought she was joking and then I realised she wasn't.

This puzzled me. Mine's no whopper, but it's not a cocktail sausage either. You know, I've never had any complaints. Up until then.

'What do you mean by enormous?' I said.

'I think it's twelve inches hard,' she said.

'Isn't that a bit painful?' I said. She had to be winding me up didn't she?

She just closed her eyes and gave a low moan, something like 'uhhhhh', clearly remembering the last time Nat had impaled her.

'Is that really the reason?' I said.

'Absolutely,' she said. She'd actually filled up with tears, maybe because thinking about Nat's mammoth schlong had made her eyes water. 'Ask any woman.'

This is something I've noticed in women – they often assume their tastes are universal. The alternative explanation – that all women are craving major meat – is not one I prefer to dwell on. She said she never seemed to meet anyone she genuinely liked who had the necessary equipment. I hadn't had a chance, our relationship had been conducted in the shadow of a twelve-inch penis.

All the frustrations I'd had seemed to come spilling out. She had said from the first that she couldn't be with me forever, she'd laid her cards on the table, how could I be angry? Easily. I was in love with her. That meant I was incapable of finishing it, no matter what she did. If she'd had any respect for me at all she would never have gone out with me for so long. By telling me she would never love me, she was just salving her own conscience, convincing herself that she'd been honest. This sort of honesty means nothing; in fact it's just cowardice. She was giving herself an excuse to behave as badly as she liked without feeling any guilt. It would have been better to have pretended that our relationship was leading somewhere and then to have finished it. At least I'd have salvaged some self-respect.

We made love for the last time, which she seemed to enjoy, despite the fact I was fucking her with what she considered a half-sized penis. We both cried. The next morning she left for work and I kissed her goodbye.

'I'll never see you again,' I said.

'Of course you will; we'll be good friends. I do really, really, like you.'

'That makes me feel worse.'

'I'm sorry, but at least now you know.'

'Can I just say,' I said, 'that in future, honesty is not the best policy. Lying through your teeth and allowing the other person some fleeting chance of psychological peace in the future might be the best idea.'

She just shrugged.

So far, I've been right, I haven't seen her again.

Within a month she was going out with a friend of a friend, Phil, a clubber, who said 'Nice one' a lot and winked when he said Hello. She always liked that sort of bloke and I heard that they had a rare click. It was love, the real two-people-who-think-as-one bit. Then in a blink they were married and she was pregnant. She moved to the country, and, the last I heard of her, she was doing a mean marrow chutney and raising her kids in a cottage. I didn't know very much about the man she married. He was affable, quite laddy, and that's almost all I could say about him. There is only one more piece of information I have – though I've no idea if it's true. It was told to me by someone who used to go to the gym with him, so it can hardly go down as reliable. However, for what it's worth, it's this: he does have a very big dick.

22 AT GRASS

If you are male, middle-class and not mental, you will eventually be promoted to a position of authority in the workplace. You'll also get rather uppity about it and start to believe it was the result of something you did, rather than being simply what happens to people of your sex and education.

So it was that, almost by default, I found myself head of a division of business researchers in central London. I was there for two years and was able to say confidently by the end of it that we provided information – to whom and about what escaped me. My division, by the way, became one of the most successful in the company. Like a typical man, I tried to take the credit, but a dog could have done it, really.

The problem was that they hadn't then hit on the idea of raiding the National Canine Defence League for managers and employees, so they employed failures like myself who were not as clever as dogs, nor as loyal.

I had a vile time when I arrived. Francesca had gone, Vanessa was no longer in my life and I was trembling from the upset. I don't think I've ever been as unhappy as I was when Francesca left. I felt like every sort of fool, that I'd wasted my time, been taken for a ride. I felt angry and used, but most of all I just missed her. I thought of nothing else but what she was doing and who she was with. I'd be at my desk in person, but in my mind I was miles away. Every time the phone rang I thought it would be her, telling me she'd made an enormous mistake and begging me to come back. It never happened.

It didn't help that I was managing a group of people who all thought they should have had my job. It was a difficult period, with the attitude of most of the staff on a scale from bored to obstructive. I couldn't complain. I'd been pretty much like that myself for most of my working life. Still, it got me down.

Allied to this, I was the manager and a good ten years older than some of the girls. I felt a definite change in attitudes towards me. When I'd last worked in a big company, women would flirt with me and ask me out. I'd been bought flowers, asked for drinks, had girls virtually scrapping in the lifts. Now I entered the dead zone. It was obvious, I was an old man. I was thirty-two and suddenly scared.

I was in fighting trim again, motivated to shift the pounds by the need for a girl. I knew exactly what I wanted – someone exactly like Francesca who loved me. I was Thai boxing, as I had been on and off for years and, annoyed by my rebellious staff, had been hitting the heavy bag nightly. I had no girl to distract me so I was in good shape, or so I thought. One of the sales guys – a contemptuous young man with Verve longish hair and a similar style – was talking about a class he had just started.

'I train with a guy called Tom Walsh,' he said.

'Oh, up at Queen's Park?'

'Yeah,' he said, 'why, do you play Badminton at the sports centre or something?'

'I used to train with him. I train with Floyd Brown now. You know, WKKC freestyle heavyweight world champion?'

'*You* are a Thai boxer,' he said, '*you?*'

I smiled, though I was dying. In my head I was still one of the boys. To him, though, I was nothing more than a dusty cardigan with leather arm patches. I wouldn't grow up, but the world had just grown me up. Someone would have to pay.

'I'll drop in at Tom's class next week,' I said, 'maybe you'd like to spar.'

'I'm not allowed to spar yet,' he said.

'Oh well,' I said, 'when you are, let me know. It'll be my pleasure.'

He looked at me as if I was a total weirdo, which in some ways I am. I was a middle manager who had just offered out a trainee salesman. I went into the loos, looked in the mirror and said 'Aaaaaaaaah!' Was that what my life had come to? I'd lost. He thought I was old and unfit looking.

How do you look at yourself in a mirror? In the most intimate way possible. You look at the eyes. They are the least changing part of the face, and it becomes difficult to see that they have taken on the appearance of currants in a ball of dough. I don't think you can really see yourself clearly. If you don't like how you look, you can always adjust the angle you're standing, ruffle up the hair, suck in the cheeks and pull in the belly. You've spent years perfecting the art of kidding yourself and you're good at it. You've got manorexia – when you look in the mirror and, no matter what your body shape, think you look OK. When you look at someone you know less well, you don't look at the eyes. You're drawn to the slightly cod-like gleam of the skin, an untrimmed mole, the bulldog cheeks. To be able to look at yourself properly you need a photo. In those I was beginning to resemble a middle-aged lady – puffy jowls and hair like a jutting toenail.

The young man's incredulity was a useful reminder that I was single and couldn't afford to be out of shape. I cut the beer and the pies, upped the training. The cabbage soup diet struck and I lost pounds in weeks and started to look a lot sharper, though I occasionally took a funny turn when working the bag.

'You've fainted,' said Callum, standing over me.

'Excellent,' I said. 'Resist that, fat.'

It was a price worth paying.

There's a myth that men aren't interested in their bodies. They're obsessed with them, it's just that they have a funny idea of what it takes to get into shape. Thinking about doing some fitness, for instance, is often seen as the same as doing some fitness. Flexing the muscles in front of the mirror is seen as the same as having developed some muscles.

Definitely starting some training tomorrow is OK, excusing the bag of cod and chips today. A run round the park (300 calories) allows six pints (1,500 calories) and a large Doner later (who knows how many calories, is there a number that big?). Three weeks of abstinence and incredibly intense training followed inevitably by a bad injury, justifies the comfort food you consume while recovering from your ricked neck.

Still, I flung myself in with the eagerness of Joan Collins at the fountain of youth.

The salesman had seen me as a middle manager, a desk jockey, a paper-tray pilot. That wasn't me. I was a literary wild man. I just happened to be working as a middle manager, behind a desk, with a paper tray at that moment.

Out on the town I was my old self. At work I was a fuddy duddy in a crap suit. The latter was my fault. I'd been inspired, if that's the right word, by a conversation with my old friend Terry Bate, who I still saw.

'I used to splash out on suits, but now I only go for cheap ones,' said the formerly trendier than thou Bate.

'Oh, me too,' I said. 'I'm man at Next nowadays.'

'Oh,' said Bate, 'not that cheap then.'

'There is no cheaper than Next,' I said.

He winked and pulled at his sleeve. It appeared to be made out of a plastic bag.

'C&A,' he said, 'seventy quid, one hundred per cent acrylic. This'll still be around when the sun explodes, it's indestructible.'

I'd reached that age too. Suddenly 'indestructible' seemed a better advertisement for a suit than 'well cut' or just 'classy'.

Two weeks into the new job and I decided to intellectually cleanse my department, importing new and more intelligent blood. I employed one very bright, working-class second-generation Greek guy and thought 'Add him to your spritzer circle' when I introduced him to my team. Someone else joined the department too.

She was a sexy blonde girl of around twenty-five, something of a Bridget Jones lookalike. She had that air to her too, a feeling that she was smiling through the interview questions, torn between being over-correct and over-frank.

'Many of your products seem like rehashes of former stuff. Is that policy or is it an accident?' she said.

'Well, I wouldn't say "rehashes",' I said.

'Oh neither would I,' she said, 'though, er, I did. What I meant to say was that you draw very strongly on your experience in the field. Very impressive brochures. Do you have a spellcheck facility here? Oh dear.'

She was much better looking than Renee Zellweger, I thought, and I found her very attractive. It may sound strange, but this prejudiced me against her. I know what I am like and, as a manager, I don't want goodlooking women working for me. That way madness and unemployment lie.

Still, she interviewed very well, and I could see she was bright enough to see straight through me.

'Are you a micro-manager?' she said.

'Well, at first I'll need to see that everything's going OK, but when . . .' I saw her smiling a knowing smile and nodding.

'Dosser,' I could see her think. 'He won't tell me what to do, and I'll have his job in ten minutes.' That suited me fine. To have my job she was going to have to work hard, which was more than I thought most other people in my department were doing.

The other thing that I found fascinating about her was that she spoke exactly like the Queen. You don't normally hear accents like that outside 1950s British films of stiff-upper-lippery. Living in Fulham, though, I had been around enough fakes to recognise it for the real thing.

She had all the qualifications and experience, she was much brighter than anyone else we had on staff, and she took the piss out of me during the interview. She'd made a good impression. On the downside she was too goodlooking and she was yet another middle-class female. I decided not to offer her the job. To bugger up the posh girl clique I ideally wanted a former French Foreign Legionnaire with an eye missing and a hobby that involved a lot of grease and swearing.

I interviewed the rest of the people, though, and had a meeting with the managing director about the appointment. She pointed out that Claire, the posh girl, was the best candidate.

'What are the reasons for not employing her?' asked the MD.

'I fear I may try to sleep with her, she will reject me, sue, I will be sacked and the only good thing to come out of it will be that it will cost the firm a lot of money,' didn't seem like a good answer. So I ummed and ahhed, looked at the

CV of a candidate who had called me 'geezer' during the interview and said I didn't know.

'We can't afford to turn down people like that on a "don't know",' said the MD.

'On your head be it,' I thought. I rang Claire to tell her she'd got the job.

'How much is the salary?' she said. 'I'm afraid I've been for so many of these things I can't remember. You know, yours is special and I'm very grateful, but how much will I be on again at Business Practices?'

'Business Solutions.'

'Quite,' she said, as if I was being difficult.

I told her how much we'd be paying her.

'Oh, that won't do at all,' she said, 'add three thousand pounds.'

'OK,' I said.

She started work, beavering away at the only desk in the building that had more crap on it than mine. She reminded me of a hamster, scrabbling wildly behind a wall of papers and files. I left her alone in work and life. I had a very 'hands off' management style, that is I didn't do anything much other than the interesting business development side of the job. It was interesting because I got large bonuses for success. Finally a workplace was offering me something I could understand.

I did look over at Claire occasionally and feel something that was more than just sexual attraction. I felt very affection-ate towards her, even when she nearly stabbed me when I borrowed her paper without asking one day. I realised I liked her, but she was going out with someone and I knew that, in Francesca's words, porking the payroll was a bad idea.

In the first year at work, I was as bored as I have ever

been. There were girls, though. My friend and lodger, Charlie, had been joined by Daphne, a Scots girl we got from advertising in *Loot*. She had a sexy friend Joan, who I'd sleep with occasionally, often after nights out or parties, and there was Cornish Rita, a multilingual barmaidy blonde with a figure like a seventies dolly bird – from men like me that's a compliment. They were both great fun, but I was still missing Francesca and kept comparing them with her. They couldn't compete because they were up against a dream. In the meantime, I was living a nightmare, increasingly desperate, increasingly picky.

I met up with Ella for a drink. She'd lost a bit of weight, glammed up her clothes and looked truly stunning in fake furs and high boots. It was the way I'd wanted her to dress when she was with me – like one of Prince's protégées, not some PR hack's bird. She couldn't dress like that for me, though, only against me, when she thought it might hurt me to see her looking so good. I don't blame her, she was owed a bit of payback. We had a miserable evening where she aired all her resentments at what had gone on between us. At the end I asked if she wanted to meet up again.

'Not any time soon, Mark,' she said, 'my life just doesn't have room for this sort of thing right now. You're a failure and I find it depressing associating with failures.' I have to point out, Ella has read this book and denies ever saying this. I think she did. If she did, she says, it was in response to my goading and spending the entire evening talking about what an idiot she had for a boyfriend. This is very likely but it's interesting that, years after we last went out with each other, we're still having a row about who said what.

'I am not a failure,' I said, 'I am a deferred success.'

'How long are you going to defer it?'

'I'll get into heaven, you see,' I said. It was only a joke but, weirdly, I thought it taught me something about the appeal of religion.

Two weeks later I was on the way home from the pub. Charlie stopped at an all night shop to get a pint of milk and, while he did, I waited outside. I'm one of those people who always carries around loads of rubbish in his pockets. My natural messiness conspires with an unwillingness to litter and I always have wodges of bills, receipts, chocolate bar wrappers, that sort of thing, on me. I took the opportunity to empty some of it out into a nearby bin. The queue was a long one, and when I'd finished emptying Charlie was still in the shop, so I mooched about a bit. It was then I remembered I had a week's travel card and had probably thrown it away along with the detritus from my pockets. Accordingly, I began to search for it. The papers had fallen down the side and I had to move a Chinese carton that must have ended up in the bin by chance, no one knowingly disposing of those properly inside the M25.

It was as I lifted the Chow Mein out that Ella's very good friend Rhona walked past. She just shook her head at me and quickly crossed to the other side of the street.

'I'm, I'm . . . aww God, I'm a tramp,' I said to the air, 'a bloody emotional tramp, that's what I am, scavenging through the bin for leftovers from the rich man's table.'

I had to admit, my prospects did not look good.

23   LOVE HAS A THOUSAND NAMES

When it comes to love, people fall into several broad types. Men are simple creatures and there are essentially only four – wankers, bastards, mummy's boys and idiots. Of course, these are more like tendencies within men than absolute categories – I myself, for instance, am largely a wanker, with a large portion of idiot, a little bit of bastard and, I'd like to think, only a pinch of mummy's boy.

The Wanker is basically someone who is deluded about the kind of person he is. He sees himself as cool, perhaps, or maybe prides himself on his arrogance because of his remarkable material success, mistaking a couple of lucky breaks for talent. He's a nightmare to go out with because you never know whether you're having a relationship with him or his idea of him. You may, if you are truly unlucky, be forced to listen to his 'big idea'. Oh, and he could walk that *Dragon's Den*, it's just that he never will.

The Bastard is self-explanatory. TV and film often accord some sort of glamour to this character. The reality is that he makes a pass at your sister, borrows money he does not return, stands you up and then whines about it when you dump him. He loves himself and has in some way formed the impression this is a good thing. It is not.

The Mummy's Boy will never find anything you do quite good enough. He has very, very high standards until it comes to his own behaviour where wheedling, grizzling and foot stamping to get what he wants are all seen as fair play. He has no idea that he could ever do anything you want to do. Prepare yourself for a life of *Die Hard* and *Seven Swords* on DVD, he's never going to act like a real man and agree to watch *Pride and Prejudice* with you. He uses his own sensitive nature as a weapon. He will often discuss his problems, but will always have 'had a really hard day' when it comes to yours. He is always comparing you to the perfect female. This may not necessarily be the mother, it could be a former girlfriend. Eventually you will find that you do have something in common with his previous girlfriend, in that you will dump him.

The Idiot says things like 'How was I to know I wasn't meant to invite my mates to our Valentine's dinner? You didn't say.' He might love you, but he has no real idea of what that means. He will crash your car, tell your mother you're a goer in the sack, reply honestly when you ask him how you look and may, if you are truly unlucky, regard himself as that most irritating species of male alive – the practical joker. This involves hiding in your wardrobe and leaping out on you as you attempt to prepare for an interview. You will smash him in the face and he will genuinely not know why.

There are categories of women in love too, at least as seen through the eyes of men. The traditional split is between Madonna and whore, but I think we have moved on a little since such value-laden titles were appropriate. Not far, though.

The biggest division today is between soul mate and sexual obsession. Which one should you go for? Do you go for the soul mate and then face a life knowing you're having 6 out of 10 sex, or the obsession and face a life of 10 out 10 sex and 5 out of 10 conversation?

You will realise the sexual obsession is a sexual obsession

the second you see her. It may take longer for you to recognise your soul mate. This will normally happen just after she introduces you to her new boyfriend, who you will think doesn't understand her like you do. She doesn't care because she'll take someone who's nice to her over someone who understands her any day.

The best thing to do is to hold out for a soul mate who is also your sexual obsession. Anyone who does this, though, should be a Buddhist, because it will take about five lifetimes for her to appear. Pursue a hobby while you wait. Knitting – you can do that anywhere.

I have spoken to many men about how they see their girlfriends and reflected on my own experience. In addition to the two categories above, there are the following.

The Runabout. I have, I hope, been out with no runabouts, but I have seen the phenomenon many times. This is the girlfriend you go out with to keep you company, go to bed with you, even meet your family while you look to trade up to a better model. Why won't he commit? Because he's not entirely given up hope of Angelina Jolie yet, although he will when you finish with him and come shaking back in fear and tears at the big wide world.

The Girl. This is the girlfriend that a boy of fifteen or sixteen chooses. The qualifications for going out with him are that she is female and she is there.

The Kook. Every man dreams of going out with a kook, that only he will understand her kookiness and that the only conventional thing about her is her love for him. Think an idiosyncratic dress sense, strange ways of speaking, life, fun, laughter, plus dreadful irritation when she just won't shut up after about six weeks of going out with her.

The Painted Wall. You think you've finished your relationship with this girl but, like a painted wall, when you look at it closely you see a bit you could have done better and go back to it, causing a bigger mess than if you'd just left it alone in the first place.

Wonder Woman. This is the girl who all your friends wonder 'What is he doing with her?' She is perfectly nice, but totally unlike you. You force yourself through six weeks of Salsa or Yoga and finally admit that you have nothing in common at just about the time your back gives out. I have spent up to three months not laughing while a girlfriend talked about 'very powerful vibration therapies', only to be undone by a smirk when invited to come Rolfing. Normally Wonder Woman appears at times of great peril – or at least stress – in your life, when you are uncommonly desperate and willing to give anything a go.

Lady Penelope. The girlfriend who is so far out of your class that you will have to restrict most of what you say to statements such as 'Yes, m'lady'. You cannot understand what she sees in you and are petrified that the same thought will occur to her. You know what happens when you are in love with a beautiful woman? Like the song says, you watch your friends. And everybody else.

Mum's Favourite. This girl is nice, down to earth, pretty and warm. Why don't you want to settle down with her? Why do you prefer

T.R.O.U.B.L.E. Unreliable, flirts with others, never gives any real hint that she likes you until she drags you back to bed. Mother meets her and says, in a tight-lipped way, that she 'knows her sort'. She lives life flat out and you keep up with her like a piece of chewing gum stuck to her wheels. If the relationship continues she will kill you, bankrupt you or break your heart. Ten years after she has chewed you up and spat you into the gutter, you will discover she has married a chiropodist and is living in Catford.

The Friend. You are friends for one reason. One of you doesn't really fancy the other one. Here's a clue. If it isn't you then it must be her.

The Mountie. Whatever you do, wherever you go, she's on your trail. You've tangled with her once and got away, but, sooner or later, she's determined that she's going to get her man.

The Arab Carpet. Arab carpets are all made with one imperfection, which is fine unless you see it, in which case it does rather nag on the eye. You know you have an Arab Carpet in that heart-sink moment when, the moon big in the heavens, the scent of the elder trees filling your soul, your mind full of her conversation, your heart pumping to the thrill of her beauty, she turns to you and says: 'Would ickle bickle Marky like to come in for a bit of coffee-woffee?'

Imperfections can, depending on your taste, include smoking, heavy perfumes, sloppy kissing, poor pant hygiene – particularly lazy bottom wiping – and irritating physical habits such as mouth breathing and ear fiddling.

The Fairy Godmother. Like the 11 o'clock Goddess, the girl who only looks good in beer goggles, but the other way round. She'll grant your wish at midnight, but the next morning all her promise turns to pumpkins and white mice. She wakes next to you and looks at you with an expression like someone seeing what Laurence Llewelyn-Bowen has done to their lounge on *Changing Rooms*. Then she is gone, never to be seen again.

The Good Time Girl. She wants one thing. You have that thing. It's altogether a beautiful thing. Often the best sort of one-night stand. You don't call, though you might like to, because she doesn't want you to. It's not that sort of thing.

The Sort of Good Time Girl. Presents herself as a good time girl but gets angry when you don't call. Why didn't you call? Not because you thought she was sexually promiscuous. You can't say. Maybe it was a little bit of neediness on her part, maybe you just didn't fancy her that much or maybe your girlfriend wouldn't like it if you did.

The Bad Time Girl. Believes that, because she has gone to bed with you once, you must now solve all her problems.

The Nutter. Self-explanatory, really. Appears normal for the first two months, then comes in one night covered in blood, baying, dressed in a wolf skin and blaming you for everything because something went wrong at work.

Some people seem more drawn to one category than to others. I have been particularly plagued with nutters. Fruitbat was one of them.

She got her name when she went out with a friend of mine because he said she was mad. He was right, in a way. There are ways of being mad, not all of them bad. There is the mad like the Northern Irish Camden boys were mad, which just involves drinking very heavily and getting into scrapes. There's mad like my friend Bomber Harris was mad, i.e., he occasionally got sectioned for the public weal, and then there's Fruitbat mad.

This is a peculiar sort of feminine nuttiness where the girl just seems to be playing by a different set of rules from the rest of the planet. It involves seeming normal for ninety per cent of the time and then taking offence at something you say. She won't tell you what it is, you have to guess. She is in a blue fit for a day and then suddenly absolutely fine. It's not PMT, it happens too regularly for that. It's more a strange instability where the person suddenly feels you're not paying them enough attention, or that you're smothering her. Everything is too much or too little and the nameless discontent that bubbles inside her suddenly settles on you.

Fruitbat was a very goodlooking, slim girl with pale skin and blonde hair. To me she seemed only a bit nutty at first. I met her at a friend's wedding. There are little signs that should put you off people. It wasn't so much a look in her eye or her conversation. It was more that several people, some of them relative strangers, stood behind her while I was chatting to her, shaking their heads, making 'back off' signs or drawing their fingers across their throats. I ignored them and by the end of the evening we were kissing. I didn't see what the problem was. We enjoyed a few dates and got on well. I had taken to dressing bizarrely out of work – big woollen coats and odd trousers – to stave off the tedium of my day to day existence. As I normally do with fashion, I got it wrong, resembling a *Playschool* presenter, or even Dave Stewart of the Eurythmics, more than I did anyone cool.

Fruitbat had a mildly successful pop star brother, a sort of Jamiroquai in even-more-miniature, who looked down his nose at me the second I sat down to allow him to do so. Still, I was in a very brief period of relatively regular drug use at the time so, coked up, I was in an affable mood. I chatted away to him one night at her flat, largely about performing in public.

I'd been doing stand-up for a couple of years until I decided I'd rather stay in with Francesca than go out making a bunch of students laugh when I'd actually like to kill them. Never mind, I had some stories and made a bit of money at it. He clearly thought I had no right comparing my experience to his. Still, he was polite as he Hoovered up my lines. He was one of those people who are so concerned about dressing and acting cool that they come full circle and reveal themselves as painfully unsophisticated. Anyone who drops the name 'Richard', and expects you to know he's talking about Richard Ashcroft of the Verve, falls hard into this camp. It's a humourless approach to life and I hate it – very likely because I couldn't be cool if I tried.

However, I have something of a death wish when I detect a contemptuous attitude in people. It may be that I have a highly refined sense of humour, or it may be that I'm just a berk, but I just have to do things to confirm and entrench their view. I do find it very funny.

'Give us that guitar,' I said, rubbing my hands. 'Do you know this one? "Streets of London"? It's a traditional air and rather appropriate to our situation, here, in Londinium town, as I live and breathe. Done in the style of Keith.'

'Richards?' he said.

'Harris and Orville,' I said, 'we're very close.'

He didn't know if I was taking the piss or not. Dave, if you're reading this, you'll just have to work it out for yourself.

Fruitbat and I went out for about three weeks, at the end of which I held a party at my house. My flatmate Daphne's friend Joan was there. I'd had a couple of flings with her, but was now trying to be committed to Fruitbat. Dave clearly regarded me as someone who buys friends with cocaine because when he turned up at the party one of his friends marched straight up to me and said,

'Dave says you've always got coke, can I have some?'

'Fuck off,' I said, as you do. I wasn't in a good mood

because, as soon as Fruitbat had come through the door, she had started chatting up a goodlooking long-haired bloke I'd never seen before. She didn't even say 'Hello' when I let her in, just giving me the cold shoulder and brushing past into the front room. It was my party. If she'd decided she didn't want to be with me she shouldn't have come. That's what I mean by mad. There had been no indication she was going to act like that on the phone that afternoon. I was miffed, but Joan was on the premises and I fancied her more so my options were still open.

'What did you say to me?' said Dave's friend.

'I said go fuck yourself,' I said, miming it in case he'd missed it. 'Sorry, gosh, I didn't mean to say that. That was a bit American. I meant go *and* fuck yourself. It's like when people say "meet with" instead of just "meet", it's irritating, isn't it?'

Musos don't generally like being spoken to in this tone and he was no exception. He flounced off downstairs to the basement like the great big girl's blouse he was and, as soon as he thought I was out of earshot, he and Dave began smashing my furniture up. We had a full disco on board, so I guess they thought they were safe because I wouldn't hear. As it was, someone came up and told me. I'm a tolerant man, but I have my limits and this was a liberty. Sorry, I was on the instant wanker powder and that was how I was talking in my head.

I glanced into the front room. The lovely Fruitbat, my girlfriend, was snogging the man with long hair. I believe the thought that came into my mind was something along the lines of 'Right!'

First things first, I had another girl on the premises, I had no more furniture. I went downstairs to find Dave and his mate giggling as they stamped on the back of one of my chairs. Two or three girls were trying to talk them out of it, but my friends were all upstairs.

'Oh no,' I said, 'I've got a much better way of smashing it than that.'

I was full of coke, so I shall try to write this as I felt it. I picked up the table, which was crowded with drinks, and charged Dave with it. He went down like the sack of shit he is and his tart of a mate ran for the exit. Dave was trapped under the upended table like a little pixie under a fallen mushroom, so I started jumping up and down on it, shouting 'If you want to smash it, smash it like this, you fucker.'

He's a small man. I am not, which meant Dave wasn't giggling any more. He was sort of whining and trying to get further underneath the table so I couldn't stamp on him. Eventually one of the girls said I was going to kill him, which was wrong, he wasn't even getting that badly hurt, just having his dignity squashed, so I stopped and went for round two with Fruitbat.

Up the stairs, she was still snogging Michael Hutchence. That's who he looked like to me. If it had happened in a pub I would have just left. The offence was unignorable, though: it had happened in my house. I went up to the couple and tapped the man on the shoulder. He turned. The poor sod was just a Fruitbat victim, he didn't know she was my girlfriend. Still, he'd have to pay. I grabbed him by both ears and thrust my tongue into his mouth, giving it the full spaniel trying to get the last bit out of a jar of marmite treatment. He fell back and just seemed to disappear. I had no idea what happened to him. Friends tell me he fell over.

I turned to Fruitbat.

'You're sacked,' I said, 'and your boyfriend's a lousy

kisser.' Fruitbat looked shocked, but before she could say anything I turned to Joan who was watching wide-eyed.

'You,' I said, 'get upstairs. I've got something for you.'

'Ooh la la!' she said in her Lancashire accent as I followed her to my room to fuck her like they used to when they meant it.

I am a complicated man and a lover of all life has to offer, the pungent and the pure. I am literate, thoughtful and kind. It's good to forget all that sometimes, though, and just be a bloke. I felt fantastic.

I was relating this story in the lift at work on the Monday. I'd given up trying to be corporate man and was finding I was getting on a lot better by just being myself. I was chatting away to Larry, a passionate Leicester City fan who would one day try to kill me after Chelsea's Erland Johnsen dived to win a penalty in the FA cup. I support the team, but I didn't tell him to do it, Larry.

Next to us in the lift was a very pretty girl with long curly brown hair. She had dark glowing skin and a face like an imp and I could see her trying not to laugh at the story.

'Is it always this exciting here?' she said in a cockneyesque accent.

'Riveting,' I said. The lift continued and I was aware I was still holding eye contact with her. She smiled at me.

'Are you new?' I said.

'First day. I'm looking for someone to show me around.'

I had a sudden flashback. There was the same quality in our voices that I'd had when talking to Catriona. I looked at her. Despite her smart clothes she could easily pass for a gypsy – one of the glamorous ones who appear in fairy tales, not the ones who filled the field where I walk the dog with old tyres.

Later in the day I was sitting at my desk writing a novel when the girl came round again, led by Dominique, the head of another department.

'This is Suzy,' said Dom, 'she's our new girl. This is Mark, he's area manager.'

Suzy's eyes goggled like the Verve lookalike's had when I told him I attended a Thai class.

'*You* are the manager?' she said, 'I thought you were a trainee like me.'

'Put it down to clean living, love,' I said.

'Yeah, right,' she said. This made me feel very good. Vervo had seen me as an old bloke. Here was a girl of twenty-two who saw me as a contemporary.

Every month work held celebrations on a Friday for divisions that had hit their targets. They were office parties like you see on the telly, that is in the office.

Wine was free and I was single so I attended a few of them.

It was here that I got chatting to Suzy again. She was funny, irreverent and bright and I liked her immediately. We'd been talking for about half an hour when one of the salesmen came shoving through, nearly knocking her off her feet and making her spill her drink all over herself She said 'Sorry!' to him pointedly, but he ignored her, just loading up a tray with drinks. The man was clearly a blister.

He came blundering back with the tray. Suzy moved smartly out of the way, but I just stuck out my foot. He went absolutely sprawling over the floor, drinks crashing down about him.

'Gosh, I'm sorry,' I said, 'are you OK?'

I was so apologetic that he actually believed I'd done it accidentally. As I helped him up I gave Suzy a wink. She was in suppressed hysterics.

'I cannot believe you just did that,' she said, snorting her wine down her nose, 'you're a senior manager. What are you doing?' She was very good at flattering you like that. I wasn't a senior manager, I was a middle manager.

I shrugged. 'It was an accident.'

'It didn't look like it.'

'I say no more without a lawyer,' I said. 'Fancy a pint?'

'Oh yeah,' she said.

I was on favourite turf, out with an attractive girl, playing up to a wild man image. It's not really me, but I can do a good impression. At the end of the evening I said 'Back to yours for coffee, then?'

'All right,' she said, 'but I've got a boyfriend.' I deliberately hadn't asked.

'He's not going to be there is he?'

'No, but you'll have to go home.'

'Isn't home meant to be where the heart is?' I said.

'I've got a feeling you'd have difficulty finding yours,' she said, 'is there an *A to Z* for that sort of thing?'

And that was it. She wouldn't kiss me on the first night, although she let me have half of her bed. I didn't know at the time, but Suzy was fairly good at manipulating men. More than that, she instinctively understood them and knew that, if she made me wait, I'd be all the keener.

In September I went to a conference in Amsterdam, which, I discovered, has some museums. They really should make more of those because I don't think most people know they exist.

I stood looking out over the waters of a canal on a late summer's day and felt great. I was about to embark on one of the most distressing periods of my life.

24 HOLIDAY ROMANCE

– AND MARRIAGE

I have acted like a nutter myself on a number of occasions.

Lois was a pretty Australian girl who was attending the conference at the same time as me. She was 5' 6" tall, dark and slim. I guessed she was of French extraction, but I think her family actually went to Australia from Scotland.

She was clearly too clever to be working for Business Solutions and had a good sense of humour that emerged in those time-wasting exercises known as 'workshops'. I felt sorry for her – coming all the way from Sydney to sit and listen about how to boost morale. I thought it must have been quite a knock to her morale.

We spoke during the course and I found her attractive, not knowing the amount of mind-warping distress we were about to conjure up between us. The course was only a two-day thing and I was disappointed that she didn't come out with the rest of the staff from Business Solutions for a meal, but she'd flown halfway around the world and needed some sleep.

I would have thought no more about her, but I bumped into her at the airport on the way back. She was coming over to London to visit friends and we chatted at the departure gate. I thought she was really nice, funny and down to earth. I was still on business, she was flying privately, so we had to part on the plane. Business class was empty, though, and I asked the stewardess if Lois could come up and sit with me. She said OK and we spent the forty-minute journey drinking champagne.

We talked about London and I said that, if she liked, I would show her around. She only had a few days, though, and I was at work, so that wasn't going to work out.

Lois was an old-fashioned girl in some ways and I could see she liked acts of gallantry, however minor. When her bags went missing at the airport I insisted on staying with her to keep her company while the baggage people looked for them. They couldn't find them so, as a compensation, I said she should take a taxi with me to her hotel and I'd cover the cost on the company. We went back to her hotel, had a few drinks and parted. The next night we met up and I ended up back in her room. We did no more than kiss, but already I knew I liked her. That was it, though, she had to go back to Sydney.

Then it struck me. I had a lot of holiday saved up and nothing to do over Christmas. I'd go to Australia for three weeks, travel around a bit and she could be my guide down under.

I spent the weeks leading up to the holiday enlivening my breaks at work by going out at lunchtime with Suzy to a greasy spoon I'd found. She went along with this down-market choice of diner – standard loss-leader behaviour – until I found a pubic hair in my beans one day and she persuaded me to shift up the road to a more modern café.

This had all the thrill of a clandestine relationship. It would have been good for neither of us to have been seen together at work. Nothing was happening, she was with her boyfriend, but it was a relief to have a friend in the office. I'd found the step up to management quite difficult in some ways and she was a connection to a time when I'd been one of the crew.

I flew to Australia at Christmas. Lois picked me up at the airport, warned me about the sun, I ignored her because it was overcast, she took me to a B&B she'd found and I discovered I was sunburned.

Never mind. By the end of the first week I was staying at her flat and we were lovers. I thought she was great. We took boats all over the city, saw the sights, met her friends, and went to fabulous restaurants.

We were doing it all in a hurry, but that didn't bother me. I took the boat from Crow's Nest to the centre one day to accompany her in to work and imagined what it would be like to commute on the waves under Sydney bridge, rather than stuck in the choking tube. I was falling in love with Lois but also with Sydney.

The Australian attitude to work very much chimed with my own – work to live, don't live to work. I liked the idea that all the builders on your new bathroom would go missing on days that the surf was good, and that you'd accept that as an excuse. I liked the way the first thing that happened when you got to someone's house was that a can of beer was put into your hand rather than a cup of tea, and that when someone said 'You can tuck it away, Mark,' they meant it as a compliment.

And I liked Lois. We were briefly together so I can't really remember much that she said, other than that she made me laugh and, despite conventional appearances, she had interesting opinions on life. The only thing that gave me pause for thought was a couple of her friends, who were nailed-on yuppies. The man was clearly very proud of his company car, something that fired my prejudices. However, other friends were down the line Aussies who took me out to see Bondi and maintained that Poms can't drink. They revised that view by the end of the evening but I have to say they gave me a run for my money.

We went down to another beach at night and drank wine overlooking the ocean in a little bay and then, joy of joys, found a fantastic fish and chip shop. In Australia fish and chip shops can be guaranteed to serve good fish and chips. It's all they exist for, so why wouldn't they get it right? The UK is full of lousy chippers. How can something that has as its sole purpose the production of chips make bad chips? It says something about the expectations of the two countries. At a picnic in a park I was amazed to see a cockatoo in a tree. It was marvellous.

I met Lois's parents. Her dad was the sort of Aussie that you don't really encounter off red soil. He was inherently conservative and quite tight laced. There is a class of older Australians who seem to fit that mould. He was old school, thought before he spoke and was slightly gentlemanly, but without the effete edges that word implies in England. If you had to go into a battle, he'd be the kind of bloke you'd be relieved to find as your NCO. He was rightly suspicious of me. I think he saw straight through me, not as a wilful deceiver but as someone much more dangerous, a man who didn't know himself. Her mum, though, was lovely and welcoming. I wouldn't have blamed them for being taken in by me, *I* was taken in by me.

I was dangerous by the time I met Lois. I was thoroughly sick of being on my own, or of being in relationships compromised by infidelity or lack of commitment. I'd been ready to settle down when I was fourteen. Now I was begging to do so. I was sick of the clubs and the parties, of asking friends if they knew anyone single and nice. I had had enough of the chase and every atom of me was ready for the catch.

I wouldn't have settled for anyone, but I would have settled for anyone pleasant, pretty and bright. Lois seemed like a dream come true and I didn't stop to think whether our personalities would click in the long term. We got on just great then though.

I went up to Cairns for a week on my own and missed her madly, sleeping in a dorm with clanking air conditioning on the 'swamp' setting, alongside five ignorant and unpleasant English backpackers. It's an Australian prejudice that Poms don't wash and this lot were doing their best not to disappoint. It was like a scene from *The Long and the Short and the Tall*. Almost without thinking, I sent Suzy a card.

'Finished with your boyfriend yet?' it said. 'You'll need to hurry up, I'm back in two weeks.'

How can I account for this behaviour? Easy. I can't. I was in Australia, having a great time with a girl I thought I was falling in love with. The fact I was sending love notes to other women was a sign, perhaps, that I wasn't.

I don't think it was cynical, though. I'd become so accustomed to failure with women that I was now lining them up two at a time, in order to have a back-up when the inevitable disaster occurred. Actually, that is quite cynical, isn't it?

I returned to Sydney and Lois and I spent four intense days together, holding hands at midnight on Circular Quay, dining in a skyscraper overlooking the harbour, taking long lie-ins in each other's arms. By the time I was ready to go we had discussed all the options for allowing me to come back to stay and decided there was only one thing for it. We must get married.

Something happens in a whirlwind romance that stops you thinking straight. You don't just fall in love with the other person but with the whirlwind itself. The idea of falling in love with your life partner after only a couple of days is very romantic and you imagine children and grandchildren, telling them 'I knew within a second of meeting her.' There's also the idea that fate owes you one and that this is it. How long have you waited? All your life it seems. How did you ever doubt it was going to work out fine in the end?

I sped home full of it, wanting to tell the world. The night I returned I had the chance to break the news to an old girlfriend who had got back in contact and said we should try to be friends. I always had one more horror lurking in the shadows for Vanessa.

Vanessa, and everyone else I knew, thought I had gone mad. There's nothing like a holiday romance to awaken the inner adolescent, though, and I thought they were all wrong.

Vanessa had a look of total bewilderment on her face, more like a parent whose child has gone off the rails again, just after she thought all that was behind him, than a former lover.

'We've only just started seeing each other again, Mark, and now this,' she said. 'Well great, you're running off with Barbie.'

Lois was actually nothing like Barbie, but Vanessa had it in her head that I was leaving her again for a pair of big tits and a short skirt.

I hadn't considered that I owed my friends anything. Part of the attraction of Australia for me was that I was sick of Britain and sick of myself. I had ambitions, I had to face it, but I would never realise them. Even though my pop-star dreams had atrophied and I now wanted to be a writer (why not a ballerina?), it never occurred to me to do the obvious and actually write something. I dabbled with writing at work, but it's not ideal to have to keep half an eye out in case you have to switch to a spreadsheet if someone comes in. All I would do if I stayed was get old, drunk and bitter talking about my potential and how no one nowadays can string an interesting sentence together. How I would have known that, I can't say. I could only bring myself to read dead writers. Anyone living just filled me with varying mixtures of contempt, envy and bile.

I also, for all my apparent arrogance, hadn't a very high opinion of myself. It never occurred to me that anyone would miss me, although I sort of knew I'd miss them. I'm very good at focusing on immediate wants and less accomplished at considering what might be best in the long term. Australia and Lois were like a pain in my breast, family and the friendships of years like a dull glow at the back of my head.

Work were unwilling to transfer me to the Australian office, as they had a policy against couples working for the same company. I took it as high as I could, to the worldwide number 2, but no one was having any of it. I had to endure a patronising lecture off one international manager, along the lines of 'When you're as old as I am, you will know about love'. He was dismissive, rude, sanctimonious and right.

I'd go anyway and we'd work it all out when I got there. I phoned Lois every night and we had long and heartfelt conversations where we said we loved each other. The thing had a momentum of its own.

None of this stopped me seeing Suzy. She was mildly taken aback when I told her over lunch that I was going, but this yielded some interesting results in the meantime. She finished with her boyfriend and we moved slowly towards a sexual relationship. Lois was arriving at Easter. Suzy had three months to get her man and she didn't rush it. Even though I was spending some nights in another girl's bed – largely chastely, snogging aside – I longed for Lois to come, along with my new life.

Then something totally unexpected and brilliant happened. I received a letter from a literary agent. She'd read an article I'd written in *The Big Issue* – on why you shouldn't feel sorry for men when their girlfriends finish with them. The gist of it was that men are swines.

The agent said she liked my writing style and asked if I'd ever considered writing a novel. I replied saying I'd done nothing but consider it. I was elated. I'd always said my talent would be recognised eventually and it seemed to me I'd been proved right. It was all I could do not to run out of the front door screaming 'You'll all pay, I am king and you will pay!' I was determined, though, to actually make it work this time and not to hear 'You should write a novel' as 'You have written a novel, it's great, you're a novelist, life is wonderful, no need for any more work.' I sprang into action and went down the pub to talk about it.

I did tell the agent – who is now my agent – that I was going to Australia. She said it would make things difficult but not impossible. It was the first bum note that had been struck concerning my emigration. I didn't have to go to wonderland, there was still a chance wonderland would come to me.

I scribbled away a bit. What should I write about? I knew – an alienated young man who's just too bloody cool to feel anything and who never connects with the world. Literary agents could never have seen anything like that before, could they? Only about five a day, as it turns out.

By the time Lois arrived I had about 1,100 words ready, the fruits of two months' labour. As a rough guide to how productive that is, I have been writing this book at around 2,000 words a day and, when I really get into it, I've done as many as 5,000, suddenly realising it's four in the morning and I last had a coffee break during *Countdown*. Let's just say I hadn't been performing the labours of Hercules.

My hero was nameless, a loner, the story began with him studying a cigarette, only at the end did you realise he was having sex while he was doing it. It was mannered tosh and I should have been horsewhipped again for it.

I had handed my notice in at work and booked my plane ticket. Then, at my goodbye party, where Claire, not Suzy, was surprisingly designated to buy my gifts, I got the call from the agent I had been waiting for.

'Hello, Mark, this is Judith.' Nowadays, after nearly ten years with her, I would recognise this brief and businesslike tone. It is not a good sign. Judith is a kind woman and if she likes something she tends to start the sentence with, 'It's me, it's brilliant. Funnier than Kafka, more depth than Ken Dodd.'

This time she said, 'I'm going to come straight to the point. I didn't like it. Not that you've written that much to like or dislike.'

'Ah. Was any of it any good?'

'I'm struggling to think of one redeeming feature,' she said.

Right, so I was off to the other side of the world carrying only the tatters of a dream. Still, it was better than no dream at all. Luckily I am a dauntless sort and asked for another crack at it, which she rather half-heartedly granted me.

I waited for Lois at the airport in a state of high excitement. Here was the woman with whom I would spend the rest of my life. She came through the gate, and stood looking for me, nervous and pale in the airport light as I realised it had all been a terrible mistake.

25   SHAME

My parents had a party for us, where I gave the worst speech of my life. I'd meant to say a few irreverent things about my dad – it was his birthday – but it came out like a character assassination.

My mum and dad liked Lois, though my nan cried because she was convinced she would never see me again. Suddenly, though, all the caution and care I had been damming up with the excitement of a new life came bursting through, like miseries after a night on the whisky. Just as I'd known she was the one for me in Australia I now knew she wasn't. I still liked her, I still found her attractive, but I just didn't want to marry her any more. It was such a terrible realisation that I could scarcely voice it to myself. Everyone had told me I was being an idiot, it was a holiday romance, the feeling would pass. I felt the hot shame of the truly wrong and could not think of a way out. So I did what I always do in such situations – nothing. In fact that's not quite true. I just trusted to my subconscious to get me out of it.

I had a good time with Lois. We went on a wonderful tour of Ireland and I waited for the magic feelings of Australia to return. The thing was, I liked her a lot. It was just suddenly so clear that I didn't love her. How could I? I'd only known her for about ten days, all told.

It became clear fairly quickly that there would be some bones of contention between us. Well, not so much bones of contention as soup of contention. When we'd been in

Australia I'd thought it a bit odd that she'd asked me to tuck in my shirt before meeting her friends. I put it down to a difference in style between the UK and Australia. In Ireland, though, she asked me if I knew you were meant to finish off your soup with the bowl tilted away from you. I said I did, but I thought it was a silly convention so I didn't do it. She said she would rather that I did. Then there was the writing – I could do it instead of getting a job, but I'd need to show her what I had done at the end of each day so she could check I hadn't been just lazing about. Then there was her attitude in the house. My house hadn't really been renovated all that much in the four years since my parents had come down for a week's blitz on the place. It was bohemian on the upstairs floors, which had all been redone and replastered, but a bit Dickensian in some of the other parts and pretty much medieval in others.

Lois, whose country wasn't that much older than the house, was shocked at its state, I think. She confined herself to my room but, when she did emerge, told Charlie, who was always more of a flatmate than a lodger, to make a better job of cleaning up the surfaces after himself in future. The second she came in she assumed a position of authority. I owned the place, had been there seven years and I didn't have a position of authority. If anyone did it was Charlie, he was the tidiest.

Then there was the cream-cake incident. I'd bought a vanilla slice from the bakery and was about to tuck in when Charlie came in.

'That looks nice,' he said.

'Keep your hands off it,' I said.

'Mark,' said Lois, 'don't you think it would be nice if you offered Charlie half of that?'

'Yes Mark,' said Charlie, with a smirk like a cat with a kipper, 'I think that would be nice.'

'I believe "Fuck off" is the apt response in these circumstances,' I said.

'Mark!' said Lois, 'give Charlie some of that slice and stop being so selfish.'

She hadn't seen at all that Charlie's demand for some of the cake and my refusal to give it to him was part of our shared humour, that he didn't expect any, nor would he expect to share a cake of his with me. To her I was being selfish and needed correcting.

These were small things, but I'm bad at being ordered about. I could easily have been wrong about her – she was nervous, with a new man, miles from home – but I thought I might be experiencing the tiny tremors that precede the big quake.

I asked one of my best friends, Mike, what he thought. 'She's nice,' he said, 'but I don't see where you fit in. She is pretty different from you.' He knew me as well as anyone and his verdict felt damning.

In Australia I'd only been able to see our similarities. In Europe all I could see was our differences. I may have been wrong – in fact almost everything I thought about Lois could be wrong, I hardly knew her – but suddenly I saw myself as a hen-pecked husband in a Sydney suburb, leading the petit bourgeois life with friends who know about what extras packages are available on BMWs. Or worse, just in a perpetual row. I only need two orders to reach for the 'Fuck off'. I couldn't do it. Actually, I could do it. Some hard courses of action that are impossible for brave men are quite open for cowards. Something major was going to have to intervene.

We were due to go back on a Thursday. On Tuesday I met Suzy for a last lunch. We sat in the crypt of the Methodist café opposite Westminster Abbey. She seemed very sad and also very different from Lois. Where Lois seemed to be evaluating my behaviour, approving or disapproving of it, Suzy appeared to think everything I said and did was wonderful. It was the classic advantage that the mistress has over the wife, though neither of the women were either to me.

Suzy had bought me an Easter egg – one of those Kinder things.

'I hate these,' I smiled.

She shook her head and laughed. 'Nobody else I know would say that,' she said. At this stage of our relationship she found this behaviour funny and iconoclastic. That would change.

'If I didn't go,' I said, 'would you, you know, want to hang around with me?'

'Sure,' she said, 'are you going to go?'

'I don't know.'

That evening I told Lois I was going out with a friend to say goodbye. It would be a boysie thing. She said she was tired anyway and wanted to sleep. I went out with Suzy in Islington. We drank buckets and ended up snogging on the street.

'Don't go,' she said.

'I don't want to,' I said.

'Well don't, this is the rest of your life. At least let's sleep together before you go.'

Suzy knew men and timed it perfectly. I did want to sleep with her, but more than that, I wanted to do something that would irrevocably sever me from Australia.

We went to the garage to buy some condoms – age had taught me greater respect for sexual health – but they were stocktaking and wouldn't sell me any. I was a bit drunk, so I held the place up and watched as the attendant's shaking hand put the condoms into the tray.

'You have,' said Suzy, in hysterics, 'just committed armed robbery.'

'Blackmail,' I said, 'not robbery.'

In fact I'd just had an argument where they said the place was closed and I said there were still flowers outside on sale. They said they weren't for sale and I said that they must be free then. I walked off with a large bucket full and they came chasing after me. After some ducking and diving I pointed out it would be easier to just take my money and hand over the condoms than chase me around the forecourt all night. They relented, I gave them the flowers, and I went home with Suzy.

Suzy seemed to think my company was very exciting and I enjoyed playing up to her image.

We made love and she looked young and beautiful in the orange light of a street lamp that was outside the window. I don't really like the expression 'make love' – that's something that's done by people who call boys 'young gentlemen' and are members of the Round Table – but it seemed like that, as if we were manufacturing something where before there had only been ingredients.

She wanted me to stay all night afterwards, but I didn't want to upset Lois, not like that anyway. I was going to say something the next day, but Lois was waiting for me, very angry.

She read me the riot act about staying out late and not telling her where I was. No one I'd ever been with had done that before, not even Ella, who would only complain if I woke her up. Thinking of Ella gave me the line I needed.

'This isn't working is it?'

Words have never come harder from my lips. I could feel her pain before I even got the sentence out. I'm not quite arrogant enough to suppose that she was going to be so upset by losing such a prime catch as myself, but to have your dreams smashed, to be rejected so far from home and from friends and family is very hard, no matter who is doing the rejecting. Then there was the social embarrassment I would heap upon her. She'd arranged a wedding venue, been measured for a dress, and was looking into booking musicians.

She made some small attempt to talk me out of it and then said she'd call a cab to stay with her one friend in London. At two in the morning she left and I never saw her again. I felt so sorry for her, but I couldn't help her.

Waves of shame came crashing down on me, smashing me out of my sleep. Every time I closed my eyes I saw her poor anguish-stricken face. For both of us, though, it had to be done. She would have been no more happy with a discontented, rebellious twit of a husband, who'd drink paint before he put it on a skirting board if he thought you were hassling him, than I would have been with her.

The next morning I sat drinking coffee from six in the morning in the kitchen. I have rarely felt so foolish, and periodically shivered when I thought of the night before. I didn't call Suzy to tell her what had happened, that just seemed wrong and disrespectful to Lois. It was a bit late for that, but that's how I felt.

At about seven Lois called and said that I'd had cold feet, it was understandable, and I should reconsider. Our plane was going at one and I should be on it. She would forgive me. I told her it was no go and we both cried. I can still make myself shudder in shame thinking about this conversation. I had treated women badly before, but this was an all-time low. I didn't consider suicide, but images of pills and ropes and falls from high towers went through my head.

I went back into the kitchen and sat crying and looking into space. At about nine I was joined by Ellen, Charlie's occasional bed partner. Charlie went out with a lot of girls that he fancied but didn't promote to the status of girlfriend because of some tiny perceived imperfection. In Ellen's case it was because she smoked.

She was actually a bit of a departure for him anyway. His taste in women was very different from mine and he favoured skinny girls. He would have fancied Vanessa, he said, but her accent terrified him. Ellen was much more my type: pretty, curvy, a bit plump, with lovely big breasts and a university arts club look to her, off the shoulder dresses, and jumpers, long skirts and big sunglasses. She was a gallery owner, bisexual, flirty and famous for her blow jobs, by all accounts capable of making a man's eyes go round like melons on a fruit machine. Charlie had once gone to bed early. Ellen, who I got on with very well, had wanted to carry on yakking to me and a few others, but she had business to attend to first. She went out of the room and was away five minutes.

When I gave her a light on her return, I noticed that her face carried a thick rope of spunk, from lip to ear. I didn't know what to say. You won't find advice on that in *Debrett's* and I know because I've looked.

She now said she had the day off so she was taking it easy. I explained what had happened and she spent the next couple of hours talking to me about it. She was sympathetic and intelligent, but all I could do was watch the clock. At one Lois would be gone and a chapter would close. Ellen is extremely bright and saw she wasn't getting through to me.

'Look,' she said, 'you're very upset and you need to forget about it for a bit. Do you want to fuck me?'

I looked at her. I did feel a rush of excitement as my eyes fell to her tits. What would she look like with one of them exposed after I'd pulled down the low side of her slanted top? Very good, I concluded. But Lois wasn't even out of the country.

'Wrong time, I think,' I said.

'At least let me suck your cock,' she said, like someone else might offer to run you home.

It was 11 o'clock.

'Actually,' I said, 'if you really want to help we can go down the pub.' I wanted a drink and I wanted to be out of the house in case Lois came back.

'You're on,' she said.

I had retained some very small sort of honour, but part of me wished later that I'd gone for it. Lois was already in my past and I felt sure that fucking Ellen with all those raw emotions going through my head would have been absolutely fantastic. She had a spectacular body and a thoroughly decadent look to her that I found very alluring. A month or two later she came to a party at our house with a girlfriend who she fucked on my bed. I accidentally opened the door and she said 'Oh, that was lucky, do come in.'

I couldn't, Suzy was downstairs, but I often ran through in my mind exactly what might have happened if she hadn't been. We shall never know, though I've considered it so much I could probably draw you a picture.

We went up the pub and drank like camels. I simply could not get drunk no matter how many lagers I consumed. I tried bitter; that didn't work either. The beers had no effect at all. One o'clock came and I felt relief mixed with ever deepening guilt. I looked out of the window at the sky. Lois was in it somewhere. I, as snakes must be, was on the earth. We drank on until about six, at which point I decided I might take Ellen up on her earlier offer after all.

We went out into the street and started kissing. Then we decided it was too cold and we should go home. I lit some candles in my room, cheesy but fun, we got into bed, and then Charlie came home.

'This is so wrong,' said Ellen as she heard him at the door.

Even though Charlie was lukewarm about her, she had designs on him as a boyfriend, and to be found in bed with one of his best friends would have been a setback in her progress to that goal. She terminated proceedings. As an aside, I don't know why he was lukewarm. She was way out of his class.

She went downstairs. Charlie came upstairs. He saw the candles.

'Awwww,' he said, 'you've been in bed haven't you?'

'No,' I said.

'I better go!' shouted Ellen from the hall.

I heard the door clunk.

'That's really fucking inconsiderate,' said Charlie.

'Don't be sanctimonious.' I said, 'If you made any sort of commitment to the girl then you'd have a case. She's not your girlfriend, you said so yourself.'

Charlie began to laugh. 'I think you're in no position to hand out lectures on commitment, cobber,' he said.

He had a point.

'You both got away lightly there,' he said. 'She wanted to be in control and you are, well, you. It would never have worked.'

'Fancy a drink?' I said.

'Yeah, why not?' he said.

So that was it, I was with Suzy. Really I should have tried to go out with Ellen, she's much more my type. Still, I didn't, and I was with sparky, mischievous Suzy, who clearly thought I was great. I didn't know that she had a way of getting what she wanted that was ten times more powerful than telling someone what to do.

26 ACCIDENTALLY CONTRIBUTING SOMETHING WORTHWHILE TO JOURNALISM WHILE WRECKING SOMEONE'S LIFE

As my relationship with Suzy began, I still saw Ella occasionally. After a period in which she had enjoyed contrasting her spectacular success to my life of industrial estate publishing and PR, we'd become good friends.

Ella didn't know it, but she was on the edge of a calamity, one that I would unwittingly engineer for her. Her boyfriend, the spectacularly successful Xavier, had decided he wasn't quite successful enough for his tastes. He had awards, but he wanted them by the bucket. His dream came true when, the year before I got together with Suzy, his latest film swept the board at international documentary festivals and won several prestigious prizes. Breathtaking footage showed Xavier driven in the boot of a car to meet a head of the Cali drugs cartel and the film followed heroin from the Colombian poppy fields, into a mule's stomach and through customs, all the way to the addict's arm. It was a masterpiece, compelling stuff.

His trusted number two, Ella, was by his side to help him with the crushing weight of medals, trophies and statuettes. She had only a small researcher's part in the English side of the film but, as a surprise, he'd billed her as the associate producer at the last minute. The fast track she'd sought was under her feet. I'd watched the film in horror. It was brilliant and I, six months away from my book deal, was still at Business Solutions. Oh God.

Ella gave me a call out of the blue one day. She and Xavier were working on his next project, but she was worried. She is a scrupulous rule follower, an i dotter of the highest order and she was worried about Xavier's approach now she was working with him more closely. She wanted me to recommend a journalist who could bring some real rigour to the reporting. Ella didn't say so, maybe she didn't even recognise it herself, but she thought Xavier was a chancer.

I recommended an acquaintance – Mike. Mike is an investigative journalist. That's what he does. He doesn't go out often, he isn't much seen in restaurants, he's not a party animal. What he is is a trained, dedicated, hound of a man who will not rest until he has dug the truth from the paving slabs with his nails if he has to. If his nails fail, he will use his teeth.

Within ten minutes of working there he was complaining to me that Xavier seemed incapable of using a notebook properly, keeping a decent filing system or doing anything that resembled what he considered journalism. Oh, two more things about Mike. One, he is an English bloke. Therefore a man strutting about telling you how great he is while wearing leather trousers really gets on his tits. Two, he speaks very good Spanish, something he never bothered to tell anyone at work because no one asked him.

So, when a Colombian girl who had been a researcher on the documentary came into the office and shouted in Spanish at Xavier 'If you don't pay me, I'm going to tell them you made it all up,' his ears pricked up, as newshounds' ears do when such alarums affright them. To put it in language Xavier would understand: 'It was the start of a sensational trail that would expose one of the greatest documentary deceptions in film history.' Mike took the researcher for coffee and, well, she spilled the beans. Xavier was, as I had noted within five seconds of meeting him, a bullshitter.

In short, he'd got a bank teller to pretend they were in the Cali cartel, drive him round Bogota for a bit, and then do an interview in his hotel room banging on about smack. Mike went to Bogotá and matched the wallpaper in Xavier's hotel room to the one in the 'secret location' of the film. The stunning and dangerous raid on the drug lord's home? A staged attack on an empty house. The heroin the mule was swallowing was in fact a tube of mints and he never got through customs anyway, contrary to what the film said. Also, Xavier had bought the plane ticket for the drugs mule to fly to Britain. This led, as Mike said, to the conclusion that either a major British TV company was in league with the Cali cartel – not very likely at all – or that there had been no contact with the Cali cartel and the man wasn't working for them anyway.

Suddenly I thought 'Yes, didn't the customs wallahs smell a rat seeing this bloke followed through by a bloody great film crew?' It wasn't shot on secret camera.

Mike spent two years researching the story, his forensic approach tearing into Xavier's 'finger's crossed' fibs at every point. By the time the process was over Xavier's reputation had been demolished in print and he left the country, having dumped Ella. The sad thing was, he was at that point the love of her life, for all his faults, and I felt desperately sorry for her, even though I was sort of pleased to have been indirectly responsible for his downfall.

What he had done to Ella was less forgivable, to me, than

faking the documentary. He had hit the very soul of her: her work. Miss Goody Two Shoes, Miss 'You Haven't Paid the TV Licence, Are You Trying to Lose Me a Job I Don't Yet Have?' was investigated too and it nearly killed her. She lost about two stones, weight she's never put back on. She was completely exonerated by the enquiry, but mud sticks and she wouldn't work for nearly two years. He could not have struck a harder blow. It was almost as if the whole relationship had been designed by some strange god to teach her a lesson – reach too high and you will be damned to the depths.

I told Ella that I'd stand by her and I'd like to think I did that. By the time the enquiry was over Mr Wonderful was back in Colombia hiding his head and I had apparently come good on my promise that success would just walk through the door one day. I didn't take any joy in it. In fact, if I'd known it was all going to come out, I would never have recommended Mike for the job. I wanted to get Xavier, but it was too high a price to pay. I loved Ella and I hated to see her so bereft.

27 KEEP ON CRASHING

IN THE SAME CAR

In fairy tales, a kiss traditionally turns a frog into a prince. In life, it often works the other way around. Suzy and I practised a sort of black magic together, where we turned each other from perfectly reasonable, pleasant people into croaking reptiles sinking in a mire of our own devising. All we had to do to get out was to let each other go, but we couldn't.

The first year, though, was great. I'd used my last bonus to fund writing my book and I'd got a deal. It seemed like a dream come true – a great girl, a job I wanted to do, a brilliant dog that we'd got from Battersea together. You can't ask for more from life than that can you?

Girlfriends often position themselves as the reverse of whatever you'd had before. She knew that my doubts about Lois had begun over her telling me what to do, so Suzy went along with whatever I liked. If things were OK by me, they were OK by her, which was OK by me. We went down to Cornwall, camping. I'd been there only a couple of weeks before with Lois. Why did I go again? Because I love the place and have a vision of me being there with the love of my life. I wanted to get on with that as soon as possible.

It was a very romantic weekend. We went with Charlie and Ellen, apparently rushing to make dinner at the pub by nine on the Friday night, but Suzy – who knew my culinary tastes – deliberately took a wrong turn so that, when we arrived, we could have a lovely dinner of crisps, nuts, scampi fries and summer ale without having to suffer anything cooked. We munched and drank in the warm evening and staggered back to the campsite hand in hand.

Suzy was with me when the book deal came through and we celebrated madly, going to Venice together. We got caught in a spectacular storm, stayed on the Lido and got fleeced at the Casino. We went to Cuba and rescued a street dog, paying for it to be treated at a vet's. I got a bad case of sunburn and was hospitalised, put on a drip full of anti-histamines. 'Do not drink alcohol for at least twenty-four hours,' said the nurse on releasing me.

'Come on,' I said to Suzy, 'let's find a bar.'

'Why?'

'Because it's a chance to get properly pissed,' I said, 'these anti-histamines double the effect of the booze.' Part of the reason we fall for new partners is because they differ from what we have had before. One of Suzy's previous boyfriends of several years had been an outwardly zany sort who nurtured a lot of fears about life and was a hypochondriac. He took his own temperature about three times a day and would never fly or go on a fairground ride. About twice a year he went to casualty, convinced he was having a heart attack. She found the idea of someone viewing a dose of intravenous medicine as an opportunity to party very refreshing.

'My last boyfriend wouldn't have agreed to leave the hospital grounds in case he had a relapse,' she said. She always said 'My last boyfriend wouldn't have . . .' with an air of incredulity, as if I was the most outrageous creature that had ever walked the earth. Of course, that made me feel pretty good.

We went up to the Edinburgh festival and had a truly

terrific time. Suzy's previous boyfriends hadn't been art tarts like myself – although one had a saxophone he couldn't play tastefully positioned in the corner of his room, so that shows some depth. She was excited to go to an event like Edinburgh and to discover a new world.

A note on previous boyfriends. It's never bothered me that my girlfriends see their exes. My attitude, with the one exception of Catriona, has always been 'If they're going to go, they're going to go.'

It's the same with ex-girlfriends. I'm still friends with most of the women I've had a long relationship with and I see no reason to change that.

Edinburgh was a whirl with Suzy. We took in show after show and laughed and laughed. It was thrilling to introduce her to a new world and I think we may have been on the edge of being in love.

Then it went wrong. The first problem was that she started to get very bad and very regular migraines. It meant we would regularly have to leave halfway through a meal or a night out, and great swathes of holidays were spent sitting in darkened rooms rather than sightseeing.

Should I have seen beyond this? Of course. Did I? Of course not. Our relationship had been based on fun, fun, fun. When that stopped we didn't have much underneath. It didn't help that I showed no signs of committing to her. Friends asked when I would be moving my lodgers out of my house. I said I wouldn't be. I liked living in a shared house, it was exciting coming home, never knowing who might have dropped round or if your planned night in front of the TV was going to be ditched because someone fancied a trip to the curry house and a few beers.

'I sometimes think you're more committed to Charlie than you are to me,' she said.

I found that a bit odd. I'd known Suzy a year at the time she said this. Charlie had been my friend for fifteen years and we'd lived together for six. Of course I was more committed to him than I was to her. That alone should have been a signal for us to end it.

It was around this time that I fell out with Charlie's girlfriend – improbably a high-flying solicitor. She was given to having screaming rows with Charlie and my strong advice was that they should split up. After one particularly grisly evening when we were out in a large group, she decided he wasn't paying her enough attention and stood stamping her feet in the street, insisting that he came home that second. I waited a hundred yards off the row for about ten minutes before I got bored and – rather ill advisedly – walked back and said 'Charlie, why don't you just dump her?'

This had the effect of pouring water onto a burning chip pan and she went berserk.

'It's him or me,' she said to Charlie. 'If you ever see him again, it's over between us.'

He tried to talk her out of it, but she was adamant. One of us had to go. I think she was a bit surprised when it was her.

Ill, and feeling unloved, Suzy became someone else when she was with me: depressed, resentful and bitter. She fell out badly with my flatmates and retreated very often into long silences. The girl who had been so energised by Edinburgh had gone, and in her place was someone who seemed like a sullen and resentful goblin.

'What do you think of that film?' I'd ask.

'It was a film.'

'What did you like about it?'

'Can't remember. The seats were uncomfortable.'

I didn't expect *The Late Review*, but you do want to feel

you can talk to your partner about something. I'm sure she did some of this to spite me because I wouldn't commit to her. Why didn't I commit? The same reason that stops everyone – I knew in my heart that I didn't want to spend the rest of my life with her.

My problem is that, just as I don't want looking after by a girl, I don't want to look after one. Some men love a woman to be dependent on them, but not me. Of course, I don't like it if she's totally independent – Ella often made it clear I was an irrelevance to her life – but I can't handle being the sole receptacle for someone's happiness. I need to feel they have a life outside me. Increasingly, it seemed, Suzy did not. Totally dependent on me, or so it seemed, she became almost impossible to finish with. If I did so, I thought and she implied, her life would be utterly meaningless.

My first book came out and we did have a great time at the launch and other parties around it. For an evening or an afternoon we were happy, and then I'd say something wrong and she would retreat into her shell again and I'd feel more alone than when I'd been single.

It was around this time I saw the last of Vanessa. She read my book and identified herself as one of the characters. I thought she was talking rubbish. Everyone I knew thought they were in it somewhere. One girl I hadn't seen for years identified herself as the lead character, Alice. 'I know I've always been your muse,' she said. It was news to me.

Vanessa was adamant, though.

'You've written about things we couldn't even discuss between ourselves,' she said.

Vanessa thought I didn't want to go out with her because I didn't fancy her. I wish it had been that easy. That can be explained, thought about and moved on from. The truth was more complicated and more difficult to grasp, even for me.

I'd just never seen her as a partner, the same way you might have an attractive sister but never see her as a partner. My mind had a block in that direction. She said we would never see each other again and I felt very sad. I also felt she would relent and call. So far she hasn't. I do miss her, but I don't know why. I don't miss the rows and her deep anger with me. In the end it was better that we stayed apart. Vanessa was right. Vanessa was always right.

Another year went by with Suzy and I was not in love with her. Every little thing she did irritated me, the way she absent-mindedly scratched her eyebrow, or twisted her hair, her increasingly monosyllabic replies whenever I spoke to her. I tried to finish with her, but she absolutely would not go.

There was always a reason to stay – she had nowhere to go, just give her a month, then a month more; a difficult period at work had begun, she was depressed over her headaches and just needed to get the next hospital appointment out of the way; not before Christmas, oh God, no don't leave her alone at New Year, not with Valentine's Day coming up and then her birthday. She presented the calendar so that there was about a three-hour period in June that I could finish with her with a clear conscience. I tried, she cried, I relented.

How did I put up with this? How did she put up with this? How did the two, bright, fun, kind, nice people who had shared such a great time at the beginning end up locked in this unbreakable embrace? It was like something from Greek mythology, a kiss we'd longed for, but from which we could now never be released.

The thing was that, in lots of ways, I didn't want to get away from Suzy. I liked her, maybe I could have loved her, but I didn't like the dependent person she became when she was with me. Nor did I have the power to change it. I thought that maybe if I acted like I loved her for a stretch, then the girl I'd known would reappear. I couldn't manage it and she didn't.

Then a letter arrived for me, via my publishers.

'So you've written a book! What a hoot!' It was from Eva. I had fucked up with women before, I thought. That, as it turned out, was just an aperitif.

28 AFFAIR

Why did I go to see Eva? Two reasons. The first was that I wanted to leave Suzy. I accused Suzy of hanging on to me, but I was as culpable. The single life is scary and one of the reasons I wasn't more insistent that Suzy went was fear of the unknown. If I left Suzy for Eva I wouldn't have to face the dark alone.

The second reason was that I still carried a torch for Eva. This meant I had, at that point, nine torches in my hand. I missed Francesca most of all, then I missed Ella, Vanessa and Anna from university too. I also still thought about Phoebe and wished she'd been able to calm down a bit. There were strange sexual longings for Rachel, the friend of Scroop, and for a couple of one-night stands with Carmen and Alice. That's probably at the high end of average of torch holding, but I don't think it's excessive.

Eva and I had remained friends for a while after university, though she was less enthusiastic about seeing me. I had the distinct impression that she regarded me and my sort as a phase she had passed. She came back from France with a middle-class boy who was holidaying as a beggar – Jean-Paul – and moved in with him. They lasted a year or two.

She still saw me but it was under the unspoken condition that I never said what was on my mind – that I was mad about her and wanted us to be together. One night, towards the end of her relationship with Jean-Paul, we met at a Greek restaurant and I tried to woo her over a meze. I couldn't tell her I loved her, because that would have ended things immediately. So instead, I had to pretend to be interested solely in sex, hoping that would be a staging post on the way to a relationship.

She'd gone into publishing but had been sacked after a month because the boss had fallen in love with her and couldn't bear her rejection. She got another job in publishing; the boss hadn't sacked her but she'd had to leave because he fell in love with her and wouldn't take no for an answer.

'I don't take no for an answer,' I said.

'It's about how you don't take it,' she said. 'You've never written me a poem.'

'Certainly not.'

'Or made a suicide attempt.'

'Really?'

'Only pills.' That doesn't really count, does it?'

'If he jumps off a building will you marry him?'

'I'll think about it if it's over twenty storeys.'

There is a particular sort of ageing bookseller to whom Eva was irresistible. They had gone to books some time in the 1960s because they thought, wrongly, that made them attractive to women, as if some of the glamour of poets (have you ever met a poet? I had one round my house once and the dog still won't go near the chair he sat on) or the vision of novelists (don't laugh) would wear off on them. So they adapted what they perceived to be the style of writers, the Gauloises and the linen suit, the Panama hat askew when pissed at Hay-on-Wye literary festival.

By some fluke they married a woman, had kids as you had to back then and, aged forty-five, it suddenly dawned on them that they weren't de facto mates of Salman Rushdie but people who sold things. 'Where did it all go wrong?' they asked. 'Where be the glamour in my life, where the danger, where the women that propped up my creaking self-esteem before I hitched myself to this harridan who just breathes out like a cart horse whenever I venture a view on anything?' Then they met Eva and flipped. She was good looking, but not intimidatingly beautiful, clearly brighter than them like a man is cleverer than a sheep, and with a sexual allure you could fall into like a hole in the floor. She also wasn't bothered with all that feminist stuff they had never got the hang of and would laugh if you said 'nice tits'. So she flirted with them a bit, and then the Grahams and the Tarquins and the Jolyons went back to their Penelopes and told them, one Merloted evening after a late night in the pub when Eva had just seemed to lift all their cares off their shoulders, 'I'm leaving you. I'll have Jonah and Nell every other weekend.' The trouble is, it was only flirting – if it was even flirting – and their lives were fucked. That happened three times, with a few variations.

'Will you come home with me tonight?' I said.

'No.'

'I won't take that for an answer.'

'You'll have to,' she said, although of course, I didn't and we finished up in bed together for about twenty minutes.

As soon as we'd had sex she got up to go.

'I can't do this, Mark,' she said.

'What do you mean? I know a mate of Paul Weller's. Get back into bed and count yourself lucky.'

'No. I'm going to have to tell Jean-Paul.'

'Are you going to finish with him?'

'No.'

Eva was quite soft-hearted and felt for Jean-Paul, even though she no longer wanted to be with him. She was in that situation so many people seem to end up in, unable to continue but scared to finish it and so behaving abominably in the hope he'd do it for her. She told him and he phoned to confront me at work – not violently but in a soulful, teary, 'why?' way.

They did split up but she made it plain that I was not under consideration as a replacement and that sexual relations were terminated.

A week or a year later, I can't remember which, she was pregnant. Another boss at work had fallen for her and she was having the baby. There was something else too, I saw it in her eyes when we met. She was changed, softer, more engaged with life and visibly kinder. She had fallen for him. He was an older man. It was obvious she'd go for someone like that, really. She liked to mess around with the boys but she was never going to spend her life with one. She had moved on from me and here would be no more mad midnight romps, everything about her attitude made that clear. Of course I asked her but this time she meant it when she said no and there was no point me giving her the old spiel. I hadn't felt bereft – our entire relationship had been on the understanding that it was never really there but, leaving her flat in east London one winter's night, I looked at her and had that feeling you get when you look at a photograph of some great time from twenty years before; that I was seeing something beautiful, life-defining and irrevocably of the past. I thought I would never see her again.

Travelling to Brighton after a break of eight years, it seemed as though there was a chance I could step into that picture and go down a road I thought she had closed to me.

The publishing bloke was back with his wife and Eva had had a second child by another man in the time we'd been apart. She'd given him his marching orders, though, and was single again. I was pleased to see she hadn't fallen into wearing the standard Brighton mother's weeds of a dull dress over leggings, but was looking glamorous in her skinny jeans and tight T-shirt.

I'd travelled on my motorbike and there had been a deluge on the way down from London. I had to get out of my soaking bike things and into my glad rags. I was taking a lot of exercise and my podge had gone, so I didn't mind dekitting in front of her and it was quite funny to see the babysitting Lesbian Admirer – Lola to friends – go scuttling to check on the kids. I'd told Suzy I was staying the night there and she had begged me not to. I said Eva was an old friend and nothing would happen. Part of the price for Suzy's residence in my life was that she put up with this sort of behaviour. I had asked her to go, I had told her I didn't love her and wanted to be free, but she wouldn't go and I didn't have the courage or staying power to make her. The result was that I did what I liked and she had to put up with it. Or not put up with it, to retreat further into her shell.

I can't like myself at this stage of my life and I have no excuse for why I acted so badly. I complained that Suzy had become depressed, but, when she looked to me for support in her illness then all she got was rejection. It wasn't far off a form of mental torture that I was inflicting on her and it was no wonder she didn't feel like being the life and soul of the party. Anyone would have reacted the same. We should just have finished with each other, but neither of us could imagine how to do it. It was a failure of bravery and of simple imagination and we both paid for it.

The only possible excuse I can offer is that being in the wrong relationship is very stressful and that, under heavy stress, you can end up behaving like someone else.

In Brighton, with Eva, the Lesbian Admirer looked after the kids and we went out. I'm being a bit hard on Lola by calling her a lesbian admirer, she was actually a very interesting and complicated woman who had the misfortune to fall in love with someone whose taste in sexual partners leaned towards the testosterone-soaked end of masculinity. Eva and I went out to a restaurant and then to a cheesy disco playing hits of the seventies and eighties. They stuck on The Clash – twice. She didn't want to dance to 'Should I Stay Or Should I Go?' but, when they put on 'Janie Jones', she was up on her feet in a second. Here was a girl to whom music meant something, who could tell the difference between a band's late period, sell-out pop and the heartfelt early stuff. Things like that shouldn't make a difference, but they do. She was dancing in front of me, smiling and laughing, that biggest of male fantasies – the girl who understands. I felt immensely flattered, it was like a dream I'd had while we were at university, that we were dancing together and that she was taking me seriously, not seeing me as some mad bloke she might just sleep with if she felt like it but as someone she was genuinely fond of, as if she felt for me what I'd always felt for her.

It seemed that all I had to do was reach out and touch her and the photo from the album would spring to life and everything would be perfect. So I did.

Then we were kissing and it seemed only an instant before we were in bed, where I felt so happy that I thought I might cry. Did I think of Suzy? Yes, for a second, but in Eva's arms I thought I had the courage to take on Suzy's tears and to end it for good.

I rode back and my bike broke down in the freezing rain. I would have been angry if I'd regarded it as a mechanical failure, but luckily I saw it as a divine judgment, so I felt I deserved it.

Suzy said nothing when I finally got back, she was friendly and more like her old self. She knew full well what had gone on, but was willing to put up with it as long as I stayed. She realised that there might be a chance I would dump her there and then, so she went out of her way to be nice to me.

So why *didn't* I finish with her there and then? Because I had already finished with her. I'd said she could live at my house until she found another flat but – the classic coward's clause – I'd said we weren't really going out with each other.

Unfortunately I am the worst sort of bastard – a soft-hearted one. You know where you are with the hard-hearted guys, but pigs like me can't bear to make a girl cry. So we just behave terribly and then are discovered. Then it's her making herself cry.

We also imagine that we are indispensable to women and that their lives will fall apart without us. It's not helped when she tells us her life will fall apart without us. So I couldn't tell Suzy the truth, preferring to keep my brutalities silent. The easy way out was 'I have met someone else and I am leaving you.' I didn't think she could stand it. She got a job in Paris, but wouldn't go if I didn't too. I thought she'd wreck her career if she heard it and, because I cared for her and didn't want to see her destroyed, I stayed with her and destroyed her more slowly instead. I had a choice between killing her with the guillotine or inflicting a death of a thousand cuts and I went for the thousand cuts.

I was in a ludicrous situation of conducting a cross-European affair, inventing excuses to return for weekends and catching the train up to Derbyshire. Eva had moved to give her kids a rural upbringing like she'd had. I can't imagine why she did that. I had whooping cough when I was a boy, but I wouldn't wish it on my kid.

So there we were in Paris, Suzy marinating in her resentment and anxiety, me longing for home, and the dog getting ticks in the Bois. Somehow, though, we conspired to enjoy it, walking beside the Seine or riding on my motorbike at midnight flat-out round the Place de la Concorde. This was the thing with Suzy, it was nearly there, love, excitement, life as it is meant to be. Except it wasn't. As they say, when it comes to a miss, an inch is as good as a mile.

I told Eva I'd finish with Suzy when her contract ended in the June and that we would be together always. So she thought I'd be pleased when she phoned to tell me she was pregnant.

29   DEEPER SHAME

Had I not been with Suzy, then I would have been reasonably pleased Eva was pregnant. It was a bit sooner than I had planned, but I'd been pretty bored with my dissolute life and was looking forward to fidelity, sobriety and children, in that order.

It stiffened my resolve and, with a week to go before we moved out of Paris and back to London, I told Suzy that I definitely didn't want to see her any more.

She took it predictably badly. I sat one evening outside a local café and watched her from a distance as she walked home from work. She didn't see me for a hundred yards and the misery on her face shamed me to my core. Was there no quick way to end it, to have her happy and me happy without her having to suffer?

It became harder to see Eva after we moved back, although why I don't know. I'd finished with Suzy and was just doing her the favour of allowing her to stay in my house, so in theory I could do what I liked. I still couldn't admit the relationship to her though, and saw Eva through invented trips to my parents and weekend motorbike events that I needed to attend.

I was feeling an unbelievable pressure and, I think, actually beginning to lose it slightly. Some people are given to mental illness and some people are not. I'm in the 'not' camp, I think, but there comes a point where there's just so much information to deal with, so many decisions to make, that your brain just shuts down. It had a magnified version of the feeling you get when something goes wrong with your computer. You've switched it off and on again, you've done what it says in the manual, you've called the helpline, you've asked friends, but still it won't do what it's meant to do and it just sits there on your desk winking at you, saying 'You'll have to do better than that!' while you beat your head with the telephone receiver.

Then, at last, a light at the end of the tunnel. Suzy arranged a flat. She would go on a three-week holiday to Peru with friends and, when she came back, she would move in to her new place. I breathed easy and felt the weight on me lift as she told me the day she would fly out of my life and leave me to my chosen destiny – September 12, 2001.

On September 11, 2001, we had twenty-four hours left together and so we thought we'd go out for one last walk with the dog. I am a sucker for this sort of thing. A break's a break and I should have spent the day on my own. It was selfish really, I wanted to remain friends in order to feel that I'm not a bastard and to continue to enjoy her company. Beneath it all I did really care for Suzy. I just couldn't see us together for ever.

Suzy was upstairs, I was downstairs, ready to go out. Suzy was looking for something and I was bored so I flicked on the TV. Oprah Winfrey was on and I watched for a while.

'Is there anything on the news?' shouted Suzy.

I flicked over to see the World Trade Center on fire. A plane had hit it, said the TV. Then, as I was watching, a second plane went into it.

'I said is there anything on the news?' repeated Suzy, coming into the room.

'Yes,' I said, with my chin on the floorboards, 'there is.'

I felt it was a shattering event and I'm still not quite sure why. We've lived with terrorism in Britain for years, I grew up on tales of the Blitz and we'd seen the whole Balkan mess unfold right on our doorstep. We were used to slaughter. In the UK we had none of the feeling of violation that they did in the US, nor the idea that we were untouchable. I think it just came down to the peculiar horror of what was done to those people and the feeling 'It could have been me on that plane.'

Naturally the personal repercussions of the attack were not first in my mind as we saw the towers collapse. Only later in the day, when all flights were cancelled, did we realise: Suzy wasn't going to Peru. The end was deferred again and it seemed churlish to ask her to leave and stay on friends' floors when the world was facing such turmoil. I think it actually made me feel protective towards her. If the attacks had been launched a day later, then who knows what might have happened. I can't remember if Suzy had been flying through the States, but anyone who had ever been on an aircraft felt a bit of a chill in those months.

I went to see Eva three days later on the Friday. I'd been feeling under pressure before the attacks, but now I was starting to experience something very odd indeed. I'm sorry to say that it was solely focused on my own situation. I began to feel that I was destined to be with Suzy forever, that it was something actually against the natural order for me to finish with her and that, whatever I did, she would never go. I was not being thwarted by the wishes of a girl but by history. This is the biggest lie ever told about love – I have no choice. Almost always, you do.

Also, this pressure had told on me and Eva. She was going through the first weeks of pregnancy and had experienced quite a personality change. She was tired all the time, irritable and simply no fun at all. This wouldn't have mattered if our relationship had been stable, but it was under enormous strain.

Eva had been a fantasy, a retreat from a difficult relationship that I simply didn't have the balls to end. Now the reality of the situation began to assert itself. I was going into a life partnership with a woman I only half knew. It had been over a decade and two children since those mad days in Eva's room and we were different people. I knew I really liked her, but was she revealing her true self to me since she'd been pregnant? Would the girl I'd known ever return? The answer is 'Yes' but it was difficult to see right then.

Just as Suzy's mannerisms had come to irritate me, now little gestures of Eva's did the same. Rubbing the inside of her wrists while watching TV, for instance. Twisting her hair in thought. I came to the conclusion that I was going nuts, developing some obsessive disorder under stress.

On top of this, even though I liked her kids, they weren't my kids. The only thing that makes children tolerable is love, you can't put up with the sheer intensity of a family relationship without it.

Still, that didn't matter. I was in, for better or for worse, because Eva was carrying my child. That, I thought, would see us through, that would lead us to where we needed to go. Her body would return to normal, her mood would improve and, through my kid, I would love her kids.

We went for the scan at the hospital.

'Well, there's nothing there,' said the ultrasound woman, in a tone that strongly implied we'd been wasting her time and that it was in some way our fault.

'I don't understand,' said Eva, 'I am pregnant, I feel pregnant.'

'Nah,' said the woman, 'it ain't developed. You'll have to have a D&C. Sorry, go to the desk and they'll book you in.'

We did get to talk to a counsellor, but neither Eva nor I are counsellor people. We said we'd be fine and left to go to drink at the pub, coincidentally where I'd picked up that accountant at the conference years before. It added to the bizarre hungover feeling that had affected me for days.

I can't remember what was said, I felt utterly numb. It wasn't that I wouldn't become a father – to be honest I had the attitude that it would be nice if it happened, but I wasn't going to weep if it didn't. It was as if my last shot at getting away from Suzy had completely failed. I felt destiny fall upon me. This was fate.

I've said before that I've relied on my subconscious to fish me out of horrible situations. It was as if my subconscious was throwing in the towel. It had said: 'You didn't have the guts to finish with Suzy on your own, you didn't even have the courage to tell her you were seeing someone else. Well, I made it as difficult as I could for you to stay with her, but now I've played my top trump and it hasn't worked. You're on your own with your cowardice.'

I went back to Eva's house. We picked up the kids from school. Then I said I had to get away and clear my head. What did *she* need? I didn't bother to think.

I got on my motorbike and rode away. She and the kids waved me off from the door of the cottage as I went. I knew in my heart it was the last time I would see them.

I called Suzy on my way back. I said I was sorry and I'd like her to stay. I'd made a mistake. I can't remember if I said I loved her or not. It seems unlikely that she would have reconsidered if I hadn't, but I truly can't recall. It was as if someone else was speaking the words.

I absolutely abandoned Eva. It wasn't that I forgot her or declined to call, it was as if a mental block had come down and she had ceased to exist in my life. After about seven weeks of not contacting her I got a letter correctly accusing me of being selfish and vile. I phoned her immediately.

'Don't worry,' she said, 'just venting some spleen. I can see it from your point of view.'

Could she? I couldn't. The thing that I'd missed about Eva, and the thing that had made me love her, was that she was impossible to abandon. She was one of those people who had sorted out her life on her own terms, on her own. She wasn't expecting me to join her as a partner, nor to move to the country. I had developed a fantasy where I had moved in, learned to ride a horse, taken the family on long walks by the river, without asking her what she wanted.

Despite the fact she'd thought she was having my kid, she had no expectation that I'd join her. We had a laugh together, I was to be the father of her baby. Beyond that, the future was up for grabs and she was just as prepared to bring up the child without me as with me. Again, I'd overestimated my importance, like a typical man.

I decided to commit to Suzy and we sold the house in London to move down to Brighton. I wanted a break with my previous life. I was psychologically incapable of finishing with Suzy so moving house seemed the best bet.

Things were no better between us there than they had been in London.

Then I got a letter.

'You've written a book!' it said, 'Good for you!'

Anna, the beautiful, frighteningly clever internationally educated girl I'd had such a crush on at university had written to me. We met up a few times and I was smitten all over again. The contrast was stark between someone who spoke of Henry Kissinger and said 'If I got the opportunity I would kill him without a thought,' and Suzy, who – as much to annoy me as anything – would never admit to having an opinion on anything other than *Big Brother*. Anna had actually done the film career, the award-winning documentaries and the invitations to international festivals and turned her back on it. It was a waste of time, she said, and had no political impact.

With anyone else you would have thought that something odd had happened, but Anna had given up the life that Ella aspired to on principle. It was perhaps because of her principles – and her brains – that she'd been able to achieve it in the first place. When I met her she was deciding what she wanted to do and was working as a temp for a while, 'to take stock'. I have never taken stock in my life and fell for her all over again.

Anna was also one of those rare people who become better looking with age. She'd lost her puppy fat and evolved a sophisticated, elegant bohemian style that you associate with certain Parisian women. Most of the handsome devils and casual beauties of my university years were looking pretty shabby by then, myself included, but not her.

What happened next remains a mystery to me. We got on well on our dates, although I did occasionally feel like a special needs pupil falling in love with his teacher, such was the disparity in IQ. We came back to my house after an evening out in Brighton where we met her brother. She said he'd really liked me and that was important to her. We started kissing passionately in my hall. I asked her to stay, but she said she had to drive back to London: I had a girlfriend and she didn't want to enter a messy relationship. I said I'd split up with Suzy as soon as she was back – she was on a girls' weekend in Barcelona. Anna said I should think carefully, but that she felt strongly for me and always had done. We kissed once more and I felt that there may just, just, be hope for me.

I finished with Suzy three days later. She had a conference in London and I suspected she'd just sabotage it by not turning up if I gave her the news before she went.

She wept and said she thought we were just back on track and said she was convinced it was another woman. I told her it wasn't.

Then she looked at my email – the password wasn't difficult to guess if you know me – and found some communications between me and Anna in which we said we should meet up with each other soon.

Even then I couldn't tell her I had fallen for someone else. I said she was just a friend and I'd been discussing the situation with her.

Suzy fled to London on the Saturday, looking as if she might dissolve herself in tears. At five she called me. He friends were having a night in, she was spoiling it for them. Could she just come down one last time? We could go out, go mad on the town like we used to and just say goodbye properly.

I made one of the best decisions of my life and certainly the best decision I'd ever made for her. I said 'Yes'.

She came back down and was in a buoyant mood. She'd clearly decided there was nothing to be gained from moping and was back to something resembling her old self, before her headaches, before me, before the silence touched her.

We went out on the town and I drank a serious amount, even for me. We finished up at a casino. The year before Suzy and I had been to Vegas and, despite being fleeced, had really enjoyed it. I'd learned to play blackjack properly to the extent that I could make £100 last for five hours or so and occasionally make a few quid. However, I was actually drunk-ish as I sat at the table, not swaying but aware that – after several bottles of champagne, a bath of Guinness and some whisky – I'd reached my limit. I drank weak lager and tried to focus on the cards.

Suzy was less drunk and in an ebullient, barbarians-at-the-gate sort of mood. Through a haze of spades, hearts, clubs and diamonds I perceived a lanky-looking bloke sitting next to her.

'Are you with anyone?' he said to Suzy.

'No,' she said. Well, technically she wasn't; I'd finished with her earlier in the day. There was some sort of scene, because form dictates you can't allow another chap to do that sort of thing, even if you actually want him to. It all calmed down, but, when we left, she nipped back 'to the loo' and got his number. Two years later she married him and was back to the happy-go-lucky, fun girl I'd first met. She was free of me.

After nearly two years of trying to give Suzy away, I'd lost her by accident.

30   OLD, FREE AND SINGLE

Anna, who was originally keen to see me, suddenly went cold and said in a phone call that we should not get together until I was over Suzy. This was a great pain to me, but I went with it. It would be a year before we would meet – for a quick meal in Battersea. We never mentioned what had gone on and I never saw her again. I still haven't a clue why that one finished.

I put down the phone to Anna and found that I immediately wanted Suzy back. This time, though, for once in my life, I recognised the feeling for what it was – fear of the dark, not just desire for Suzy.

I was finally on my own and tried to take the opportunity to breathe in for a bit. Even I couldn't bear to go out hunting for another girl so quickly. Instead I tried to develop a gambling habit, maybe feeling my portfolio of vices was naggingly incomplete. I failed. One evening I sat in a tiny, grimy, smoke-stained casino at the blackjack table and immediately hit an awful run of cards that set me back £150. I stumped up another £50 and spent the next seven hours winning it all back. I emerged into the morning light precisely £5, two really weak warm lagers, a terrible cheese sandwich and a chest infection to the good. I'd have been better employed working in McDonalds – or writing, I could have done that. And that was a good night.

Really I think my brief gambling habit was just a way of trying to put off the inevitable – the beginning of a trawl for another girl. I was deeply tired of the chase, but I knew nothing else. It was my default mode, just what I did. Trying to fight it made as much sense as a dog not wanting to be a dog. My desires were unimportant. Looking for a girl had been my function in life for twenty-five years. I wasn't suddenly going to develop an interest in staying in watching TV.

Eventually I discovered internet dating, where you find your life so depressing that you think 'I know what would cheer me up! I'll turn myself into a commodity!'

My image of these dates isn't of chatting to strangers in unfamiliar bars, but of the dead air of the cavernous platform at Farringdon station at 11.25, just one underpaid Pole in the cappuccino stall for company, as I waited for the train back to Brighton. I'd met some girl from the internet and we'd immediately realised we weren't for each other. An hour, maybe two or three, of chat later, looking through the compartments of each others' personalities for a match with increasing desperation, like someone who is sure they have packed their passport somewhere in their bag but can't find it, we separated and I went to catch the Thameslink back. After that, I attended two speed dates – both at Turnmills nightclub in Farringdon – and was back on the station at midnight again.

I saw myself on the same platform at fifty and at sixty, maybe seventy. Where would it stop? How many more times would I raise my hopes? I needed to give up, but I just couldn't.

I joined the Sussex Arts Club in Brighton, thinking that it would give me access to a new group of friends who might be impressed that I was a writer and introduce me to some interesting women. On the first night, a Thursday, I sat with my friend Mike at 9.30 in the long bar. There was one other person in it and he, annoyingly, was a man.

'Never mind,' I said, 'someone else will turn up in a minute.'

Ten came and went. Finally, at about ten past ten I saw a shape move across the glass at the front of the building.

'Here we go!' I said, anticipating a stampede of modern-day Whistlers and Wildes pursued by Tallulah Bankhead and Sarah Bernhardt.

A man poked his head around the door.

'Taxi for Nigel!' he said.

The bar's only other occupant got up and left. The trove of impressionable arty French girls I'd expected was going to be delayed by some time, it seemed.

I went to one speed dating event to discover everyone was under twenty-five. I was cheered to gain four ticks from women who wanted to see me again, but less cheered when I saw who they were. Then I went with my lodger Sarah to a small event in Brighton. She very charmingly refused to talk to anyone because she didn't fancy them and then bawled out the organiser in front of the assembled men for charging so much and providing such mingers. She was an interesting girl.

'What are you looking for in a man?' I said.

'Tall, trendy, *must* be trendy, goodlooking, probably a DJ or club promoter, probably wears . . .' She mentioned some trainers I've never heard of.

'How about his personality?' I said.

'Oh, I don't give a shit about that,' she said, like I was nuts.

At this event I saw one bright hope. There was a stop-a-clock-gorgeous Asian girl about five women away from me at the start. I had already anticipated and discounted the mail-order-bride jokes. I would marry her and then people could joke all they liked. I'd be the one with her on my arm.

I later found out she was from Thailand. She looked as if she could have been on a tourist brochure to advertise the place. I looked at the competition – flabby men in open-necked shirts and chinos, the financial adviser at leisure look. One was even in jeans and a suit jacket. I wasn't going to lose to Top Gear lookalikes. There was no competition. I was in if I played my cards right.

I went through a couple of interesting but not for me girls and finally got to this flower of the east.

'Hi, I'm Mark,' I said, trying not to feel like a sex tourist. She was only about twenty, I saw when she got close, and utterly beautiful. She smiled at me and nodded. She liked me, I could tell.

'What's your name?' I said.

She smiled and nodded again.

There was an uncomfortable pause.

'You are?' I said.

'English. No,' she said.

'Right,' I said, suddenly feeling as if our five-minute slot might seem a very long time, never mind the lifetime I had planned. Somehow, and I've no idea how, I got her nationality out of her. She spoke two words of English, both of which she'd used up as soon as she met me.

There were evenings, though, of wading through unsuitables, giving and receiving our stories for examination and judgement and then rejecting each other. I couldn't bear it, to look upon a room of eager dates and see no one I fancied, or to see someone I fancied but who, by their dress, was just culturally entirely different to me – too neat, too career-ie, too not me. This sounds snobbish, but at least I finally knew what I was looking for.

Here then, is my perfect woman. After all the years, I knew what I liked. This is it. She would be between 5′ 3″ and

5′ 5″, be curvy without being fat, slim without being thin. Hair colour doesn't matter at all. She would be very intelligent, sexy and fun and stable enough to take me for what I am. She must be independent and neither clingy nor aloof. She must not be tactile. That is, holding hands in public is fine, kissing or stroking with people around isn't. Without wishing to go personal ad on the whole thing, she must also enjoy theatre, books, film and, though it pains me to say it, walks in the country. She must be a very good conversationalist and, try to keep your dinner down, just a li'l bit crazy. I wouldn't really care what job she did, she could work at Tesco's or live off daddy's money. It's just that culturally we'd need to click. I was beyond the stage of expecting her to like all my favourite bands and books, but we'd need to be on the same page when it came to what we liked to do and to talk about. It's just that I've found the sportswear girls with the over-tight hair don't like to go to the theatre that often and the trust fund girls don't want to meet your mates in old men's pubs.

I drew up an ad for Udate one day, listing my likes and dislikes, and was about to post it on the internet when I got a call out of the blue.

'Hi, Mark, it's Claire here, I'm going to be in Brighton for the day on Tuesday and I require you to take me to lunch.'

Who was it? Oh that Claire, from Business Solutions. She'd remained friends with me and Suzy, but I hadn't seen her for a couple of years.

'Other friends out?' I said. 'Am I third on the list?'

'Fourth. All the others are at work during the day.'

'Fine. Where?'

'That Havana restaurant's nice,' she said, 'oh and I think you should pay, it seems apt.'

'Right, Al Fresco's it is.'

'Is that as nice as Havana's?'

'It's a lot nicer for the person paying,' I said, 'and it's got a sea view.'

'I approve of the sea,' she said, 'you may take me there.'

Claire was a notorious eccentric, but beyond that I couldn't really remember that much about her. I knew tales of her forgetting that she'd come into London in her car, going home to Cambridge and then suddenly remembering it was back in town, getting a taxi back to London and then somehow threatening legal action on the pound that – absolutely incredibly – made them give it up free, parking up for a celebratory drink and then having to get a hotel for the night, at which point the car was towed again.

I could remember that she was very pretty, about 5' 4", curvy without being fat, slim without being thin. She was blonde, intelligent, sexy, fun and posh. Also she was very independent, enjoyed theatre, books, film and walks in the country. She was a very good conversationalist and quite a lot crazy. We often used to discuss film and theatre when we were at work and she had similar, but not the same, tastes as me. At the extremes, I liked *The Day Today* and she liked *The Vicar of Dibley* – because, she says, it's so realistic (you figure) – but there was a lot of ground in the middle we shared. Culturally, we were on the same page.

I was a bit irritated by her call, though. While she was on the phone – we talked for a couple of hours by mistake – the profile I was about to post on the internet expired, meaning I'd have to do the whole thing again. God does occasionally send me messages, though not of the 'kill them all' variety, and this, it turns out, was one.

Claire came down. Originally she'd planned to stay with Suzy, but Suzy had a bit of a fit when she learned Claire was planning to lunch with me. She said she didn't want to see her. Suzy had continued her slight obsession with me, even though she was by now seeing her future husband. I don't mean that she wanted me back, but that she was over-interested in what I was up to and still thought she had a hand in my destiny. Maybe I wasn't completely over her, either, even though I'd spent the best part of two years trying to get her to leave. We went for a drink and she confessed that she'd slept with someone on a business trip to New York. At the London conference when I'd been seeing Anna, she'd been sleeping with an American who was visiting for a week. It was, she said, an act of revenge for being ignored.

'That's a relief,' I said, 'because it means I can tell you about Eva.'

I did and she was amazed.

'Whatever I try to do to you, you can always trump it, can't you?' she said.

Strangely I was furious that she'd slept with someone else, more out of a sense of wounded pride than anything. I spent several nights composing long speeches in my head where I would call him and tell him to fucking watch himself, that I was coming to New York and that, if he had any sense, he'd get himself a gun pronto. Luckily this stupidity faded, as did my anger. How could I complain? And yet I did.

I didn't see what the fuss was about with Claire, though. She didn't fancy me and I knew that because . . . Actually, how did I know?

We went to Al Fresco at lunch and the smart Havana in the evening, a modern American-style place where you might expect to see Edward Hopper sketching in the corner. I discussed my relationship with Ella. We'd been back in contact and had mulled over getting back together again. We'd slept together and tentatively moved towards making a go of it. Should we have kids? It looked like the game of musical chairs that was our love lives was coming to a close and we were the only ones left in the ring. I bent Claire's ear on the theme.

This was my prelude to asking her if she wanted to go to bed with me that evening. She, unsurprisingly, rejected me, saying that wasn't what she'd come down for. It was a pity. I knew I really liked her, but she also knew too much about me. My past had caught up with me, I thought, and would rob me of someone who might, just might, be the one for me. When you've looked for the one for so long, though, you're used to the idea that you're going to be disappointed.

There was always Ella. Maybe that would work out in the end after all.

31   ONE LAST GO

Ella and I lasted two dates. The first one was fantastic. We went for dinner, slept with each other and spent the next day strolling in the sunshine on Parliament Hill, London laid out before us like a bright future. On the next date, we went to see a lecture on the South Bank, a comedy thing with Christopher Guest out of *This Is Spinal Tap*. In the audience was Matt Lucas, then only famous as Vic Reeves's drummer. I couldn't place his name or who he was when he asked a question. Suddenly it came to me.

'That's Matt Lucas,' I said, 'the baby off Vic Reeves.'

'I know who it is!' hissed Ella, 'for God's sake, I know who it is.'

I thought I was drawing her attention to someone of interest. In fact, to Ella's ears, I was telling her she was still a naïve little Kettering girl who couldn't possibly recognise the hip and trendy of the capital without them being pointed out to her.

I hit the roof because I hate being misunderstood and we just about managed a truce after lunch in the South Bank complex. Then we walked along the river. It was a glorious summer day, the sunlight playing on the water and St Paul's rising above us magnificent and bright, my very image of a perfect afternoon. That's when she finally lost it with me.

'You're not even looking at me when you speak!' she said.

'No,' I said, 'I'm looking at Wren's masterpiece, one of the great sights of Christendom on a rare and clear day on the Empire's river in the greatest city on earth. I know what you look like.'

We argued terribly all the way back home and then dived into our trenches. She started work when she got in, tapping away at her computer and smoking as if it was going to be banned at any minute. I drank a quick twelve-pack in my boxer shorts watching the football. Then we had a proper row to the recipe we'd devised together all those years ago, the one where you end up rowing about the row itself, the 'you said, no you said' row that is as tiring as it is interminable. We slept in separate beds, both feeling utterly misunderstood, hard done by, exhausted and friendless. In the morning we awoke and called it quits, had breakfast and fell to our separate lives.

We both wanted to move on to the next stage, kids – a house in the country, nights in helping with homework rather than nights out up west – but, though we were desperate, we weren't yet abject. We loved each other and, finally, left each other.

I was beginning to feel old. I was thirty-nine, which feels like a sneaky forty, a forty that won't own up. That is old for a man, despite what the style pages would have you believe. Newspapers and magazines are full of articles about the appeal of the mature male. Do you know why? Newspapers and magazines are edited and published by mature males. Those pieces come out normally just before the fashion editor has her pay review. Hollywood actors can be appealing well beyond forty? Why? Because the old sods who own the studios want to portray them like that. Does anyone really think that Marlon Brando was more attractive at fifty than he was at twenty-two? The fat Elvis of Vegas rather than the svelte boy of *Jailhouse Rock*, anyone?

I began internet dating in earnest. I had anticipated I'd be meeting a parade of sag-eyed losers who would be grimly growling into their spritzers, and sucking on their Virginia Slims while their lipstick rode up their wrinkles. I'd have to sit listening to them moaning about what their ex-husbands did to them. It didn't particularly put me off, I quite like women like that.

What I got I couldn't believe. Woman after woman after woman – 23, 27, 23, 26, 22, and, in one case a 20-year-old – who were so goodlooking I nearly left the bar the second they walked in. I hadn't a chance, I thought. And yet I had.

How a girl like Daisy had to advertise on the net to get a date I shall never know until my dying day. She was a mature student, 25, studying the MA in Utter Crap at Sussex University. Something about post structural elements of . . . oh, I lost interest. The morning that she woke up in my bed she took a photo of herself on my phone. I showed it to a friend.

'My God!' she said, 'she's a Persian princess.' She really did look like it.

We'd exchanged emails through a dating site and then met in a bar near my house. As soon as she walked in I thought 'No hope, Fatso, buy her a drink, stop wasting her time and go home.'

We had two drinks and she said she'd like to see where I lived. Ten seconds after we came through the front door she was down to her yellow fishnet tights in the middle of the rug. I know this is the sort of story normally seen in a certain kind of men's publication, normally beginning with the words 'None of your readers will believe this but . . .' It's true though, and it happened to me.

She said she wasn't looking for a boyfriend, but hadn't had sex in a year. There, right there, young men is your ruin – the case against you spelled out in dusky skin, perfect breasts, long dark straight hair, and those dark eyes with the petulant 'I want it' expression. Could not one of you bring yourselves to talk to this girl and give her what she was clearly looking for? Some of you must, or what hope the human race?

Men didn't approach her, she said. They should have been throwing themselves from the balconies. I came to the conclusion there was something wrong with modern manhood. Still, that suited me fine.

We slept together and she said she'd like to get to know me, but didn't want to go out with me because she didn't fancy me. She was quite firm about that.

'You've got a funny way of showing it,' I said.

'I suppose so,' she said, putting her hand back inside by boxers.

Actually, things didn't go that well on our first time together, or at least there were bumps in the road.

'Talk dirty to me,' she said.

My experience of this had been formed by Francesca and honed on women such as Cornish Rita, who used to like to shout 'I'll be your whore, I'm such a fucking slut,' at the moment of bliss.

Accordingly I set off on the sort of thing these girls seemed to like: plenty of rude words, instructions of what to do, explicit requests . . .

That sort of thing is of obvious appeal to vicars' daughters and they respond with the conspicuous pleasure their mothers do when judging the Handsome Hound competition at the local fête.

As I launched into the spiel, however, Daisy's eyes began to widen. I took this for a good sign before she started to shake her head and said 'That's disgusting! And I'm not a tart! I haven't done this for a year.'

'Sorry,' I said, 'I didn't literally mean you were a tart, it was just a figure of speech, you were only a tart for the purposes of this fuck, a tart of convenience, so to speak.'

'My God, I've never heard anything like it.'

'Sorry, I was just testing boundaries.'

'You mean you had further to go? My God, I thought you were just going to say something nice about my tits.'

'Well, I'd quite like to come on them,' I said, by way of an olive branch.

'That's better,' she said, 'carry on like that – but don't touch my tits, it's a myth women like that.'

Still, I don't think she did really fancy me, though I thought she looked fantastic.

Every time we went out it was a race to get three glasses of wine into her before she went home. At three glasses of wine she became very horny and took me back with her. It was quite exciting because every time was like a first date, and I'd always wonder if the evening would finish the way I wanted it to. Eventually she lined someone else up, and I made a complete idiot of myself after we came back to her flat and she said it was definitely over between us. We'd had a couple of ales and I started banging on her door shouting 'I'll make you fancy me, I'll lose weight, I'll go to the gym, I'll change my T-shirt twice a week, you wait and see.' I didn't really see much of her after that.

I wasn't just chasing Daisy for sex, though. I really wanted a permanent girlfriend. I found her a little bit irritating and naïve but, by that stage, I thought irritating and naïve were worth putting up with if I was ever to find a life partner. She was beautiful, generally good company – especially when she had a couple of drinks and relaxed – and I thought we might have managed to make a go of a relationship.

Then there was Carla, a very pretty tall girl with short blonde hair and a spectacular body. I met her at a club. The second I saw her I approached her. There was a scrum of men of her age beside her, propping up the bar talking about their hairstyles. It made me weep and laugh all at the same time. She was lovely, really good fun, kind and affectionate. I really liked sleeping with her. She had the very sexy habit of coming in and taking off all her clothes. We'd sit drinking wine and watching a film, even having dinner on one occasion with her completely naked and me fully clothed. I remember taking her from behind as she played the piano once, which I think we both enjoyed very much. Apparently the well-built, handsome 23-year-old man at the bar who she was looking at before I fell upon her as the wolf upon the fold had something better to do than that. I'd love to know what it was. Buying hair gel, probably or standing in front of a mirror wearing a hood and convincing himself he looked tough. I thought she was too nice for me, though, not enough bite to her. I was wasting her time by going out with her so I stopped seeing her.

Then I slept with Milly, a journalist and author who had been sent to interview me a few years before. She was in town and asked if I wanted to meet up. We'd got on well the first time we met, and it helped that she was a goodlooking blonde with a hint of the Kate Mosses to her. I met her at lunchtime and was due to meet Ella for a drink in the evening. One thing led to another and we were still together when Ella turned up. Ella and I weren't going out with each other, but she was still pretty miffed to find another woman with me. When Milly went out for a second, Ella gave me an ultimatum – come to dinner with her or she was going. She went. At eleven, after ten hours of drinking, I called Ella to ask if it was OK if Milly and I crashed at her house. She told me to fuck off and get a room, which we did.

We had an evening of spectacular sex – it turned out that

she had come to lunch wearing the full stockings and suspenders kit, but in 1940s light brown rather than an obvious black or white. We had to wait until 6 a.m. when a grocery store opened to get any condoms, and so we had six hours of enforced but very enjoyable foreplay. I found her very sexy but she was going out with an older man and lived miles away.

The next time I saw her was at a literary knees up. She'd invited me there and I made the mistake of assuming she would immediately want to sleep with me again. As soon as I saw her, before the canapés had even finished, I asked her if she wanted to come upstairs with me. She said 'no'. I think my keenness put her off and I was left alone in the expensive hotel room I'd booked solely for the purpose of sharing it with her. It was a low point. I'd consoled myself that, though I couldn't find love, I was living the sort of life that would be envied by many men. Lying on the overpriced bed of the luxury hotel, coked up so I couldn't go to sleep but with absolutely nothing to do, I couldn't think of many people who would envy me.

I had a fling with Charley, a small, intensely pretty, curvy, dark-haired girl I met through a friend. She was great fun in and out of bed with a real verve for life. Again, I didn't want to go out with her long term, so I did her the favour of finishing with her and not just keeping her hanging around until Miss Right turned up. She was a lovely girl who anyone should have wanted to go out with, but I didn't. I'd managed to blend a desperation to settle down with a new fussiness. It wasn't a combination that looked like yielding good results any time soon.

There were stranger girls who were best avoided.

There was Tracey, who looked like Inga but was a lot odder. She was twenty-one, a secretary at an architect's practice, and went out on one date with me during which she told me a strange story about being abducted by architects. It might have been true, but it just didn't sound it. At about 8.30 she asked to go back to my house, where we had some very brief and functional sex. Then, at nine, she said she had to be somewhere else. It was so weird that I almost thought she was going to ask me to pay her.

Jezebel, which was sort of the name the next girl gave herself, was funny and interesting when we talked through the dating site. She was a good writer too – her emails were stylish and funny – and I was hopeful approaching the date. I met her in London and she announced she was a witch, which I thought rather dull. She had a sort of unquestioning acceptance of all things alternative – tattoos, piercings, modern art, magic, alternative medicine. I argued with her a bit about that and had the strange feeling she was trying to wind me up.

Never mind, we went back to my friends' house where I was staying – they'd said I could bring someone back if I got lucky – and she started making the most enormous row. 'Stop,' I said. 'You'll wake the kids.' 'Make me,' she said. 'Oh God, you're not a dull little sub are you?' I said. 'Fuck off!' she shouted.

Still, I went up and made a half-hearted attempt at sexual domination. It was OK, I suppose. I seemed destined to be pursued by the S&M crew and, while I wasn't going to join them, I didn't mind beating them. If there was nothing else to do. Jezebel was quite attractive and I couldn't see why she was single. Surely she could get some spotty warehouseman to tell her she'd been a naughty girl and stomp about in crap studded leather boots while she ate out of a dog bowl. What's wrong with men today?

32 IN THE FAMILY'S WAY

The biggest indictment against modern men was undoubtedly Tanya. Tanya was a Bosnian girl of about 5′ 10″, willowy slim and really, really beautiful. When a girl has been told she looks like a Bond girl so many times that she has a joke ready for you when you do so, then I think you can say she is a sort.

I have said that my biker girlfriend Debbie was intensely pretty, that beauty does not belong to teenagers, that Debbie had the sort of face that is rendered by popular and sentimental artists. Tanya was not pretty, she was beautiful. She had the sort of face that inspires the Whistlers and the Beardsleys.

I have a print of John Singer Sargent's *Madame X* on my wall. Every time Charlie came to my house he launched into the same diatribe about how he couldn't believe Tanya was so vain as to have herself photographed in that mannered profile. I reminded him every time that it's a hundred-year-old painting, but we got the same rubbish on each visit.

Now, I can see why men wouldn't approach a girl like that. She's intimidating, she's probably got someone and he's probably called Dmitri, is worth a fortune in oil and has enemies who have a strange habit of turning up dead.

So, there is an excuse. However, when she is sitting on her own at a table *in the middle of a singles' ball*, then it is now or never boys. It's a once in a lifetime experience, Eminem is playing in the background telling you it's ready to blow, whoa, and you know that this is a unique opportunity, it ain't coming back. What's the worst that can happen? She can say 'Get away from me you filthy pig, I wouldn't look at you if you were the last man alive,' and then start throwing chairs at you, and one might strike you on the head, and a photo of you being carried to the ambulance might appear in the local paper under the title 'Sex Pest Vanquished'. It's not that bad is it? Worse things happen at sea.

I saw her from about thirty yards away and there was a streak of fire across the dancefloor behind me by the time I got to her.

'Hello,' I said.

'Hello,' she said and smiled.

I looked around the table and under it and then up to the ceiling. I tapped at the table and then got up and examined the chair. I don't normally do this sort of thing, but the idea had come into my head so I thought I might as well use it. In fact, I had never used a chat-up line before as I regard them as the province of unholy cheese merchants, but for some reason one popped out of me.

'What are you doing?' she said.

'I'm looking for booby traps. The only reason I can imagine a girl like you is sitting on her own in a place like this is if a big weight's going to fall on whoever sits next to her. I was half expecting to be swept up into the rafters by a lasso. You're not in cahoots with a Wily Coyote with a big load of dynamite are you?'

She laughed. I didn't know at the time, but Tanya was an absolute sucker for being told how goodlooking she was. It was easy to do, she was very goodlooking.

'That's a new one,' she said.

'You're right, I just made it up for you.'

This corn went down very well. I had long learned from my mistake with an Argentinian girl I tried to chat up on holiday once. She was gorgeous, blonde with golden skin and sky-blue eyes, like one of those women who rather improbably falls in love with Captain Kirk in episodes of *Star Trek* with titles like 'In Arcadia Also'. I went about ingratiating myself in the best way an English boy knows how – by being relentlessly sarcastic to her. After listening to my gob for about an hour she wailed in a thick accent 'Why are you tormenting me? Is it the Malvinas?'

No girl likes a smarm bucket, but it shows a bit of self-confidence and old-fashioned charm to tell her she's attractive. Plus it clarifies your intentions. You're not looking for a friend.

Then another drop-dead-gorgeous girl turned up. It was Tanya's sister. And still around us was a thirty-foot exclusion zone for men. If I'd been there with the Falls Road boys I used to hang around with in Camden, I'd have been beating them away with an axe. It would have been like one of those nineteenth-century paintings *Horatius on the Bridge*, one man's bloody sword arm raised against the barbarian hordes. Have you seen *The Vikings* with Kirk Douglas when the bloke jumps into the pit of wolves? That would have been the scene. There, though, I had the girls to myself. I was in loserville and I had to get out before I got stuck there.

Across the dancefloor my friend Jenny, who I'd gone in with, was being chatted up by an advertising bloke. His opener? 'The band are shit aren't they? The food's bollocks as well. And this champagne's like piss.' Ooh, Cary Grant must have been rolling in his grave.

Tanya's sister turned out to be married, she was just keeping her company there. That cleared up some confusion, at least. Amelia had a more idiosyncratic look to her, dark and sparkly, but equally goodlooking. I would have had difficulty choosing which one to make a play for, but luckily the decision was made for me. Otherwise I could have split my attention and ended up with neither.

I immediately saw that these were rather old-fashioned girls and that Tanya needed to be approached in the old-fashioned way. Accordingly, I was ultra polite and ultra courteous and wouldn't allow either of them to fetch a drink for the entire evening.

When I was at the bar a man approached me. He had his shirt tucked into his trousers in that middle-aged way that made his hips look too wide, as if he'd have difficulty in turning.

'Do you need any help with those two girls?' he said. 'It might be easier for you if I came over and took one off your hands. Could you introduce me?'

Again, I had to think of an Irish chap I'd known in Camden called Paul Murphy. You would very likely have found yourself superglued to the bar when you tried to return with the drinks, only to see him strolling towards the girls with a bottle of bubbly as you struggled to free yourself. There would be no 'Could you introduce me?' In fact, had I seen Murphy there, I would have been tempted to throw a blanket over Tanya's head and to have tried to smuggle her out.

As it was, I just growled at the man in a way that actually made him flinch. I meant it. In my mind, I was a lion and he a low, scavenging jackal.

Tanya was very interesting. She told me all about how she'd been marooned in the UK by the Balkans war, how her family had spent the whole of the conflict trapped in Sarajevo, and how she'd worked to get a good job over here to send money back to them. It was an insight into another world that left me feeling as if I knew nothing of life at all. She'd faced more challenges by the end of her teens than I had in my entire life, and she'd come through them remarkably well.

One girl – remarkably only one – I'd been out with had complained that I never asked her anything about herself. I'd thought this was because she never said anything interesting. Tanya, however, was not the sort who needed an invitation to take the lead in a conversation. She didn't push herself forward, but neither did she want to be coaxed out. She had an absolute expectation that she would be heard and that she had valuable things to say. I instinctively found myself more in the role of listener than talker.

I didn't ask Tanya for her number at the end of the evening, I gave her mine. I thought it was less intrusive and, besides, I couldn't face dialling to find I'd been put through to the Sunshine Retirement Home for Discarded Relatives.

She called halfway through New Year's Eve and I asked her to come over to a party I was having. She said she wouldn't, but she'd see me the next week. In a way this turned out very well. Charlie was being chatted up by an attractive girl, Georgina, who'd come with some mutual friends. She'd spent the early part of the evening talking to me and I thought I detected some interest. As soon as he appeared though, she said something about his 'cat-like grace', and left me at the buffet like a browsing hippo. Charlie has a deep inability to take any sort of decision, however. He was at the tail end of another relationship at the time and couldn't make up his mind whether he should jump ship. At the end of the evening – five in the morning – I went round to check if everyone had bedding.

'Well, I'm sleeping on the sofa,' said Charlie.

'Where am I sleeping?' said Georgina.

Charlie, in a move only he could make, shrugged his

shoulders. This was meant to be an alluring little come on but to her it looked like 'I couldn't care less.'

She frowned a deep frown and I said she could share half my bed, if she liked. Charlie didn't say anything because he decided he would try to stay loyal to his girlfriend. Georgina lay on the other half of the bed for around five seconds before I put my arm across her, and then we ran through the full programme of *The Lovers' Guide*, including the bits that are illegal to show in England, in a twelve-hour session that finished with her in hospital in a diabetic coma. She was OK in the end, thank God. I said I'd go in to see her the next day and her friends all said 'It must be love.' I think this is why I am quite dangerous to some women. To me it was a common courtesy, to the girls a sign that I was serious. As it was, she was discharged early so the issue faded.

Charlie later went out with her for four years, and we agreed that, if they did ever get married, I would have a very good best-man's speech beginning with the words 'I well remember when I first met the bride.'

Georgina and I did see each other a couple of times after that, but by then I was on the way with Tanya so I decided not to pursue things. It wasn't just that Tanya was such a beauty, though that definitely helped. She was very different from me – it was probably a greater cultural difference that she liked Rugby than that she was a southern European – but that was the appeal. I'd tried it with women of my own background – the band-mad pub girls and the rock-chicks and the working-class/lower-middle-class babes I'd had so much in common with – and it had failed to fly. I'd thought my ideal girl was a literate ladette and arty beer monster who I could take to long evenings in the pub and club with my friends.

Perhaps a girl who didn't necessarily expect to be my

friend, but seemed to want – I might have been wrong – an older kind of relationship based very much on mutual respect and courtesy, would be the one. One advantage was that she was very clear what she expected from the relationship: respect, admiration and I suppose eventually love. It was also interesting that she wasn't going to leap into bed with me, or even go much further than a peck on the cheek for the first few dates. This contrasted strongly with some English girls who, though aware their blood sugar is at dangerously low levels, are willing, if not keen, to let you fuck them into a coma within thirty seconds of meeting them. Not that I'm knocking that.

It did help too that rooms tended to go quiet when she came in. She didn't have the spectacle-bending sex appeal of some women, but had more the sort of beauty that would cause old men to start crying rather than spill their pints.

There are some rather dubious pleasures to be gained in going out with a beautiful woman, and the jealousy of other men is certainly one of them. We went to Sean's wedding together and met up with Terry Bate. He collared me alone at one moment.

'That girl's very good looking isn't she, Mark?' he said, his lip twitching. 'Yeah, you lucked out there, didn't you? Hmm. Who would have thought it?'

'Me,' I said.

Terry was happy with his wife but, as someone very concerned with face and status, he knew that there is no more face to be had than that deriving from arm candy. In some indefinable way I was saying I was better than him and I could see it tweaked his anger.

I really thought for a while that I might make a go of it with Tanya. The only thing I objected to was her occasional baby-talk habit, where she'd say something in a squeaky little voice. Virtually everyone I've known who does this is in fact hard as nails underneath, and she proved true to type.

I broached the subject of 'ickles' and 'ahhhs!', trying to explain that they make my blood run cold. Her expression suddenly darkened, like a Japanese warlord contemplating his foe.

'If you don't like it,' she said, 'there are ten more in the queue. I remind you again that I am more used to going out with very handsome men.'

But, as Leonard Cohen said, for me she would make an exception – while I played my cards right.

She did teach me some things about myself. I have a tendency to showboat and, when she forgot to get a paper from the shops and asked me to go back for it I said 'Ahh!' and mimed slapping her. She got her assessment bang on. 'You are trying to demonstrate to the people in this pub that you are the dominant partner in this relationship,' she said. 'It's the gesture of a bully disguised as good fun.'

I had to admit, she was right, although I'd never have seen it unless she'd pointed it out to me. She also had some observations on my friendships with other men.

'You and your friends seem to be in a permanent compe-tition to see who can say the funniest thing,' she said. Er, that'll be men, then. I had no idea what else conversation was meant to consist of.

Still, she seemed to like me well enough and I really liked her. She had a very funny habit, for one so goodlooking, of absolutely refusing to be photographed unless given time to put herself into a pose. So every snap I have of her, she is sitting bolt upright with a look of engaged intelligence on her face, rather like a Victorian portrait. She told me stories of her youth under communism and gave me a glimpse of another life, another world. Beyond this we just got on and

I felt comfortable in her company. There is an expression 'the ugly ones try harder'. I certainly did with her.

Everything seemed to be going well when I was invited on holiday with her, her sister and her brother-in-law. I thought they were all good fun, so I agreed. We would go to Dubrovnik for a week and then travel down to the Croatian coast to meet her brother, who she hadn't seen since before the conflict. I should not have gone for many reasons, mainly because I was the only non-family member. A recently acquired boyfriend has no place butting in on this sort of event.

The first week was like a dream. When we moved on from Dubrovnik, some Italian men we met on the boat to Split could have been a lesson to the UK wallflowers on what it takes to get the girl you want. Two of them, who pounced on the sisters in the ten minutes I was away at the bar with Tanya's brother-in-law, simply would not leave when we got back. Despite the flashing of a wedding ring, despite Tanya pretending to go to sleep, despite the presence of a sixteen-stone brute of a boyfriend, they kept at it all the way to Split. It was quite entertaining, really.

I knew it was going to be difficult from the first second I met her brother. He was welcoming and pleasant, but definitely had the air of a patriarch about him. The father of the family was dead and her brother emanated a strongly protective air towards his sisters. The look he gave me seemed to say 'Welcome, I'm pleased to meet you. I'm also very much watching you.' I can't blame him, it's a natural way to feel when the last time he saw the girls they were teenagers.

At the resort the family were more interested in seeing each other than eating in restaurants on the sea front, which was more my thing. So we spent most evenings with Tanya's sister-in-law cooking for us in a small apartment where her brother would attempt to smoke all the cigarettes available on mainland Europe in one evening. I think he must have been on about 120 a day.

It was nothing he did or said, but I was beginning to feel like something of a ponce. I would say I was a vegetarian. There would be no comment on the subject. No comment at all. Then he would suddenly say, out of the blue, 'It is the grenades that terrify me. If we were sitting here and one went off it would clear the whole street.'

'From just one hand grenade?' I'd say.

'Not hand grenade!' he'd say, as if I'd made an idiotic blunder, 'tank grenade. Hand grenade is like nothing. Tank grenade brings the terror.'

'Righty ho,' I'd say and then struggle to see where the conversation was going after that.

To be fair to him, he'd been through an unimaginable horror. For several years he'd only been able to use one side of his apartment during the day because if he went near the other one he risked sniper fire. Hunting parties of Serbs would come in at the weekend. They'd down tools in Belgrade or leave their offices and drive to Sarajevo to kill and to loot. I'd not realised how much war is about robbery before. The experience had made him ten times the man I am, but a lousy light conversationalist.

In my imagination, every time he looked at me he was thinking 'What is my sister doing with this portly prancing popinjay?'

Everything around him seemed to go wrong for me. It was like when you've made a bad impression with a teacher at school and then they always seem to find you in some compromising situation that looks like your fault but in reality was nothing to do with you.

The stress made me act like an idiot. I have never in my

life, before or since, quibbled a bill. Why I chose to do so with Tanya's family will be explained to me by that celestial bouncer St Peter, just before he tells me I'm not getting in. We went for a meal, the bill came and was split. Suddenly I said 'Hang on, I didn't have the fish.' The table went briefly silent and then burst into life as Tanya's brother and sister redid the bill to remove the offending fish from my tally. I immediately said I'd been joking, but the damage was done, there was no way I was ever going to be able to pay for the fish. It was like being in some hellish farce, struggling to make yourself understood but being thoroughly unable to do so.

I have my own ideas why I did this. First, beer. I perhaps thought it was funny. Second, stress. I was in the middle of a contract wrangle and was temporarily skint. Maybe that was at the back of my mind. Also, I was nervous. When nervous, shut up, that's my advice to me, but I don't follow that advice.

Finally, maybe it was my old subconscious butting in again. Tanya was never the girl for me: I'm just not an 'always on best behaviour' bloke. I'm not an old-fashioned gentleman, no matter how much I wish I was, as I think readers will by now agree. My back brain just said 'Once again I shoulder the responsibility of digging you out of the swamp into which you have placed yourself,' saw the bill, and went for it.

Tanya has high standards in a man and it was the beginning of the end. I went snorkelling, impacted wax in my ear, and had to go to the doctor's. Tanya's brother said nothing, but his expression seemed to say he had seen men put up with worse. He had. It still hurt, though.

Then I made a comment about his German football shirt.

'Don't wear that if you come to England,' I said, in a japey way.

Darkness gathered to his jowls.

'The Germans were great friends to us,' he said. 'Once some Serbs had an artillery piece up on the hill. For week after week they plagued us. Only the German tank commander had the balls to countermand his orders and intervene. Ten tanks turned to the hill and when they had fired, the hill was gone. It was the sweetest sound I heard in my life.'

'Wear it if you want to then,' I said.

I offered to pay for a night-time glass-bottomed boat ride, in a ham-fisted attempt to win back some of the respect I'd lost over the fish. We had been queuing for half an hour when a German teenager pushed in front of us. His family followed. No Englishman can bear a queue jumper, but I bit my tongue. When he sat in the boat he turned to us and said, in that utterly charming Prussian aristocrat's manner that we English have so admired for centuries, 'The boat is full. You must get the next one please.'

He had his feet over two seats and so I suggested he moved.

'The boat says it is for six, you are too many,' he said.

I explained to him, politely and firmly, without anger, that unless he wanted to get a very close look at the fish indeed he should move his fucking legs.

'Cool it!' said his dad. If there's one thing guaranteed to make the simmering tensions of a terrible holiday explode it's being told to 'cool it' in a mittel-European/American accent.

'Teach your son some fucking manners,' I said, 'or some-one else will.'

Across the language barrier, though, and only half hearing, Tanya's brother could not be expected to understand what was going on. He already had a certain view of me owing to my football shirt comment; without a grasp of an Englishman's deep respect for first come first served, he just saw me abusing a German teenager and his dad like a cowardly hooligan. We took the trip; there were no fish.

Then there was a mix-up when I thought I was being asked what I wanted to do that evening and, in good faith, said I wanted to go for a pizza in a courtyard overlooking the sea. I'd had enough of sitting in a smoking booth with an atmosphere you could almost literally cut with a knife. Apparently I hadn't understood that I was meant to say I'd like nothing more than to eat again in the smoking booth. I went for a pizza, to discover the rest of the family had opted not to join me. Tanya sat in silence, drinking only water while I finished. Then we went back to the others. The holiday was beginning to turn from a disaster into a nightmare.

Tanya didn't really speak to me for the rest of the trip, other than to make me apologise to the villa manager for being noisy when coming back late one night, and I knew my borrowed time had run out.

She finished with me the evening after we got back. We went to see *Pirates of the Caribbean* and then she made me walk the plank. That's the best I can do, that's as cheerful as I can sound about it. I felt awful, alone again and just out of ideas. I'd tried every type of woman and failed. The one for me was the one for someone else, she'd gone, probably years before while I was acting like an arsehole with unsuitable girls. I just felt like giving up there and then, saying 'That's it, I'm off to a monastery.'

Tanya fired a last shot: 'I couldn't bring myself to have sex with you any more. I have no respect for you. I feel as though my ovaries have shrivelled.'

'I get the picture, love,' I said.

'There you are, always joking,' she said. 'You can't make a joke of everything.'

I had to admit that, on that occasion at least, she was right. She started crying and said we could try to be friends.

I passed on that one. As a matter of policy I wasn't going to let her finish with me the easy way, and anyway, what does 'friends' mean? Could I see myself saying 'Gosh, I'm glad your ovaries are feeling OK again, now you've met lovely Tom. I bet you're enjoying a fantastic sex life. Good on you!'

I went home and phoned Charlie.

'Don't worry,' he said, 'there are plenty of other very intelligent Bond girl lookalikes in the sea. Ooh, hang on, now I come to think of it, there aren't are there?'

I had to laugh. Tanya was wrong. You can make a joke of almost everything. It's just a matter of trying. You can make a joke of your life if you keep laughing hard enough.

33 CLAIRE

This story does not deserve a happy ending, but it gets one. If I was writing it as a novel I would think that the protagonist carried too many sins to be forgiven. Some twist of fate should emerge to rob him of what he wanted.

I have only one excuse and it's pretty weak. I think I am typical in most of my behaviour. Some of the things I have done frighten me when I look back on them. How can I have been so unclear? How can I have been so changeable, so directionless and emotionally unformed? The only defence I can give is that there are an awful lot of people like that. I said it wasn't a very good excuse.

I am certainly not unique. If anything makes some of the stories here scary, it's that they are ones that are lived, with minor variations, by millions of men across the planet. I am not violent, a belittler, a wilful abuser of any sort. I never set out to hurt anyone, I'm not looking to control or to be controlled. I like women and I want those in my life to be happy. I might not be what you'd call *very* nice, but I think I am nice-ish.

I was weary after I finished with Tanya, bone sick of the chase. I had resigned myself to the thought that I would never meet anyone and a peculiar calm descended on me. Free from the hunger for a partner, I felt lighter in myself, as if an oppression had lifted. I would, I decided, cultivate friendships with women, sleep with some occasionally, but the acquisition of a life partner would no longer be my only aim. I could be friends with any woman I got on with, go to bed with those that would have me, but the strains of representing someone else and being represented by them would be absent.

I went to the theatre with Claire, but she had made it very plain we were just friends. I also went up to stay with her and slept in her overheated box room alone.

She made me hoot – she was someone even more absent-minded than me, going out without closing the front door, never knowingly turning off a light and, thank God, with only a two-year-old onion in her fridge. No forcing home-made muck on you and talking about Jamie Oliver from her. She went out for every meal, just like I did. We walked the dog out to Grantchester, got stuck in the mud by the river, drank in the long shadows of the pub garden, went to the theatre in the evening and stayed up eating curry and talking until late in the morning. We had forty-eight hours together that weekend and it seemed we tried to use every one of them.

I found her incredible. She was extremely bright, very funny, full of talk about plays and galleries, but with huge holes in her cultural knowledge. We saw a poster with a goodlooking young man on it.

'Who's that,' she said, 'I know him. That's Eric Cantona, isn't it?'

'It's David Beckham,' I said.

This was so refreshing. During the ladette phenomenon of the 1990s women had found it fashionable to talk about football, and we'd all had to endure them calling it 'footie'; comments such as 'I hope the other team scores a goal now, I feel sorry for them'; and 'I'm supporting Liverpool in this match.' Claire couldn't even name you three football teams, like a proper girl.

We were similar to each other but different, which I think

is important. It means you have some finding out to do. Also, you're not going to argue about whether Bowie finally lost it on 'Let's Dance' or 'Tonight'. Claire had two CDs, one of them by a bunch of Pan pipers she'd heard in the park. It made me admire her tremendously. She didn't give a stuff about being trendy: if she liked Pan pipers, she was going to listen to Pan pipers. Obviously, that didn't stop me throwing the CD away. When she found out a year later, she thought it was funny and filled me in on the 'inexplicable' disappearance of my favourite ten-year-old furry overcoat.

Because Claire had turned me down twice – I'd made one pass at her when I was going out with Suzy, when she'd visited to ask me to contribute to a business project she was doing, and one when she'd come down to visit as a friend – she was off limits. Two Noes are enough for any man. If you require a third, you're a stalker. I really liked her, though, and it was good to enjoy female company without all the pressures of a relationship.

I went to a party in London and met up with an old friend, a very pretty Irish girl called Chloe. She was just back from overseas, an ex-indie-kid like me, and I had always fancied her. We ended up snogging and snorting coke in a friend's kitchen. I wanted to go home with her, but she wouldn't let me.

'You've got a girlfriend anyway,' she said.

'No I haven't,' I said, 'unless I'm being unusually unobservant, even for me.'

'That's how you speak about this girl Claire,' she said.

'She doesn't want me,' I said.

'The way you talk about her, I'd make her want you, if I were you. I'd make this your last cheap blow job. You're getting too old, kid. Even I only half fancy you nowadays; what must the younger girls think?'

Under other circumstances I might have pursued Chloe, rung her up in the week, arranged to meet just for a drink, but I didn't bother. On paper she'd got the lot. In fact she had the lot, it was just that I didn't want it.

Chloe thought I was getting too old to score with girls, but I knew that I could continue as I'd continued for quite a while, meeting girls at parties, through the internet or in clubs, having a wild week, month or a year, hoping this was the one, but finding she wasn't and moving on. Against myself, I'd actually become quite good at seducing women – I'd had a lot of practice – and was facing a totally unwanted life as a middle-aged Lothario. There isn't a lot to meeting women. I think there are five rules.

1. Wash. Amazing how many men overlook this basic move. Clean teeth that have seen a dentist within the last six months are a must too.

2. Approach her. Let her reject you, don't reject yourself before you even speak. 'Hello' is your best chat-up line. It doesn't matter if you're nervous. That's not an excuse. Unexploded-bomb men are nervous; they still do their jobs.

3. Be broadly positive and talk about them. However, there is a limit. Don't say stuff like 'I notice you leave your home at 7.15 a.m. each day and return between 8 and 8.30 p.m., apart from on Tuesdays when you go to yoga.' That won't work.

4. Relax. This doesn't mean get pissed. It means try to act like your life doesn't depend on making her your girlfriend, even though we all know it does.

5. That's it.

But even if I could continue to meet women, work my lines, make them laugh and take them to bed, I was tired of it all. In truth, I'd been tired of it since I was fourteen. I'm the marrying kind. I never set out to sleep with more than one girl; just ineptitude and immaturity had meant I'd never held one down.

This is why it always makes me laugh when I see that women are putting babies on hold to concentrate on their careers. Women are marrying later because men are, on the whole, idiots like me. It's nothing to do with their jobs. Women don't have to marry the first half-passable goon that comes along; they'll dump him and move on to a two-thirds-passable goon, and then back to a quarter-passable goon, and so on as they seek for a wholly passable non-goon. They have choice in everything else, why not men? Men are fools, liars, self-deceivers and frauds, and a woman may have to wait a long time for one that deserves her.

There in the kitchen with Chloe, I didn't know that I would take her advice. That was my last cheap blow job, though it wasn't that cheap because I've always been very fond of Chloe. It was also, by coincidence, my last line of coke. The next woman I would kiss would become my wife and I would have something so much more important in my life than a transitory thrill.

Claire came down to see me a few days later and we went to walk the dog on Hove Lawns. It was a bright blue day, white sails on the sea and the dog hammering after his ball with a wild glee. I turned and looked at her and had a strange realisation. There was no one in the world I would rather be with. That awful line I'd thought about Julie Christie all those years ago came into my head – the one about her eyes having stolen the colour from the sky. It felt true, though.

But she didn't want me, did she?

With anyone else I would have given up, moved on, found

someone else. Claire was different, though, and, as much as I wanted her as a friend, I thought it worth risking losing her for good rather than hide my feelings. I tried to think of the future without her. I couldn't. It was literally unimaginable.

A week later we went to the theatre again, some strange play about divorce and murder. We had a wonderful time, but I didn't want to look at the play, I wanted to look at her. Obviously I didn't want her to think she had some ice cream on her, so I restrained myself from staring at her like a dog at a sausage. It wasn't that easy, though. We went for coffee afterwards – coffee, with milk and no alcohol – and rushed to meet our divergent tubes.

On the Piccadilly platform I had to give it one last go. I had no sense of the future, no idea that I was picking a destiny. I just felt like kissing her.

'Might I have a kiss?' I said.

She pecked me on the cheek.

'A proper one?'

Claire looked at me with her big, deep-blue eyes and said in a low, soft voice 'I don't think that would be appropriate.'

The train was coming, the crowds moved by. It felt like a metaphor for my entire life, seeing something I wanted for a second before it was swept into chaos.

She got on the train and I watched her go.

'Ring me,' she said, and I noted how she didn't make that irritating telephone shape. She was the one and she was gone. I didn't feel myself infatuated; I didn't think she was great apart from one thing; I wasn't in love with her mind more than her body or the other way round. I just knew, in a very strange way, that I would never be happy with anyone else.

The next day I was on the train up to London again to see a friend. I didn't want to call in the morning because I didn't want to seem too keen, but I couldn't let it stew either. I summoned up my courage and phoned. I didn't get the result I was looking for.

'Ah, yes, Mark,' she said. 'Bad tidings, I'm afraid. I do find you attractive . . .'

That sounds like good tidings, I thought, though wait for the chop of the 'but'.

'But I'm not looking for that sort of relationship with you at all. I just don't think we're looking for the same thing.'

'You mean you're looking for casual sex?' I said. 'I think that's disgusting.'

'No, I am not looking for casual sex. I do not understand the concept of casual sex. It repulses me.'

'If you prefer it formal I can wear a dinner suit,' I said. 'I have spats if they're required.'

'That might be nice, though spats are never required by anyone but the dustbin man. But no. It's just . . . I prefer to stay as friends.'

Oh my daughter, see how I had to fight to bring you into existence? At least put that into the picture when you're beating me over the head with this book.

'OK,' I said. Did I like her enough just to want to be her friend? Definitely. Also, I knew men, I knew what losers I was up against. OK, I'm a loser myself, but there are degrees of loserdom. I just knew she fancied me, knew it like I know my name. You can tell by the way a girl stands next to you. Claire wasn't a breast pusher, like Phoebe or Catriona, one of those girls who almost stand on tiptoes and crane their neck. She wasn't like Ella, who had showed that she liked me by pushing me into a hedge, or an eye softener like Eva, who's attraction was signalled by a change in the quality of her attention. She was like none of those. I couldn't say what it was; sometimes she turned away slightly, as if shielding herself from my gaze.

You might think this is a sign she's not attracted, but it's more that she is attracted but isn't sure you're the right one for her. If you're not attracted to someone, then why turn your breasts away from them? Who brought breasts into it? It certainly wasn't me. Must have been her.

Other times she would look at me directly, but not in the 'You reckon you're pretty cool but I could have you' way of Catriona – just in a way that made me think she was looking right into me. No one had ever looked at me like that before, possibly because I'd never looked at them in that way.

Whatever she said, I knew she was attracted to me. My certainty was backed up by something Suzy had said years before, in passing, that Claire thought I was goodlooking. I might have been slightly on the turn, but not nearly as much as some blokes of my age. Most of my friends, the former golden youth, by then looked like scarecrows, corpses or Shakespearean drunks. Own hair, own teeth, regular exercise, a nice layer of drinker's fat pushing out the wrinkles. I could have passed for weeks younger than I was. She had to still like me – didn't she?

We kept talking. It was a hesitant conversation that sounded as if she wanted to cut the embarrassment and get off the phone, but she didn't get off the phone and we went on for half an hour. She apologised and said she didn't really know why she was turning me down. I said not to worry, I was going to try a traditional remedy for a broken heart.

'Not bloody homoeopathy? You do know it's just water in a fancy bottle?'

'I do,' I said, 'not homoeopathy, which isn't traditional anyway, it was dreamt up by a charlatan at about the time of Waterloo.'

'Christian Hahnemann, 1807, nearer the time of Trafalgar,' she said. 'So what is the traditional cure?'

'Suicide.'

'Well, you'll be missed.'

'That's my line,' I said. Actually, it's Charlie's line.

'Not any more,' she said. 'Look, do you want to come up this weekend? You can stay in the box room again.'

'I'm not actually going to commit suicide, in case you were thinking of selling tickets,' I said. 'I am a hardy beast and shall stroll on loveless, daunted but just a little wiser.'

I don't know if it was the mention of love, even when twinned with 'less', but when I arrived something had changed.

Claire was embarrassed and halting, two qualities I rarely associate with her.

'What I said on the phone,' she said, 'forget it completely.'

'What did you say?'

'That I didn't want to go out with you.'

'You tell me to forget it and now you're reminding me.'

'Shut up,' she said.

We stood in silence for a minute.

'You may kiss me,' she said. So I did and it transformed me.

That's how I felt. I'd got the one, the girl who when she shines, she shines for you, the girl who makes you laugh and, more than that, makes you smile when you think of her, and who makes it not matter what the rest of the world throws at you, because you've still got her. I'd wanted a girl to rescue me from the mundane, someone to eat iced rowan berries with in frost-enchanted forests, but I didn't need that any more. With a kiss Claire had destroyed the mundane for me. If I had to choose between a night in the winter palace with Dr Zhivago's Lara and an afternoon with Claire drinking tea in the Copper Kettle I'd go for the latter.

Beneath these feelings was an undercurrent of relief. It

was over, the journey that had begun when I was fourteen, the madness of the twenty-five-year search was done and I felt so happy as we kissed that first time that I nearly started to cry. For the first time in my life, the future felt like something that might happen. Before, it had just been a series of looming shapes in the dark. Women, as I have said, have shocked me, but this was the biggest shock of all. I felt saved.

It shouldn't have taken Claire to give my life meaning, I should have been able to do that on my own. I couldn't though, and she had. This is the final category of girlfriend – The One – and I felt very lucky to have found her. That's not lucky as in 'blessed', though I did feel that, but lucky as in someone who has just bent to tie his shoe and hears a bullet whistling past him where his head had been.

Years before Ella had accused me of being unambitious. As I held Claire in my arms I realised that the reverse was true. I'd been ludicrously ambitious in the only field that ambition really matters – love. All the miseries I'd had, the discontent and the self-doubt, had all been because I was failing in the one area of human endeavour where I truly wanted to succeed. I was never going to be self-sufficient, happy on my own. Some people just aren't built like that and, if you're not, no amount of therapy, religion, New Age nonsense or self-help is going to change you. So what happens? You become that bitterest of creatures – the disappointed romantic. Or you get lucky.

My mum had been right. I needed a good woman to settle down with, needed one like a toy robot needs batteries: I just didn't work without one. The trouble was that I hadn't understood enough about myself to know what that woman might be like. No wonder I'd never managed to make a go of it before.

'What was the problem?' I said.

'Some of my friends thought you might be slightly unreliable.'

'What do you mean, unreliable?'

'That you might see other women.'

I was outraged. Where did they get an idea like that from? I wanted names, numbers, descriptions.

'Calumny! Identify these slanderers!' I said.

'Everyone.'

'Absolutely everyone?'

She thought for a moment.

'Yes. Apart from me. Luckily that's the vote that counts.'

There was no sense between us that this was anything other than the real thing. We weren't going out with each other, we weren't giving each other a try. We both knew, right from the second the idea occurred to us, that we were playing for keeps.

Claire even got on with my friends.

'Johnny Morris, that one,' said Mad Bomber Harris.

'What?'

'She's a keeper.'

You maybe have to be a certain age to get the analogy, but it meant a lot to me.

Within six months I had proposed, in an old-fashioned pub called the Cambridge Blue, oars on the wall and Old Murderer on tap from the cask. It's the kind of place I would have wanted to firebomb a year before, or to shoot the regulars as they asked Doreen to direct them to the blackboard and run them through the guest ales, but now a substantial part of my anger seemed to have left me and I really liked it.

We were at a table full of lesbians who overheard and drank a toast to us like in a Richard Curtis movie. Later they got chatting to us, realised they didn't like me and asked

Claire if she was sure she was making the right decision. We left before it started going Tarantino.

We got married in May 2005 on cup-final day at a little church in a tiny village in Cambridgeshire. I had decided to forgive Jesus for the last twenty-five years and offer him another chance. So far he's taken it.

Ella was there, as was Phyllis. Suzy decided not to make it, but she sent a card. She was with someone who loved her and, free from the yoke of me, back to the bright, funny girl I'd known when I'd met her. Claire's old boyfriend Sam was there, too.

Claire was typically late. Very late, because it was raining – a proper summer deluge. I struggled to keep rather banal thoughts about the cleansing of sins out of my head, but they did keep intruding. I didn't know, but it was almost true. Something had changed inside me. After the honeymoon I even lost my appetite for drink and haven't bothered to touch a drop since. That is very strange, considering drinking was not only my hobby but my talent too. Some women had tried to change me. Claire had managed it with no effort at all. Why would I want to spend time in a pub with a bunch of cronies when I could spend it with her? Why would I want to drink, when we had so much fun sober?

I was looking down the aisle at the door and my uncle said 'Don't worry, she'll be here.'

He didn't know me. I knew she'd be there, I had no doubt at all. I was just wondering if two of my friends from Coventry were going to make it in time. They did.

This is going to sound like I'm making it up, but I'm really not. When she came into the church the clouds parted and the place filled with light. Claire looked like the queen of the May, a plain white flat-fronted dress like Guinevere might have worn, a garland of flowers in her hair.

It's a cliché, but I've never seen anyone look so beautiful. I half expected her to point at me suddenly and laugh, to reveal that it was some set-up, a lavish practical joke at my expense. It really did seem too good to be true.

She came up to the altar and, on impulse, I kissed her as she approached. I think I wanted to make sure she was real.

'Mark, will you take Claire to be your wife. Will you love her, comfort her, honour and protect her, and, forsaking all others, be faithful to her as long as you both shall live?' said the vicar.

'Absolutely one hundred per cent yes,' I wanted to say, but I contented myself with the words I'd been waiting to say since I was fourteen.

'I will.'